Social Impact Measurement for a Sustainable Future

Richard Hazenberg
Claire Paterson-Young
Editors

Social Impact Measurement for a Sustainable Future

The Power of Aesthetics and Practical Implications

palgrave
macmillan

Editors
Richard Hazenberg
Institute for Social Innovation and Impact
University of Northampton
Northampton, UK

Claire Paterson-Young
Institute for Social Innovation and Impact
University of Northampton
Northampton, UK

ISBN 978-3-030-83151-6 ISBN 978-3-030-83152-3 (eBook)
https://doi.org/10.1007/978-3-030-83152-3

This Palgrave Macmillan imprint is published by the registered company Springer Nature Switzerland AG.
The registered company address is: Gewerbestrasse 11, 6330 Cham, Switzerland

Acknowledgements

Social impact measurement remains a nascent field, despite the growth in methodologies and reporting over the last two decades, driven by global frameworks such as the Millennium and Sustainable Development Goals. For those that read this book, it will become clear that the Editors believe that this is a crucially important area, not just in terms of ensuring methodological robustness and validity of data (albeit these are important areas), but also in safeguarding those for whom social impact measurement is allegedly designed to support (i.e. the most disadvantaged globally). Issues of power, engagement, networks and ethics come to the fore here, as the world seeks to find ways to develop sustainably, and also effectively measure the progress in this area. We as Editors are hugely indebted to the authors who have contributed to this book. Each individual is an expert in their field and their contributions within their chapters cover important philosophical, methodological and practical areas with regards to social impact measurement. Without their thoughtful considerations as presented here, this book would not have been possible. Further, we would also like to express our gratitude to those authors and/or publishers cited in this book, who have granted permission for their important work to be included in this edited volume. We hope that this text can act as a clarion call for the social impact sector more widely, by illustrating the best practice (and challenges) that are emerging globally with regards to sustainable development and the measurement of social impact. It is no exaggeration to say that the next few decades represent a critical juncture in the development of humanity, as well as the survival of the global environment and modern society as we know it. The field of social impact measurement has a critical role to play in ensuring that these future years are not wasted.

Contents

Notes on Contributors

Katie Barnes (MA (Cantab), FRSA) is a researcher and consultant with interests in urban and place-based development, systems behaviours and strategic responses to social disadvantage. As a member of the University College London (UCL) research team on the five-year *Liveable Cities* programme, Katie researched evolving city governance and policy-making models and frameworks, collaborating with research colleagues across four universities. She is a Visiting Fellow at Sheffield Hallam University and Associate Director of Sonnet Advisory & Impact CIC, a consultancy specialising in impact-based planning, design and measurement, and has led a number of high profile and influential impact and strategy projects, notably in the social housing, health and social care sectors. Katie has a strong belief in education as an enabler of future opportunities and is CEO of an education charity in East London.

Jo Barraket is Distinguished Professor and Director of the Centre for Social Impact Swinburne at Swinburne University of Technology in Melbourne, Australia. A political sociologist, Jo has research interests in the social economy, the intersections between state and civil society in the conduct of new public governance, and the social impacts of social innovation.

Oanh T. Cao is the lecturer of Faculty of Business Administration, University of Economics and Business, Vietnam National University

Hanoi. She received the PhD degree from the University of Northampton, the United Kingdom in 2019. Her research interests are social impact, social value creation, social enterprise, social entrepreneurship, social innovation, and public service delivery. She also has practical experience in working with small social enterprises through Thriive project, a pay-it-forward program, in Vietnam.

Heui Jae Choi is a student of a master's course at Business School, Sungkyunkwan University, South Korea. Her research focuses on the social impact of platform businesses, and social entrepreneurship. She is running a project for achieving the social responsibility of university with college students as she is interested in incubating college students to be social entrepreneurs.

Jim Clifford (OBE, MSc, FCA, FRSA) is a Visiting Fellow at Sheffield Hallam University, and the Founder and CEO of Sonnet Advisory & Impact CIC, a consultancy specialising in impact-based planning, design and measurement. Over the last ten years he has designed programmes and measured impact in the UK and beyond in place-based and community development, housing, children and young people, domestic abuse and violence, health, social care and transport. These have included the Adoption Bond – the first social impact bond originated in the social sector – a proposed redesign of the funding of women's refuges, which was picked up in the UK Government's subsequent white paper, and the local and National impact of problem debt on Individuals and Communities, which contributed to legislative change to control payday lending. He has published work on impact measurement, and social investment. In 2014 he co-chaired the European Commission group that developed the 'GECES' standards for impact measurement, and later served on the G8 Social Impact Investment Taskforce. Amongst other roles in public reviews and enquiries, in 2018 Jim was a member of an independent commission on post-18 skills development in the UK, where he advised on impact and potential economic gain.

Ericka Costa is Associate Professor of Accounting, University of Trento. She is international associate for Italy at the Centre for Social and Environmental Accounting Research (CSEAR) networks and co-director of CSEAR Italy. Ericka participated in several research projects on accounting and social accounting for nonprofit organisations and she has attended national and international conferences. Her research interests are focused on investigating sustainability accounting and corporate social responsibility for both for-profit and non-profit organisations. She has written and published a number of chapters in books, articles and papers for national and international journals and conferences. Her research has appeared in international publications, including Accounting, Auditing & Accountability Journal, Critical Perspective on Accounting, Accounting and Business Research, Voluntas, Service Business and Sustainability Accounting and Management Journal.

Aurora Elmes is a Research Fellow at the Centre for Social Impact Swinburne, Swinburne University of Technology. Her current multi-year evaluation research focuses on the effects of a work integration social enterprise on employment, social inclusion and wellbeing outcomes. Since 2016, Aurora has worked on multiple social enterprise research projects about impact measurement, resilience and resourcing.

Kelly Hall is a Senior Lecturer at the University of Birmingham. Her principal research interest is social care, and her current research explores the contribution of social enterprise to social care. Kelly's previous research has explored social innovation, market shaping and micro enterprises in the social care sector. This largely policy driven research has also included the impact of public service mutuals and has evaluated key governmental policies, including the 'Care Act 2014' and 'Right to Request/ Right to Provide' programmes. She is primarily a qualitative researcher drawing on narrative interviews to understand the lived experiences of individuals and communities.

Richard Hazenberg (BA, MA, PhD) is a Principal Researcher and Research Leader of the Institute for Social Innovation and Impact at the University of Northampton. Richard has research interests in the areas of social innovation, social finance, public service innovation and social impact. He has contributed to international/national government policy through papers, conferences and roundtable meetings (including the European Commission; OECD; Cabinet Office; and HM Treasury).

Richard is on the editorial board of the Social Enterprise Journal and is a reviewer for a number of international peer-review journals.

Chantal Hervieux is Associate professor at Saint Mary's University in Halifax, Canada. She is the Director of the Centre for Leadership Excellence (CLE), and the founder of its Impactlab. Dr Hervieux's research interests lie in social impact assessment, network relationship mapping, social and sustainable entrepreneurship, social innovation systems, and ethical responsibilities of organisations. Her work has been published in the Journal of Business Ethics, the Social Enterprise Journal, Business Ethics: A European Review, Qualitative Research in Organizations and Management and the Journal of Enterprising Communities: People and Places in the Global Economy.

Kiros Hiruy is a Senior Research Fellow with the Centre for Social Impact Swinburne at Swinburne University of Technology in Melbourne, Australia. Kiros is a Development Anthropologist with extensive experience in evaluation and project management. His research interests include impact assessment and evaluation, research for development, and migration and development. Kiros has over 20 years of experience conducting program design and evaluations, international evidence reviews and capacity building project for communities, governments and non-governmental organisations across Africa, Southeast Asia, the Pacific Islands and Australia.

Linda Odhiambo Hooper (BA, MSc, completing PhD) is a doctoral researcher at the School of Applied Social and Policy Sciences at Ulster University (SASPS). Her work looks at the impact of Social Innovation on the welfare in low-income and middle-income countries. Her analysis of the impact of interventions aids organisation to identify impact as well as the intended and unintended outcomes of policies and interventions. Originally from Kenya, Linda engages and consults internationally on with all actors involved in livelihood support within the international development framework. The gender dimension is key to her work as poverty disproportionately affects women.

Andrew Joyce is a Senior Research Fellow with the Centre for Social Impact Swinburne at Swinburne University of Technology. Andrew's work at the Centre focuses on evaluation and his research interests include the use of continuous quality improvement models and the role of evaluation within practice and policy settings. Andrew has a history of both academic and industry positions including roles in community health, schools, and local government.

Philip Kinghorn is a Senior Research Fellow in Health Economics at the University of Birmingham. Philip's primary research interest relates to the conceptualisation, assessment and valuation of outcomes for inclusion in economic analysis. In particular, Philip has an interest in the Capability Approach and its use within health economics to assess broad quality of life outcomes. This has led Philip to working in areas such as supportive end of life care and social care.

Won Jun Lee is a professor at SKKU Business School, Seoul, South Korea. He has served as the editor-in-chief for Asia Pacific Journal of Information Systems. He is currently the chairperson of Entrepreneurship Major and also serves as the director of Entrepreneurship & Innovation Center at SKKU. His publications have appeared in journals such as Decision Sciences, Information & Management, Production and Operations Management, and Computers in Human Behavior. His current research interests include issues related to digital transformation, team entrepreneurship, and entrepreneurship education.

Ari Margiono is the head of the Center for Innovation, Design, and Entrepreneurship Research at Binus University – International in Jakarta, Indonesia. Ari received a PhD in Management (Entrepreneurship) from Queensland University of Technology, Australia; and he has been publishing a number of research on social entrepreneurship and digital transformation topics in reputable international journals. Prior to his stint in the academia, Ari worked in the UN systems and in a few international NGOs.

Margaret C. McKee is an Associate Professor in the Department of Management at Saint Mary's University, and teaches and researches in the areas of leadership, governance, business ethics, and corporate social responsibility. Margaret's recent research focusses on the role of business schools in educating the next generation of responsible leaders, and assessment of the nature and impact of organisational initiatives for PRME and the SDGs. She has presented her work at the Academic of Management and Society of Business Ethics Conferences, and been published in the Journal of Business Ethics, the Journal of Leadership, Accountability and Ethics and the International Journal of Management Education.

Tirta Nugraha Mursitama is currently the Vice Rector of Research and Technology Transfer and the head of the Centre for Business and Diplomatic Studies (CBDS) at Binus University, Indonesia. He received his master's degree in 2004 and doctorate in 2007, both in management, from the Graduate School of Management, Gakushuin University, Tokyo, Japan. He received his second doctorate in Politics and International Relations from Padjadjaran University in 2016. He was a visiting fellow at the School of Marketing, Management and International Business, Australian National University in September–November 2011.

Alex Nicholls (MBA) is the first tenured professor in social entrepreneurship appointed at the University of Oxford and was the first staff member of the Skoll Centre for Social Entrepreneurship in 2004. His research interests range across a range of topics within social entrepreneurship and social innovation, including impact measurement and management; social and impact investment; the nexus of relationships between accounting, accountability, and governance; public and social policy contexts; and systems change and social movements. To date Nicholls has published more than one hundred papers, working papers, book chapters and articles and six books. Most appear in a wide range of peer reviewed journals and books, including six papers in the Financial Times Top 50 journals.

Jarrod Ormiston is Assistant Professor in Social Entrepreneurship at the School of Business and Economics, Maastricht University. Jarrod's teaching activities focus on social and sustainable entrepreneurship. His research focuses on working with social enterprises and impact investors to enhance their impact, and understanding the role of emotions in entrepreneurship. Jarrod has worked as a consultant to the Australian Government, the OECD and United Nations on entrepreneurship and education. Prior to his work at Maastricht University, Jarrod worked as a lecturer at the University of Sydney, as an analyst at Deloitte and in various management roles in the Australian and Latin American nonprofit and education sectors.

Junsu Park is a research professor in the BK21 research group for humanistic future studies and social entrepreneurship, Sungkyunkwan University, South Korea. His research focuses on individual and contextual factors associated with social performance and its relation to financial performance among social enterprises.

Claire Paterson-Young (BA, MSc, PhD) is an Associate Professor at the University of Northampton. She has extensive experience in researching the social impacts of social inequality and social disadvantage. Claire has experience in ethics and is a member of the West Midlands Police and Crime Commissioner Ethics Committee, Health and Research Association Research Ethics Committee and the University of Northampton Research Ethics Committee. She is an Associate Editor for the Journal of Child and Family Studies and has published in numerous international peer-reviewed academic journals.

Caterina Pesci is Assistant Professor of Accounting, University of Trento (Italy). She held a PhD in the University of Parma (Italy). Caterina's research interests are at the intersection of financial and non-financial reporting and revolve around accountability, sustainability, financial and non-financial reporting of both for profit and nonprofit organisations. She participated in several research projects and she has attended national and international conferences to present papers on the results of these research projects. She has written books, chapters in books and papers that have been accepted for national and international journals and conferences. Her research has appeared in international publications, including Accounting, Auditing & Accountability Journal, Critical Perspective on Accounting, Accounting and Business Research, Managerial Auditing Journal, Journal of Management and Governance, Sustainability Accounting Management and Policy Journal.

Joanne Qian-Khoo is an economist with extensive experience in program design, monitoring and evaluation, and impact assessments in development settings. As a researcher and practitioner, Joanne has designed and conducted numerous program and project evaluations and impact assessments, and developed impact evaluation frameworks for multi-stakeholder initiatives, NGOs, social enterprises and philanthropic organisations. Her project experience extends to poverty reduction, inclusive finance, consumer empowerment, social performance management, and corporate social responsibility gained from work in Australia and overseas. At the Centre for Social Impact Swinburne, Joanne's research has focused on social impact measurement, evaluation approaches, social economy and inclusive employment.

Michael J. Roy (PhD) is Professor of Economic Sociology and Social Policy at the Yunus Centre for Social Business and Health at Glasgow Caledonian University. He is internationally respected for his research on social enterprise, health, and wellbeing, on 'ecosystems' of support for social enterprise and social entrepreneurship, and for his critique of innovative funding mechanisms such as Social Impact Bonds. He is Editor-in-Chief of Social Enterprise Journal and Associate Editor of the Journal of Social Entrepreneurship.

Jieun Ryu has been working in the social enterprise and social impact field as a researcher, educator and business advisor for 15 years. Previously, Jieun served as a Lecturer and a Researcher in Social Innovation and Impact at the University of Northampton, where she led social enterprise related modules and managed social innovation and social impact relevant projects. Jieun also taught several social entrepreneurship and sustainability related topics at different universities such as Warwick Business School, where she received her PhD. Her work has been published as journal articles, book chapters, and research reports.

Simon Teasdale (PhD) is Assistant Vice Principal Social Innovation, and Professor of Public Policy and Organisations at Glasgow Caledonian University. His research focuses on the intersection between public policies and organisational behaviour. He is particularly interested in how social innovation policies are enacted through discourse and financial incentives, and the complex ways in which practitioners seek to negotiate and informally amend such policies.

Roosalina Wulandari specialising in crisis intervention and trauma recovery, co-founded Lentera Sintas Indonesia – a social organisation that provides psychological assistance for victims of sexual violence in Indonesia. Wulan currently is a PhD candidate at the University of Indonesia with a research interest in religious intolerance and collective identity. As a seasoned clinical psychologist with years of experience working for national and international humanitarian agencies, Wulan is currently also a Counseling Section Head at Binus University International.

Edward Yee works at the intersection of finance and social impact to drive social change. He has had leadership roles in non-profits, founded start-ups, and is running his current venture, Givfunds. Edward co-founded Givfunds to help neglected social enterprises gain access to catalytic capital at scale. He has worked at various levels of the global impact investing sector, from systems change at the Global Steering Group for Impact Investment to consulting for global impact funds and performing academic research on the sector in Oxford. Edward is a Rhodes Scholar, Forbes 30 U30 Awardee, World Economic Forum Global Shaper, Kairos Society Global Fellow, and a Diana Award Recipient.

Acronyms

ALRI	Acute Lower Respiratory Infection
ASCOT	Adult Social Care Outcomes Toolkit
AVPN	Asian Venture Philanthropy Network
BSC	Balanced Scorecard
CBA	Cost-Benefit Analysis
CBPR	Community-Based Participatory Research
CEA	Cost-Effectiveness Analysis
CEDAW	Convention on the Elimination of all forms of Discrimination Against Women
CERITA	Community Empowerment for Raising Inclusivity and Trust through Technology Application
COPD	Chronic Obstructive Pulmonary Disease
DFID	Department for International Development
ESG	Environmental and Social Governance
EVPN	European Venture Philanthropy Network
FAO	Food and Agriculture Organization
FPIC	Free, Prior and Informed Consent
FSC	Financial Services Commission
GECES	Group d'Experts de la Commission sur l'Entrepreneuriat Sociale
GIIN	Global Impact Investment Network
GIIRS	Global Impact Investment Rating System
GSK-SI	GuideStar Korea Social Impact
HYES	Healthy Years Equivalents

IAIA	The International Association for Impact Assessment
IAR	Impact Accelerating Report
IFC	International Finance Corporation
IFRS	International Financial Reporting Standards
IMP	Impact Management Project
KIBO	Korea Technology Finance Corporation
KODIT	Korea Credit Guarantee Fund
KPIs	Key Performance Indicators
MGS	Millennium Development Goals
MoEL	Ministry of Employment and Labor
MOI	Means of Implementation
MRE	Milled Rice Equivalent
MSP	Measurement of Social Performance
MSS	Ministry of Small and Medium Enterprises and Startups
NEPA	National Environmental Policy Act
NICE	National institute for Health and Care Excellence
NSIF	Non-Profit Organisation's Social Impact Framework
OECD	Organisation for Economic Cooperation and Development
OS	Outcomes Star
PbR	Payment by Results
PPP	Public-Private Partnerships
QALY	Quality-Adjusted Life Year
QoL	Quality of Life
RCTs	Randomised Control Trials
REDF	Roberts Enterprise Development Fund
RSPO	Roundtable for Sustainable Palm Oil
SAA	Social Accounting and Audit
SASC	Social and Sustainable Capital
SCBA	Social Cost-Benefit Analysis
SCRQoL	Social Care-Related Quality of Life
SDGs	Sustainable Development Goals
SEEES	Social Economy Enterprise Evaluation System
SEIF	Social Enterprise Investment Fund
SHG	Self Help Groups
SIB	Social Impact Bonds
SOBI	Social Binis Indonesia
SOPOONG	Social Power of Networked Group
SROI	Social Return on Investment

SVA	Stakeholder Value Added
SVC	Social Value Creation
SVI	Social Value Index
SVLK	Sistem Verfikasi Legalitas Kayu
SVVMM	Social Venture Value Measurement Model
UN	United Nations
UNCED	United Nations Conference on Environment and Development
UNICEF	United Nations Children's Fund
VAWG	Violence Against Woman and Girls
WELLBY	Well-Being-Year
WHO	World Health Organization

List of Figures

List of Tables

1

Introduction

Claire Paterson-Young and Richard Hazenberg

1.1 Introduction: Social Impact and Social Value

Social impact and social value as concepts are ambiguous, which creates challenges in the field of social impact measurement (Emerson, 2000; Maas, 2014). Increased attention on understanding social impact and social value has been driven by developments in the public and third sectors (i.e. funder requirements on measuring impact), government policy (i.e. the Public Services 'Social Value' Act of 2012 in the UK being a prime example) and European Methodology on social impact measurement (Clifford et al., 2014). Interpretations and definitions in social impact measurement vary, with research (Maas, 2014) illustrating subtle differences in the terminology around impact, output, effect and outcomes.

C. Paterson-Young (✉) • R. Hazenberg
Institute for Social Innovation and Impact, University of Northampton, Northampton, UK
e-mail: claire.paterson-young@northampton.ac.uk; richard.hazenberg@northampton.ac.uk

R. Hazenberg, C. Paterson-Young (eds.), *Social Impact Measurement for a Sustainable Future*, https://doi.org/10.1007/978-3-030-83152-3_1

Despite differences in definitions, the fundamental principles for social impact measurement are evident in the definitions provided by Clifford et al. (2014). Social impact was defined by the Group d'Experts de la Commission sur l'Entrepreneuriat Sociale (GECES) as "*The reflection of social outcomes as measurements, both long-term and short-term, adjusted for the effects achieved by others (*alternative attribution*), for effects that would have happened anyway (*deadweight*), for negative consequences (*displacement*), and for effects declining over time (drop-off)*" (Clifford et al., 2014:12). This definition outlines the short-term and long-term outcomes of measurements, allowing for identification of adjustments for alternative attribution, deadweight and drop-off (Hazenberg & Clifford, 2016).

The practice of social impact measurement has grown exponentially, and this book seeks to explore developments in social impact measurement approaches and offer a critique on the use of social impact measurement in modern society. It seeks to uncover the tensions inherent in social impact measurement, especially between creating and measuring social value creation. As the world becomes ever more globalised in its focus to deliver sustainable solutions to social and environmental problems, frameworks such as the United Nation's Sustainable Development Goals (SDGs) provide opportunities through which to assess and compare impact globally. This United Nations SDGs, introduced in 2015, outline 17 global goals designed to improve outcomes for all by 2030. Constructive critiques of global frameworks are required to ensure that they do not misinform stakeholders, disenfranchise the disadvantaged and exacerbate existing social problems. This book is separated into four distinct sections: 'The how, what, why and whom of Social Impact Measurement', 'Agency, expertise and partnerships', 'Politics and public good', and 'Power, accountability and ethics'.

1.2 The How, What, Why and Whom of Social Impact Measurement

Social impact measurement has foundations in modern scientific enquiry, with explicit attention on measurement outlined in the U.S. Agency for International Development in 1971 and Claude Bennetts hierarchy of program effectiveness in 1976 (Knowlton & Phillips, 2013). Developments in social impact measurement have been revisited with the amplification of social impact measurement, both within academia and within policy and practice. Chapter 2 outlines the potential for development in the social impact measurement sector moving forwards, in a way that will set the scene for subsequent chapters. It examines the social impact measurement sector, outlining complexities in establishing a consistent and common definition of social impact measurement. Despite ongoing definitional issues in social impact measurement, significant progress in the coalescence of social impact framework and approaches are evidenced in the development of global standards in social impact measurement (i.e. GECES) and global targets for sustainability (i.e. United Nations SDGs) [Relevant SDGs: SDG17: Partnerships for the Goals].

Building on the historical development of social impact measurement, Chap. 3 explores the growing demand for effective social investment, transparency and accountability, the need for social impact measurement has become more critical than ever. It offers an anthropological critique of current approaches and identifies strategies and tools that empower and place people at the centre of social impact measurement. Arguing that such approaches can help map the contribution of social investment at all system levels (micro, meso and macro) to the United Nations' SDGs [Relevant SDGs: SDG16: Partnerships for the Goals]. The book's first section ends with a chapter investigating 'Why and what to measure?'. It explores how the United Nations SDGs (United Nations, 2015) seek to make the world a better place but setting Goals alone will fail to achieve that end. This chapter explores the role of social impact measurement in evidencing goal achievement, with emphasis on the role it plays in telling us what is working, why it is working and how far it we have progressed towards goals [Relevant SDGs: SDG17: Partnerships for the Goals].

1.3 Agency, Expertise and Partnerships

Agency, expertise and partnerships are core elements in social impact measurement, with approaches to social impact measurement generally focused on social enterprises and hybrid organisations. This section begins with a chapter on the challenges in establishing ways to measure social impact, theoretically and empirically, especially in measuring the impact on gender. It seeks to understand the approaches to social impact measurement, focusing on pro-social behaviours, with an emphasis on gender. It reflects on the experiences of female participants living in low-income areas in Kenya, highlighting issues with discrimination, unfair norms, decision-making, sexual and reproductive issues, political participation, leadership, unpaid work among others. Drawing on empirical data from interviews with participants, this chapter illustrates the challenges of addressing social issues and the need for concrete efforts to bridge theory and practice in developing suitable approaches to social impact measurement [Relevant SDGs: SDG5: Gender Equality; SDG17: Partnerships for the Goals].

Social impact measurement has a myriad of approaches, with Chap. 6 exploring the competing discourses of impact measurement forwarded by impact investment funds in the United Kingdom. It examines the ways in which impact investors justify and explain their use of impact measurement practices on their websites and in their annual report and impact reports. Through examination of the ways in which impact investors justify and explain impact measurement practices, it highlights the need for organisations to appreciate the multi-disciplinary nature of impact measurement as they strive to address the UN SDG*s* [Relevant SDGs: SDG17: Partnerships for the Goals]. This section concludes with a chapter investigating the role of stakeholders and beneficiaries in social impact measurement. It investigates multi-stakeholder approaches to social impact measurement, acknowledging the role of such an approach in fostering approaches to measuring outcomes associated with the SDGs [Relevant SDGs: SDG17: Partnerships for the Goals].

1.4 Politics and Public Good

Social impact measurement has a political dimension, with the politics and public good of social impact measurement, across the globe, explored in this section. Chapter 8 focuses on social impact measurement in Indonesia and argues that despite a shift from a state-centred to private sector focus on social impact measurement (including the third sector), the involvement of beneficiaries in social impact measurement is often sugar-coated, if not neglected. It outlines the need to revisit strategies and policies regarding social impact measurement in Indonesia, providing recommendation for the government, the private, and the third sectors [Relevant SDGs: SDG17: Partnerships for the Goals]. Turning our attention to Vietnam, Chap. 9 examines the social impact measurement approach to community library services, with consideration towards the limited resources of both government and the community. It seeks to investigate the partnership between the community, third sector organisations and the government in public service delivery in relation to the contextual factors that affect social impact creation in developing countries. Such collaboration and customer-centric approaches are required to empower public service design, which is essential in social impact measurement [Relevant SDGs: SGD 4: Quality education, SDG 11: Sustainable cities and communities, and SDG 17: Partnerships].

The political dimension of social impact measurement in South Korea, with several government departments such as the Ministry of Employment and Labor (MoEL), Ministry of Small and Medium Enterprises and Startups (MSS), and Financial Services Commission (FSC), involved in developed social impact assessment tools, is explored in Chap. 10. Social impact assessment tools enable the monitoring and evaluation of organisations; however, there have been limited efforts to classify these tools in Korea. Chapter 10 seeks to categorise the social impact assessment tools in Korea, using seven variables: Data typology; Impact typology; Purpose; Model complexity; Sector; Time frame; and Developer (Grieco, 2015). It outlines the tension between different stakeholders in defining social impact in Korea, contributing to supporting policy-makers and organisations in identifying suitable social impact assessment tools [Relevant SDGs: SDG16: Peace, Justice and Strong Institutions; SDG17: Partnerships for the Goals].

The commodification and financialisation of everyday life are intertwined with the concept of 'social value', which hinders the development of common social impact measurement approaches. Chapter 11 draws on Karl Polanyi's concept of 'fictitious commodification', focusing on social impact measurement approaches including Social Return on

Investment. It outlines the implications of impact measurement and the need to shape an economy in the ashes of the old [Relevant SDGs: SDG3: Good Health and Wellbeing; SDG 11: Sustainable cities and communities; SDG17: Partnerships for the Goals]. Chapter 12 investigates the effectiveness of impact measurement tools on social care interventions. It identifies commonly used measurement tools in social care, specifically the English Adult Social Care Outcomes Toolkit (ASCOT) designed to measure care-related Quality of Life and used by the Department of Health and Social Care for the English Adult Social Care Survey. Through examining commonly used measurement tools, it recommends improvements in measuring social care outcomes and its relationships with the SDGs [Relevant SDGs: SDG4: Good Health and Wellbeing; SDG11: Sustainable Cities and Communities; SDG17: Partnerships for the Goals].

1.5 Power, Accountability and Ethics

Social impact measurement can promote transparency and accountability (Zahra & Wright, 2016); however, procedures for social impact measurement are often under-conceptualised. This creates ambiguity over social impact measurement resulting in questions over power, accountability and ethics. Chapter 13 focuses on advances in impact measurement and management practices, with emphasis on impact materiality. Impact materiality enables an understanding of impact risk and the role of beneficiaries and end-users in the measurement process. It shows that impact measurement and management practices can adopt evidence-based through following the Hierarch of Evidence Model [Relevant SDGs: SDG8: Decent Work and Economic Growth; SDG17: Partnerships for the Goals].

Understanding impact materiality in impact measurement creates opportunities for enhancing measurement practices. Chapter 14 builds on our understanding of impact measurement with attention on the SDGs. It argues that siloed solutions to the wicked problems, outlined by the SDGs, may not provide the desired impact, and could even have unintended, negative effects. Through investigating the food system in Sub-Saharan Africa, this chapter shows that siloed solutions and policies, without consideration of interacting issues, have the potential to cause unintended impacts, including gender inequality, hunger and poverty [Relevant SDGs: All SDGs].

Sustainability has strong grounding in ethics, with the Brundtland Report (1987) outlining the fundamental principles for sustainability based on social justice, poverty and equality. Friction arises in world of impact measurement, with the process for developing suitable conventions and standards complex. Chapter 15 investigates these complexities, with emphasis on the ethical issues associated with social impact measurement. It argues that the processes for collecting data (to measure social impact) can result in ethical violations that directly impact individuals and society. It investigates the core ethical principles associated with social impact measurement, creating an 'Ethical Framework for Social Impact Measurement'. Creating an 'Ethical Framework for Social Impact Measurement' promotes transparency and accountability, whilst promoting best practice in impact measurement [Relevant SDGs: SDG16: Peace, Justice and Strong Institutions; SDG17: Partnerships for the Goals].

1.6 Conclusions

Social impact measurement is used to identify a 'whole picture' of the impact of services and interventions on beneficiaries and wider society. Scholars highlight the fact funders place emphasis on social impact measurement, finding that social impact measurement and evaluation are an expectation from funders (Stevenson et al., 2010; Chapman et al., 2010; Ogain et al., 2012). These expectations are strengthened with legislation (i.e. The Public Services (Social Value) Act, 2012) and guidance (i.e. GECES) that place emphasis on organisations to identify the economic, social and environmental benefits of services. This means organisations are under pressure to evidence the social impact of services and interventions which creates a need for resources that outline valid and reliable social impact measurement frameworks and strategies.

The processes of social impact measurement are also intrinsically tied to the UN SDGs 2030 framework, with a need to capture, measure and disseminate the economic, social and environmental impacts of the public, private and third sectors towards achieving these goals. This book aims to address this need by producing a resource for organisations (in several fields) that will highlight valid and reliable social impact measurement frameworks and strategies and how these can be linked into the SDGs. It focuses on four distinct areas: 'The how, what, why and whom of Social Impact Measurement', 'Agency, expertise and partnerships', 'Politics and public good', and 'Power, accountability and ethics'. In doing so, it seeks to move on discussion around social impact measurement beyond normative considerations of methodological efficacy, to also consider the wider impact of the measurement itself, particularly for those disadvantaged communities around the world most in need of highly impactful sustainable development.

References

Brundtland, G. H. (1987). *Our Common Future*. Report of the World Commission on Environment and Development, United Nation.

Chapman, T., Robinson, F., Brown, J., Crow, R., Bell, V., & Bailey, E. (2010). *What Makes Third Sector Organisations Tick? Interactions of Foresight, Enterprise, Capability and Impact*. Northern Rock Foundation.

Clifford, J., Hehenberger, L., & Fantini, M. (2014). *Proposed Approaches to Social Impact Measurement in European Commission Legislation and in Practice Relating to: EuSEFs and the EaSI*. European Commission Report 140605 (June 2014). Available online at http://ec.europa.eu/internal_market/social_business/docs/expert-group/social_impact/140605-sub-group-report_en.pdf and http://ec.europa.eu/social/main.jsp?catId=738&langId=en&pubId=7735&type=2&furtherPubs=yes

Emerson, J. (2000). *The Nature of Returns: A Social Capital Markets Inquiry into Elements of Investment and The Blended Value Proposition*. Harvard Working Paper Series, No. 17 Social Enterprise Series, Boston. Available online at http://www.blendedvalue.org/wp-content/uploads/2004/02/pdf-nature-of-returns.pdf

Grieco, C. (2015). *Assessing Social Impact of Social Enterprises: Does One Size Really Fit All?* Springer.

Hazenberg, R., & Clifford, J. (2016). GECES and the Valid Measurement of Social Impact in the VCSE Sector. In R. Gunn & C. Durkin (Eds.), *Social Entrepreneurship: A Skills Approach* (2nd ed.). Policy Press.

Knowlton, L. W., & Phillips, C. C. (2013). *The Logic Model Guidebook: Better Strategies for Great Results* (2nd ed.). Sage Publications.

Maas, K. (2014). *Classifying Social Impact Frameworks.* [online] Available online at: http://tcbblogs.org/public_html/w*p*-content/uploads/TCB_GT-V1N2-14.pdf?width=100. Accessed on: 9 Sept 2015.

Ogain, E. N., Lumley, T., & Pritchard, D. (2012). *Making an Impact.* NPC.

Public Services (Social Value) Act. (2012). Available online at: https://www.legislation.gov.uk/ukpga/2012/3/notes/contents

Stevenson, N., Taylor, M., Lyon, F., & Rigby, M. (2010). *Social Impact Measurement (SIM) Experiencing and Future Directions for the Third Sector Organisations in the East of England.* Working Paper. Social Enterprise East of England.

United Nations. (2015). *Transforming Our World: The 2030 Agenda for Sustainable Development.* https://sustainabledevelopment.un.org/post2015/transformingourworld. Date Accessed 9 Apr 2021.

Zahra, S. A., & Wright, M. (2016). Understanding the Social Role of Entrepreneurship. *Journal of Management Studies, 53*(4), 610–629.

Section I

The How, What, Why and Whom of Social Impact Measurement

2

The Development of Social Impact Measurement

Richard Hazenberg and Claire Paterson-Young

2.1 Introducing Social Impact Measurement

The social impact measurement sector has grown exponentially over the last few decades, going from a niche area to one that is deeply embedded within government policy, investor behaviour and third sector management (as well as growing in the private sector). The growth of Corporate Social Responsibility (see Chap. 8 for further information on Corporate Social Responsibility), Environmental and Social Governance (ESG), green investing, impact investing, as well as new policy mechanisms such as Payment by Results contracts (PbR), Social Impact Bonds (SIBs) and outcomes-based commissioning have all played a part in this growth. This growth in pluralistic policy mechanisms, investment markets and a

R. Hazenberg (✉) • C. Paterson-Young
Institute for Social Innovation and Impact, University of Northampton, Northampton, UK
e-mail: richard.hazenberg@northampton.ac.uk; claire.paterson-young@northampton.ac.uk

R. Hazenberg, C. Paterson-Young (eds.), *Social Impact Measurement for a Sustainable Future*, https://doi.org/10.1007/978-3-030-83152-3_2

growing awareness of the need for sustainable growth, have all combined to drive interest in social impact measurement (Kah & Akenroye, 2020).

As we now enter the third decade of the twenty-first century, the growing importance of global sustainability frameworks such as the United Nations' Sustainable Development Goals (SDGs) (UN, 2021) means that social impact measurement frameworks will become increasingly important. However, there remains key barriers to embedding social impact measurement with a plethora of different frameworks available, a lack of definition as to what constitutes social impact and an often top-down focus on social impact measurement that disempowers the very beneficiary groups that such measurement should support. The aim of this chapter is to provide an introductory overview to this complex area, by exploring what constitutes social impact, what 'best practice' looks like in social impact measurement and identifying some of the key frameworks that currently exist for measuring social impact globally. The chapter will end with an exploration of the potential for social impact measurement moving forwards. In doing so we aim to provide a base for the subsequent chapters that follow, which will each explore different facets of the social impact measurement debate globally with regards to the SDGs.

2.2 Defining Social Impact

At the turn of the millennium, research recognised that there was a lack of understanding as to what social value and social impact constituted (Emerson, 2000), whilst agreed upon definitions of social impact were not in place (Sairinen & Kumpulainen, 2006). Whilst this definitional ambiguity has changed in recent years as definitions and research into social impact and social value have emerged (Clifford et al., 2014; Hazenberg & Clifford, 2016; Jain et al., 2019), it must be acknowledged that the very nature of social value/impact remains socially constructed (Burdge & Vanclay, 1996). This fluidity in meaning explains why different approaches to impact measurement have been developed over the years, ranging from Social Return on Investment (SROI) (NEF, 2021)[1] through to social accounting (Rawhouser et al., 2019).

Social impact was defined by the Group d'Experts de la Commission sur l'Entrepreneuriat Sociale (GECES) as "*The reflection of social* outcomes *as measurements, both long-term and short-term, adjusted for the effects achieved by others (*alternative attribution*), for effects that would have happened anyway (*deadweight*), for negative consequences (*displacement*), and for effects declining over time (drop-off)*" (Clifford et al., 2014:12). Further, social value was defined by Jain et al. (2019:10) as "*…a value that demonstrates change(s) in the live(s) of an individual or groups of individuals when tangible and intangible resources are employed at grassroots level by social actors, ultimately creating social change within the* society". What these definitions have in common is a shared focus on how changes occur in the lives of individuals or groups of individuals (communities or society); where they differ is that the former is focused on quantification of said change, whilst the latter is focused on the process of driving that change[2]; this makes social impact measurement a process of assessing changes rather than structures (Burdge & Johnson, 1998).

The concept of social impact and its measurement is therefore deeply embedded in social value creation processes, as well as research methodologies that seek to quantify change and explain it with regards to the null hypothesis and wider societal antecedents. This combination of approaches has been encouraged by policy-makers globally, with examples such as the Public Services (Social Value) Act 2012[3] in the UK pushing the agenda of social value in public service commissioning and delivery. Globally, the Organisation for Economic Cooperation and Development (OECD) (2019) have identified 590 policy instruments, designed to support the growth of impact investing and measurement. Therefore, it is clear that the agenda for social impact measurement is one that is growing politically, which further aligns with the SDG framework

[1] See https://www.nefconsulting.com/our-services/evaluation-impact-assessment/prove-and-improve-toolkits/sroi/ for more information on SROI. SROI mechanisms can also appear in cost-benefit analysis also.

[2] See Jain et al. (2019) for an overview of the social value *creation* process as a model.

[3] The Public Services (Social Value) Act 2012 obliges public service commissioners to *consider* social value in the commissioning and procurement of services.

from the United Nations and the outcomes for these that sit under each SDG (UN, 2021).

The proliferation of these top-down policy mechanisms does not however, come without its limitations. These top-down approaches (as will be discussed several times later in the book) can come at the cost of bottom-up innovation, reducing local relevance and hence buy-in, and disempowering the very people it is intended to support. This limiting of bottom-up engagement could potentially stifle bottom-up social innovation, which has been shown in prior research to offer more impactful solutions than top-down driven innovations and linked to community empowerment (Kruse et al., 2019; Mulgan, 2019). This can often fly-in-the-face of what Nicholls (2018) identified as social impact measurement's purpose of identifying beneficiary engagement and empowerment (see Chap. 3 for a discussion of this area), whilst at the same time ensuring that social impact measurement becomes a tool of entrenching existing privilege for those that hold power (Voltan & Hervieux, 2017). It is these contradictions that can detract from the benefits that impact measurement can bring around legitimisation and enhanced understanding of what works.

2.3 Social Impact Measurement and the SDGs

Whilst the definitional aspects of social impact are contested, the actual process of developing and conducting social impact measurement has evolved considerably in recent years, as best practice models and frameworks have emerged; whilst definitions of the constituent elements within social impact measurement have also arisen. This development has been underpinned by the work of the European Commission's GECES subcommittee (Clifford et al., 2014), alongside prominent scholars such as McLoughlin et al. (2009), as well as the development of global frameworks by key stakeholders (for example, the Global Impact Investment Network's Iris+ approach),[4] albeit the work of many others has also fed into this progress.

[4] See: https://iris.thegiin.org/

Theoretically, the key overarching element of social impact measurement involves the development of a Theory of Change (Carman, 2010), a process particularly popular in international development work (Arensman et al., 2018), which can be defined as a causative logic model that demonstrates the links between inputs and activities, and the changes that these deliver to individuals, communities and societies (Clifford et al., 2014). Within this Theory of Change are embedded five key constructs as defined by the GECES report (Clifford et al., 2014, p. 6):

Inputs:	What resources are used in the delivery of an intervention?
Activity:	What is being done with the 'inputs' (i.e. the intervention)?
Output*:*	How that activity touches the intended beneficiaries?
Outcome:	The change arising in the lives of beneficiaries and others.
Impact*:*	The extents to which that change arise from the intervention.

This approach to identifying the key elements of Theory of Change built upon the work of McLoughlin et al. (2009), who first identified outputs, outcomes and impacts. Outputs pertain to direct outputs of a programme; an outcome represents positive/negative changes to individuals state of being; whilst impact is the wider benefits to society of the outcomes delivered (ibid.). When measuring these outputs, outcomes and impacts, it is important to also consider 'deadweight', that is the null hypothesis (what would have occurred anyway); 'alternative attribution', that is what outcomes and impacts are directly attributable to factors outside of the intervention in focus; and 'drop-off', relating to the decreasing outcomes and impacts derived over time (Clifford et al., 2014). When these Theory of Change factors (Inputs, Activities, Outputs, Outcomes, Impacts, Deadweight, Alternative Attribution and Drop-off) are combined, it creates a holistic social impact measurement framework (see Fig. 2.1). The reality of course is that this is rarely the case, with resource issues relating to finance, knowledge, capacity and time all constraining the alignment of these variables.

There are also considerations when developing a social impact measurement framework related to what the overall goal of the impact measurement work is. Indeed, this is critical for any organisation to understand in order to better identify what resources they can and should commit to

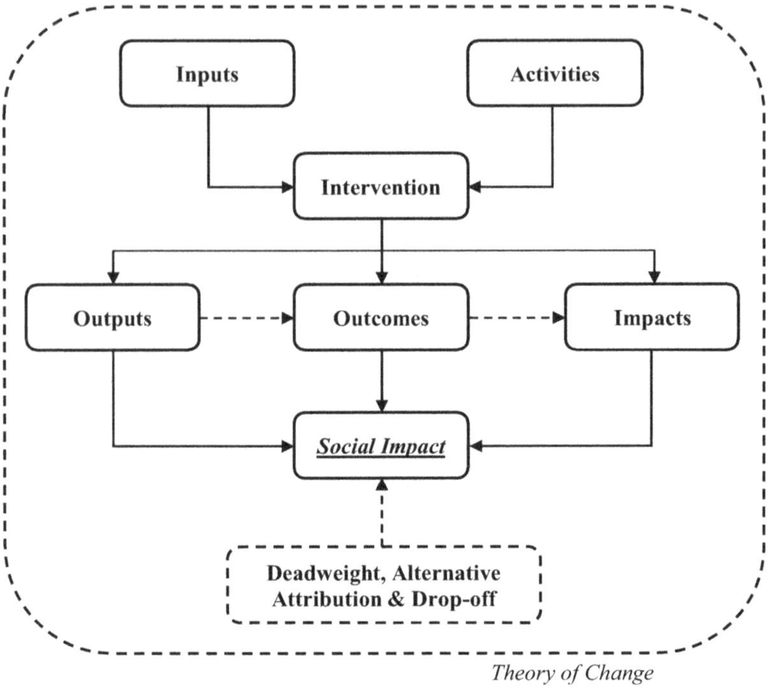

Fig. 2.1 A holistic social impact measurement framework

social impact measurement. As an example, if an organisation wishes to develop a short, non-rigorous infographic report to present internally, then there is probably little point in engaging in a holistic social impact measurement framework as outlined above. However, if an organisation needs to present reliable and valid data as to the efficacy of its interventions vis-à-vis current traditional interventions (for example in healthcare), then a holistic social impact measurement framework utilising aspect such as control groups (deadweight) will be required. This is why Clifford et al. (2014, p.7) identified within the GECES report the five steps to undertaking social impact measurement, which clearly identify the need to: (1) *Identify objectives:* What are the objectives of the impact measurement (i.e. organisation and partners)?; (2) *Identify stakeholders:* Who are the beneficiaries and who provide resources?; (3) *Relevant measurement:* Understand the theory of change and then utilise relevant indicators to capture this; (4) *Measure, validate and value:* Assess whether outcomes are achieved and whether they are recognised by the various stakeholders; and (5) *Report, learn and improve:* Ensure the dissemination of and meaningful use of the data gathered and findings produced to internal and external stakeholders/audiences (ibid.).

The development of impact measurement approaches built in this rigorous methodological approach is increasing as the sector develops, and the growing popularity of the United Nations' SDG framework (UN, 2021) means that many organisations are seeking to align the outputs, outcomes and impacts that they measure with the key performance indicators identified within each individual SDG.[5] The SDG framework contains 17 goals, which within them contain 169 individual performance targets (Fisher & Fukuda-Parr, 2019), pushing statistical and impact data from a regional/nation-state mechanism to one that seeks to drive global transformation (Reigner, 2016). Given the global prominence of the SDGs and the way that increasing numbers of organisations in the public, private and third sectors are aligning with them, we are likely to see more and more social impact measurement frameworks that feed into SDG agendas. This focus on the use of social impact measurement as a means to assess transformative outcomes aligned to the UN SDGs has been recognised already in prior research (Paterson-Young & Hazenberg, 2020) and is an area that is only likely to grow as we move towards the 2030 SDG milestone. However, given the above focus on social impact measurement framework development and the SDGs, it is incumbent for us to consider what existing social impact measurement frameworks seem best placed to offer rigorous approaches, specifically when considering the focus within the SDGs on partnerships (SDG17: Partnerships for the Goals) and the need to engage and empower beneficiary groups in social impact measurement (Nicholls, 2018).

[5] These 17 SDGs and the indicators within them can be found at https://sdgs.un.org/goals

2.4 Existing Frameworks and the Future of Social Impact Measurement

Noya (2015) in a policy paper produced for the OECD identified that there are three main types of impact approach that tend to align with different stakeholder groups. First, there is 'cost-benefit' analysis that tends to be employed within the public sector (ibid.), to understand how the costs of interventions or policies can produce wider benefits for the state and reduce long-term costs. This approach to impact measurement is often seen employed in outcomes-based commissioning contracts and to a degree also in Social Impact Bonds (SIBs), with providers working together alongside the state to deliver services with a specific outcome focus linked to payments (NHS Confederation, 2014). Second, Noya (2015) identified the 'rating' impact assessment, that is focused on calculations related to returns on investment. This approach is often linked with private investors through mechanisms such as impact investment (Noya, 2015) but can also be found in cross-sectoral partnership approaches such as Social Impact Bonds (SIBs).[6] Approaches to impact measurement including Social Return on Investment (SROI) (NEF, 2021) are often utilised within such evaluations. Third, there is the Social Accounting and Audit (SAA) approach, which is a beneficiary approach to social impact measurement focused on stakeholder outcomes and satisfaction (Noya, 2015). This type of approach tends to be implemented in community settings and civil society and can mix quantitative assessments with qualitative based narrative overviews (ibid.).

It is not the purpose of this chapter to explore these different types of meta-approaches nor individual frameworks in detail; this has been done elsewhere by other scholars and pertinently, subsequent chapters within this book provide interesting overviews of different frameworks, sectors and approaches. Rather, it is important to acknowledge that these approaches are grounded in different logics, tend to be pushed by

[6] Social Impact Bonds are mechanisms for funding public services delivered by third/private sector delivery organisations, whereby payment for the service is dependent on the delivery of certain outcomes, and the upfront funding of these services is paid for by social investors (UK Government September, 2017).

different stakeholder groups, and have different positive and negative aspects depending upon what you are measuring where, and for whom. What this demonstrates though, is that the social impact measurement sector is heterogeneous, with a multitude of different approaches and frameworks within these, making the choice of approach and the metrics within them difficult for stakeholders. Indeed, in a meta-analysis of the academic literature focused on social impact measurement between 1996 and 2016, Rawhouser et al. (2019) identified 273 papers, of which 71 had a core focus on social impact measurement itself. Their conclusions from this review were that social impact measurement remains a fragmented area of study, that emerges across multiple sectors, leading to confusion and a lack of clarity over what can and should be measured. The UN's SDG framework could provide the holistic, global overview to this area that would pull together social impact measurement work centred around its 169 key indicators (Fisher & Fukuda-Parr, 2019). If approaches to measurement were aligned with the SDG framework, and also followed the best practice guidance as described by GECES (Clifford et al., 2014), then cross-comparison of social impact measurement data would be made much easier.

2.5 Summarising Social Impact Measurement

The social impact measurement sector and field of inquiry is certainly complex and given the varying types of impacts that can be delivered across sectors (the 17 SDGs provide evidence of this), it is no surprise that consistent and commonly accepted definitions have yet been identified. In the same way that Nicholls (2010) argued that social enterprise was a pre-paradigmatic field over a decade ago, the same can be argued of social impact and social impact measurement today, with ongoing definitional issues affecting scholars' and practitioners' ability to engage in meaningful social impact measurement. However, progress is being made, with a coalescence globally around certain frameworks and approaches (for example: SROI; IRIS+; GECES) and the growth of global sustainability targets as embedded in the SDGs. Whilst the focus of this book is on the SDGs and their relevance for social impact measurement (and certain specific social impact frameworks), this is not to say that one must accept the SDGs as purely positive in driving the sustainability and social impact measurement agendas. Our job as scholars, practitioners or wider stakeholders in the social innovation ecosystem is to critically assess new opportunities, in order to understand the strengths and weaknesses of different approaches. This is certainly the positionality adopted in this book as can be seen in subsequent chapters, with contributing authors demonstrating the inherent problems related to global sustainability agendas, common social impact measurement standards, and top-down approaches to driving sustainable growth and the measurement of its impact. As Grieco (2015) argues, a one-size-fits-all approach to social impact measurement is problematic and can actually lead to the disempowerment and disenfranchisement of the very beneficiary groups it is intended to serve. Nevertheless, the growing popularity of some social impact measurement frameworks, combined with global standards such as GECES and the UN SDGs, provides us with a unique opportunity as we enter the third decade of the twenty-first century, to take social impact measurement from its pre-paradigmatic state and turn it into a developed field that can truly support sustainable growth.

References

Arensman, B., Van Waegeningh, C., & Van Wessel, M. (2018). Twinning "Practices of Change" with "Theory of Change": Room for Emergence in Advocacy Evaluation. *The American Journal of Evaluation, 39*(2), 221–236.

Burdge, R., & Johnson, S. (1998). Social Impact Assessment: Developing the Basic Model. In R. Burdge (Ed.), *A Conceptual Approach to Social Impact Assessment* (pp. 13–29). Social Ecology Press.

Burdge, R., & Vanclay, F. (1996). Social Impact Assessment: A Contribution to the State of the Art Series. *Impact Assessment, 14*, 59–86.

Carman, J. G. (2010). The Accountability Movement. *Nonprofit and Voluntary Sector Quarterly, 39*(2), 256–274.

Clifford, J., Hehenberger, L., & Fantini, M. (2014). *Proposed Approaches to Social Impact Measurement in European Commission Legislation and in Practice Relating to: EuSEFs and the EaSI.* European Commission Report 140605

(June 2014). Available online at http://ec.europa.eu/social/main.jsp?catId=738&langId=en&pubId=7735&type=2&furtherPubs=yes

Emerson, J. (2000). *The Nature of Returns: A Social Capital Markets Inquiry into Elements of Investment and The Blended Value Proposition*. Harvard Working Paper Series, No. 17 Social Enterprise Series, Boston. Available online at http://www.blendedvalue.org/wp-content/uploads/2004/02/pdf-nature-of-returns.pdf

Fisher, A., & Fukuda-Parr, S. (2019). Introduction—Data, Knowledge, Politics and Localizing the SDGs. *Journal of Human Development and Capabilities, 20*(4), 375–385.

Grieco, C. (2015). *Assessing Social Impact of Social Enterprises: Does One Size Really Fit All?* Springer.

Hazenberg, R., & Clifford, J. (2016). GECES and the Valid Measurement of Social Impact in the VCSE Sector. In R. Gunn & C. Durkin (Eds.), *Social Entrepreneurship: A Skills Approach*, 2nd Edition Policy Press.

Jain, P., Hazenberg, R., Seddon, F., & Denny, S. (2019). Social Value as a Mechanism for Linking Public Administrators with Society: Identifying the Meaning, Forms and Process of Social Value Creation. *Journal of Public Administration*. https://doi.org/10.1080/01900692.2019.1660992

Kah, S., & Akenroye, T. (2020). Evaluation of Social Impact Measurement Tools and Techniques: A Systematic Review of the Literature. *Social Enterprise Journal, 16*(4), 381–402.

Kruse, D. J., Goeldner, M., Eling, K., & Herstatt, C. (2019). Looking for a Needle in a Haystack: How to Search for Bottom-Up Social Innovations That Solve Complex Humanitarian Problems. *Journal of Product Innovation Management, 36*(6), 671–694.

McLoughlin, J., Kaminski, J., Sodagar, B., Khan, S., Harris, R., Arnaudo, G., & McBrearty, S. (2009). A Strategic Approach to Social Impact Measurement of Social Enterprises: The SIMPLE Methodology. *Social Enterprise Journal, 5*(2), 154–178.

Mulgan, G. (2019). *Social Innovation: How Societies Find the Power to Change*. Policy Press.

New Economics Foundation. (2021). *Social Return on Investment*. Available online at https://www.nefconsulting.com/our-services/evaluation-impact-assessment/prove-and-improve-toolkits/sroi/

NHS Confederation. (2014). *Beginning with the End in Mind: How Outcomes-Based Commissioning Can Help Unlock the Potential of Community Services.* NHS Confederation/PriceWaterhouseCooper Briefing Note 274, September

2014. Available online at https://www.pwc.co.uk/assets/pdf/beginning-with-the-end-in-mind.pdf

Nicholls, A. (2010). The Legitimacy of Social Entrepreneurship: Reflexive Isomorphism in a Pre-Paradigmatic Field. *Entrepreneurship Theory and Practice, 34*(4), 611–633.

Nicholls, A. (2018). A General Theory of Social Impact Accounting: Materiality, Uncertainty and Empowerment. *Journal of Social Entrepreneurship, 9*(2), 132–153.

Noya, A. (2015). *Policy Brief on Social Impact Measurement for Social Enterprises*. OECD Policies for Social Entrepreneurship. Available online at https://www.oecd.org/social/PB-SIM-Web_FINAL.pdf

OECD. (2019). *Social Impact Investment: The Impact Imperative for Sustainable Development Highlights*. OECD Development Co-Operation Directorate. Available online at https://www.oecd.org/dac/financing-sustainable-development/development-finance-topics/Social-Impact-Investment-2019.pdf

Paterson-Young, C., & Hazenberg, R. (2020). Transformative Outcomes: The Use of Social Impact Measurement. In W. Leal Filho, A. M. Azul, L. Brandli, A. Lange Salvia, P. G. Özuyar, & T. Wall (Eds.), *Encyclopaedia of the UN Sustainable Development Goals: Peace, Justice and Strong Institutions*. Springer.

Public Services (Social Value) Act. (2012). *UK Government Legislation*. UK Public General Acts 2012c. Available online at https://www.legislation.gov.uk/ukpga/2012/3/enacted

Rawhouser, H., Cummings, M., & Newbert, S. L. (2019). Social Impact Measurement: Current Approaches and Future Directions for Social Entrepreneurship Research. *Entrepreneurship Theory and Practice, 43*(1), 82–115.

Reigner, M. (2016). *Implementing the 'Data Revolution' for the Post-2015 Sustainable Development Goals – Towards a Global Administrative Law of Information*. World Bank Legal Review, 7. Available online at https://papers.ssrn.com/sol3/papers.cfm?abstract_id=2720597

Sairinen, R., & Kumpulainen, S. (2006). Assessing the Social Impact in Urban Waterfront Regeneration. *Environmental Impact Assessment Review, 26*, 120–135.

UK Government. (2017, September 26). *A Guide to Social Impact Bonds*. Available online at https://www.gov.uk/guidance/social-impact-bonds#what-are-social-impact-bonds

United Nations. (2021). *Sustainable Development Goals.* Available online at https://www.un.org/sustainabledevelopment/

Voltan, A., & Hervieux, C. (2017). *Social Impact Assessment of a Community Engagement Initiative.* Paper Presented at the 9th International Social Innovation Research Conference, Swinburne University of Technology, Melbourne, 12th–14th December 2017.

3

Placing People at the Centre of Social Impact Measurement: Current Approaches, Challenges, and Future Directions

Kiros Hiruy, Aurora Elmes, Joanne Qian-Khoo, Andrew Joyce, and Jo Barraket

3.1 Beneficiaries and Impact

The demand for accountability, transparency and legitimacy from funders and policymakers coupled with organisations' interest in understanding the contribution of their interventions on society has fuelled interest in social impact measurement (Kah & Akenroye, 2020). The assumption is that organisations' investment and activities create a social impact that alters how people live, work, play, relate to one another, organise to meet their needs, and cope as members of society, and that such impact is measurable (IAIA, 1995).

Regardless of the different definitions and conceptions (outlined in Chap. 2), social impacts can be both positive and negative. That is, they

---

K. Hiruy (✉) • A. Elmes • J. Qian-Khoo • A. Joyce • J. Barraket
Swinburne University of Technology, Hawthorn, VIC, Australia
e-mail: khiruy@swin.edu.au; aelmes@swin.edu.au; jqian@swin.edu.au; ajoyce@swin.edu.au; jbarraket@swin.edu.au

R. Hazenberg, C. Paterson-Young (eds.), *Social Impact Measurement for a Sustainable Future*, https://doi.org/10.1007/978-3-030-83152-3_3

can empower or disempower beneficiaries and have a beneficial or an adverse effect on their well-being. Consequently, the role of social impact measurement is to measure and demonstrate the (positive and negative) social outcomes or impacts created by organisations for intended beneficiaries and society (McLoughlin et al., 2009). In such processes of measurement, in theory, people are expected to be at the centre. However, the scope and complexity can differ based on the contexts under which social impact measurement is carried out, its purpose, and who conducts it. For instance, a multinational corporation can conduct social impact measurement as part of its internal procedures but can a consultant employed by proponents seek development approval from regulators. Organisations trying to assess the value of their investments or comply with regulatory or funding requirements and researchers with an academic interest may conduct social impact measurement. While each of these actors has legitimate grounds to conduct social impact measurement, and the different applications are valuable, undertaking social impact measurement requires consideration of its intended purposes (Vanclay et al., 2015).

Typically, social impact measurement is understood as an activity or process touted to assess intended beneficiaries' participation and empowerment (Nicholls, 2018). However, evidence suggests that current social impact measurement practices do not always put people at the centre or adequately address the power relations of the different actors involved (Chouinard & Cousins, 2015). Although social impact measurement may hold explicit participation and empowerment goals, it remains questionable whether it can adequately address power relations and imbalances. Moreover, the intended beneficiaries' participation often remains limited to their involvement as data sources (Chouinard & Milley, 2018). Thus, a people-centred approach is needed to ensure that social impact measurement enables people's participation and empowerment, particularly marginalised groups. A people-centred social impact measurement is one that not only enables the voices of intended beneficiaries to be brought into the evaluation process but also one that empowers and recognises that intended beneficiaries (marginalised communities and individuals) are evaluators and legitimators of the delegation of power in the process (Erfani, 2020; Herbert, 2005).

This chapter offers a critique of current approaches. It identifies methods, frameworks and tools that empower and place people at the centre by integrating 'local voices', questioning assumed values, and attending to local contexts. The chapter promotes the potential of participatory approaches and advances the need for power analysis in social impact measurement, recognising the hiatus between the intention and practice of social impact measurement regarding the empowerment of beneficiaries and other stakeholders. The chapter also argues that such approaches can help map the contribution of social investment at all system levels to the United Nations' Sustainable Development Goals (SDGs), particularly SDG16 (the promotion of peaceful and inclusive societies that provide access to justice for all and builds inclusive institutions at all levels).

3.2 Current Approaches in Social Impact Measurement and the Scope of Stakeholder Engagement

With the growing demand for effective social investment, transparency and accountability, the need for social impact measurement has become more critical than ever, attracting the interest of practitioners, policymakers and academics who are keen to measure social impact or value. Despite a broad range of frameworks, finding a universal approach or standard for measuring social impact has been one of the challenges in social impact measurement, at least for the last thirty years (Gibbon & Dey, 2011). There are a couple of reasons for this. Firstly, social impact measurement is underdeveloped conceptually (Rawhouser et al., 2019). Secondly, in practice, social impact measurement is expected to meet various stakeholders' needs and strategic objectives such as developing organisational performance, attracting investment, and obtaining legitimacy (Nicholls, 2009; Noya, 2015). However, Social Accounting and Audit (SAA), Balanced Scorecard (BSC) model, and Social Return On Investment (SROI) are the most common approaches used in impact assessment in the social sector (see Gray, 2001; Zappalà & Lyons, 2009; Grieco, 2015). This section discusses these widely used methods and how they engage stakeholders.

SAA is an accounting framework that estimates the present social value created by an organisation through a project or an activity (Gray, 2001; Pearce, 2001). SAA employs qualitative and descriptive statistical data to assess the organisational mission and stakeholders' expectations (Zappalà & Lyons, 2009). With a clear stakeholder engagement plan and step-by-step guidance, SAA promotes transparency and organisational learning (Pearce, 2001). However, as Gibbon (2010) notes, SAA can be problematic in practice as social accounts can be used to support individualistic or hierarchical accountability rather than informal and broader accountability to beneficiaries and the community.

The BSC model refers to strategic management tools that enable an organisation to manage and communicate impact drivers (Grieco, 2015; Olsen & Galimidi, 2008). BSC models provide analytical and visual tools to help managers briefly look at different business areas and translate their visions. It mainly focuses on four interconnected analysis areas – financial perspectives, customer perspectives, business processes, and learning and growth (Grieco, 2015). The idea is that by focusing on factors that influence social impact and revenue, companies can improve their organisations' effectiveness. For a discussion of the pros and cons of BSC, see Hoque and Kaplan (2012).

SROI is a mixed-method approach that measures the social value created by a program or organisation by engaging stakeholders and monetising the intangible social, economic, cultural, and environmental outcomes. SROI is presented as a single ratio of the Present Value of Benefits to the Present Value of Investments. Its simplicity, comparability, and effectiveness as a communication tool have made SROI appealing to policymakers, funding agencies and investors (Gray, 2001; Maier et al., 2015). However, as Gray (2001) argues, the apparent simplicity can render the exercise of measuring impact meaningless and misleading by reducing the impact into a single figure. Gibbon and Dey (2011) questioned the value of reporting a figure critiquing the subjectivity of monetisation. Others have also indicated barriers around complexity and costs (Millar & Hall, 2013) and questioned commensuration, standardisation and quality assurance in SROI (Maier et al., 2015).

Despite methodological differences and uses, the three frameworks involve stakeholders in managing, measuring, and communicating social

Table 3.1 Processes, components, and principles of SAA, SROI and Social Enterprise BSC (Kay, 2011; Nicholls et al., 2012; Somers, 2005 [italics are added by authors])

SAA	SROI	*Social enterprise* Balanced Scorecard *(BSC Model)*
SUMMARY OF PROCESSES AND COMPONENTS INVOLVED AT EACH STAGE		
Clarifying the purpose ***Stakeholder analysis*** ***Key Stakeholders*** *Confirming the scope and building a plan* ***Consulting stakeholders*** *Collate/analyse data and create draft social accounts.* *Audit findings and create final report.*	*Establishing scope* ***Identify stakeholders*** ***Decide how to involve stakeholders*** Starting from Impact Map, identifying inputs , outputs, and outcomes Developing indicators, collecting outcomes data, and valuing outcomes. Calculating impact and accounting for deadweight, displacement, attribution and drop-off. Present and future value projections and ratio calculation. ***Reporting to stakeholders***	Identify desired outcomes and (state social goals) Address financial sustainability perspective including revenue and costs. ***Include Stakeholder perspective***: ***Customers*** ***Users*** ***Employees*** ***Community, Beneficiaries*** ***Suppliers, Distributors, Partners*** Address internal process perspective including areas for improvement and information sharing. Measure impact, communicate internally and externally, noting resources that could support improvement.
PRINCIPLES		
Clarify purpose *Define scope* ***Engage stakeholders*** *Determine materiality* *Make comparisons* *Be transparent* *Verify accounts* *Embed the process*	***Involve stakeholders*** Understand what changes Value the things that matter Only include what is material Do not over-claim Be transparent Verify the result	**Include stakeholder perspective:** Customers Users Employees Community, Beneficiaries Suppliers, Distributors, Partners

value or impacts created. Table 3.1 outlines the processes and principles of these frameworks, with stakeholder participation elements appearing in bold.

Whilst Pearce and Kay (2008) identified stakeholder engagement as one of the common principles underpinning the practice of both SAA and SROI, they also flagged that the two have different starting points regarding stakeholder engagement. SAA starts from articulating the organisation's vision, mission, objectives, and activities and then conducts stakeholder analysis to map their relationships with the organisation and identify key actors to consult during the social accounting process. For SROI, identifying and involving stakeholders primarily serves to link stakeholder outcomes to the activity under analysis. Similarly, the BSC model approaches the stakeholder mapping analysis by expanding the customer perspective in the original Kaplan and Norton BSC (Somers, 2005).

Overall, these methods consult stakeholders to understand the organisation's impact and how it is achieving its social goals and creating social value. For example, described as stakeholder-informed instead of stakeholder-led, in SROI the opinions of stakeholders are considered essential to determine the significance of outcomes , while other factors also play a role (Nicholls et al., 2012,). Nicholls (2009) noted that a "top-down" approach in the social sector is focused on adopting business models and reporting practices, while a "bottom-up" approach leans towards facilitating greater stakeholder engagement in designing the reporting practices that affect them. Nevertheless, what entails stakeholder participation is worth more attention. As Bryson, Patton, and Bowman (2011) note, the selection and engagement of stakeholders itself involves the exercise of power and judgment on the part of evaluators. Further, they argue that inadequate consideration of stakeholders' perspectives, interests and power dynamics can compromise the social impact measurement process (Bryson et al., 2011). The answer to this may involve recognising the power dynamics among stakeholders and making it visible throughout the social impact measurement process of planning, designing, implementing, and reporting impact measures – a practice inherent in a people-centred approach (Bryson et al., 2011; Dart & McGarry, 2006; Erfani, 2020).

3.3 Towards People-Centred Social Impact Measurement: Legitimising Social Value

The participation and empowerment of the intended beneficiaries are desired impact measurement goals (Vanclay, 2003). However, despite good intentions and promises, social impact measurement does not always facilitate beneficiaries' participation and empowerment. Some critics argue that this is due to the complexity of the conception of power and the difficulties in translating 'empowerment' into practical actions (Bebbington et al., 2007). Regardless, there is a need for social impact measurement to move from intention to action in facilitating beneficiaries' participation and empowerment. This section presents how power analysis and participatory methods can facilitate empowerment and place people at the centre of social impact measurement.

As defined earlier, a people-centred social impact measurement approach enables beneficiaries' participation and empowerment, recognising them as active participants, evaluators, and legitimators of what is measured (Erfani, 2020; Herbert, 2005). Such an approach can ensure responsive, inclusive, participatory, and representative decision-making at all levels (SDG target 16.7), which can be mapped into SDG16. This is different from what Dart and McGarry (2006) call people-centred evaluation, which encourages the inclusion of beneficiary voices in the evaluation design to create a shared understanding of changes and who is affected by those changes. Theirs is an extractive process whereby program staff capture intended beneficiaries' voices to design program logic rather than including them as participants and legitimators, as demonstrated in a wool research project evaluation (see Dart et al., 2011).

A people-centred approach recognises the power dynamics in the social impact measurement process. It provides opportunities for beneficiaries to engage in the design, implementation and reporting of social impact measures as evaluators and legitimators, rather than participating only as consultants or data sources. This is a significant departure from current practices focused on consulting stakeholders, as discussed in the previous section. Thus, in operationalising a people-centred approach, it is crucial to recognise who the actors are, their roles, the resources they bring into the social impact measurement process, and their influence on the process itself.

3.4 Power in Social Impact Measurement and the Power of Social Impact Measurement

The social impact measurement process often involves at least three categories of actors (stakeholders) – the sponsor or client (mainly funding agencies), the evaluator, who can be external (a consultant) or internal (project staff), and the intended beneficiaries. The different actors (stakeholders) have different power positions (Eliadis et al., 2011). Each actor plays different roles and brings different resources to the social impact measurement process. Thus, understanding the power dynamics is essential to a people-centred approach.

However, as the concepts of power is contested, it is crucial to articulate what we mean by power and empowerment. A single and agreed-upon definition of power does not exist. In this chapter, following the theoretical explication of empowerment based on Weberian concepts, we adopt Giddens definition of power as relational, involving transformative capacity and domination (Giddens, 1982, 2016). Transformative capacity refers to individuals or groups of people making a difference to a pre-existing situation or their capacity to transform the structure to bring about social change. Empowerment theories and practices are based on this transformative capacity (Gaventa, 1982). Structures are rules and resources that actors (stakeholders) draw upon to produce the intended outcomes. The rules can constrain or enhance actors' actions, and resources can make their actions possible. This understanding is vital in analysing the empowerment of intended beneficiaries when conducting social impact measurement.

The International Association for Impact Assessment (IAIA) indicates that the primary focus of development should be positive outcomes, such as capacity building, empowerment, and the realisation of human and social potential (IAIA, 1995). The primacy of the intent to empower communities is stipulated in some of the principles. For example, the Principle of Subsidiarity suggests that decision making power be decentralised or taken as close to the intended beneficiaries as possible. In social impact measurement, this includes local people having an input into what needs to be evaluated and legitimising the evaluation results. The guideline also considers community participation as a vital part of the social impact measurement processes. However, there is no instrument to mandate such a practice.

The IAIA guidance notes that most social impact measurement consultants advocate support for communities, but still recognise the disproportionate influence proponents might have over the community (Vanclay et al., 2015). Thus, the guidelines suggest that in contexts with low trust between the actors, the proponent need to provide funding to the beneficiaries to commission their impact assessment consultants. This represents a tangible example of how rules (who is invited to conduct social impact measurement) and resources (distribution of funding for social impact measurement) can constrain or enhance participation and empowerment. The idea is that a community-based assessment would inform the community, and arguably, this model would support a negotiation process that is consistent with the spirit of free, prior, and informed consent (Vanclay et al., 2015). Overall, the IAIA guidance states that a social impact measurement process should contribute to the beneficiaries' empowerment and to attaining other social goals such as equity and human rights should underpin all actions.

The IAIA guidance outlines several key concepts central to understanding the issues involved in managing social impacts, including social licence to operate, free, prior and informed consent, a human rights-based approach, and human rights diligence. These lofty goals are directly or indirectly related to participation and empowerment. However, there is no guarantee that these goals will occur. In practice, the context (including legislative requirements and norms of practice) under which social impact measurement is carried out, and the position and resources of the evaluator(s) and the sponsor(s) can explicitly or implicitly, intentionally or inadvertently affect the beneficiaries adversely. There is a possibility that social impact measurement can be used as a tool to legitimise certain political and ideological positions and disempower intended beneficiaries unless the power dynamics in the evaluation process and the consumption of its results are fully understood and recognised, and corrective action is taken proactively.

Premised on this concern and recognising that social impact measurement is not value-free, we propose using power analysis in social impact measurement. Understanding the power dynamics and the local contexts that influence social impact measurement decisions, questioning assumed values, and integrating 'beneficiaries' voices' into the process through genuine participation can place people at the centre of social impact measurement. This requires shedding light on the nuances of power play in social impact measurement, which can be accomplished by making each actor's position and power visible. By asking the right questions, it is possible to clarify the power relationship among the different actors. Understanding the power dynamics offers opportunities to ensure that power imbalances are dealt with, and people and their empowerment are placed at the centre of the process (Bryson et al., 2011).

3.4.1 Why Is Power Analysis in Social Impact Measurement Important?

By making formal and informal power relations among actors visible, power analysis can help stakeholders understand the different forms of power that may undermine communities and reinforce marginalisation. Once this is understood, evaluators, sponsors or other stakeholders can take corrective actions to shift relations and empower people to attain their goals. This may include changing existing institutional arrangements or systems and dismantling possible barriers to the beneficiaries' cooperation and full participation (Gilchrist, 2000). Thus, power analysis lends itself to systems-analysis of social impact. It requires a holistic view that involves engagement with and acknowledging the larger and nested systems in which individual interventions or organisations operate. An integrated power analysis can also enhance the value of social impact measurement and create opportunities for well-informed decisions to be made, thereby contributing to the empowerment of vulnerable groups in the community – and hence to SDG16 – by facilitating responsive, inclusive, participatory and representative decision-making.

3.4.2 What Can Be Done? Elements of the Framework to Analyse Power Relations

Power analysis can be integrated into the social impact measurement process as an additional instrument to support participatory and representative decision-making in social impact measurement. The proposed framework/tool for power analysis is partly drawn from institutional analysis (Dimaggio, 1988; Ostrom, 1998; Zucker, 1988). Empowerment is about changing institutions that affect communities' lives (including the intended beneficiaries of social projects). Institutional theorists define an institution as norms or organised external patterns of action; and as formal internal structures or aspects of organisations (Dimaggio, 1988; Zucker, 1988). Thus, in social impact measurement, empowerment is premised on understanding the context, the action and interaction of the various actors involved.

The socioeconomic and political context, including pre/existing institutional arrangements, social situations and norms can influence actors' behaviour in the social impact measurement process. Understanding how empowerment can occur in social impact measurement requires identifying each actor involved, their roles and positions, and how they interact with each other. By observing the patterns of interaction, it is possible to analyse emerging power relations, institutional arrangements, and outcomes. In the social impact measurement process, the different actors' intentions and actions and their interactions determine what is valuable and measured. Thus, it is worth documenting the exchange of information and knowledge throughout the process. It is also essential to give meaning or validate results through the various actors' interactions (Chukwu, 2017). The legitimation of results has implications for beneficiaries' empowerment as it requires actors to reach a consensus to create shared meaning. It implies that beneficiaries' empowerment is contingent on the collaboration or agreement of other actors such as evaluators and sponsors (funders).

3.4.3 Important Questions to Ask

For practical purposes, we suggest understanding the contexts and institutional arrangements that govern the social impact measurement process, actors and their roles (position), and the knowledges and resources that actors bring to the social impact measurement process. Table 3.2 presents some suggested questions that help clarify and make power relations visible and provide relevant targets and Means of Implementation (MOI) for SDG16. The questions are mapped against possible SDG16 questions. For other examples of tools that could be used to establish and map the power relationships, influence, and interest levels of different stakeholders, see Bryson et al. (2011).

3.4.4 The Utility of the Framework

The framework can offer a way to systematically identify the power relationship among actors to create an opportunity for negotiations. The power relations can be analysed at each stage of the social impact measurement process to allow learnings to be documented continuously. It can also be presented as a supplementary document of social impact measurement for decision-makers. However, adding another tool to an already busy evaluation process can also add cost, which may have an undesired impact on the community/beneficiaries. There is also a question of relevance (measuring what matters) and accuracy (what is represented/ missed).

3.5 Participatory Methods

Participatory evaluation methods are conceptualised in various ways, and there is no consensus on what participatory evaluation methods involve (Cullen et al., 2011). However, two main streams of participatory evaluation can be found in the literature. The first is practical participatory evaluation, which stresses that stakeholder participation (of intended beneficiaries and others) is for practical purposes, such as enhancing

Table 3.2 Questions for social impact measurement power analysis

Elements	Social impact measurement power analysis questions to ask	Relevant SDG16 related questions	SDG16 relevant target and Means of Implementation (MOI)
Context and institutions	*What is the regulatory context?*	*Are the laws underpinned by a human rights-based approach? Do the laws and policies promote inclusiveness and participation.?*	*16.b Promote and enforce non-discriminatory laws and policies for* sustainable development.
	What is mandated through existing institutional arrangements, including laws?	*Do institutions effectively discharge their mandates in service of the public?*	*16.6. Develop effective, accountable and transparent institutions at all levels.*
	Do disadvantaged/ beneficiary communities trust formal institutions?	*What are people's actual perceptions and experiences of formal institutions'* accountability *and* transparency*?*	*16.6.*
	How does social impact measurement *action?*		
Actors and their interaction	*Who determines what to measure?*	*What specific strategies are implemented to ensure the participation of* marginalised groups *in the* decision-making *process?*	*16.7. Ensure responsive, inclusive, participatory, and representative* decision-making *at all levels.*
	Who is measuring what?	*Who in the community is and who is not involved in the* decision-making *process at all levels?*	*16.7.*
	Who validates what is measured?		

(*continued*)

Table 3.2 (continued)

Elements	Social impact measurement power analysis questions to ask	Relevant SDG16 related questions	SDG16 relevant target and Means of Implementation (MOI)
Knowledges and resources	*Whose knowledge matters/what counts?*	*Does the process embody the 'people-centred' nature of the* 2030 Agenda *and its commitment that 'no one will be left behind'?*	*16.7 Ensure responsive, inclusive, participatory, and representative* decision-making *at all levels.*
	What is the role of local/indigenous knowledge?	*Are governments more inclusive of people in all aspects of their* decision-making *processes?*	*16.7.*
	What kind of resources does each actor bring?		

evaluation relevance, ownership and utilisation. The second is transformative participatory evaluation, which has core principles of promoting social justice and seeking to democratise social change by empowering marginalised community members (King et al., 2007). Either of these can be applied to social impact measurement. Stakeholder participation can occur across the evaluation spectrum from design to data collection and analysis – but proponents argue that participation should (at the very least) involve project stakeholders beyond being data sources (Cousins et al., 2016; King et al., 2007).

Cousins et al. (2016) note that justifications for participatory evaluation often fall into one or more of the following categories: practical (aiming to enhance the quality and usefulness of social impact measurement processes or outputs); political (seeking to transform existing power relations); or philosophical (understanding meaning). The practical and political justifications align with the two streams of participatory evaluation identified. In contrast, the third (philosophical) justification points toward power and voice considerations –how meanings are constructed with or without the people involved in a program. Some scholars note that participatory evaluation is more suited to formative or process evaluations – where learning and program improvement in the focus, rather than summative evaluations – where accountability or impact assessment is the focus (Cousins et al., 2016; Cullen et al., 2011).

The purposes of participatory evaluations influence the processes followed. Transformative participatory evaluation that aims to empower participants and influence power dynamics will involve different activities than a practical participatory evaluation that aims to improve the validity and usefulness of the evaluation itself (Cullen et al., 2011). For example, practical participatory evaluation can occur without addressing or altering the power dynamics; however, for transformative participatory evaluation, the explicit goal is to address power imbalances (Baur et al., 2010; Greene, 2006). Therefore, the kind of participatory evaluation approach undertaken will vary depending on: the evaluation goals; who has decision making power about how the evaluation is conducted; the diversity of people directly involved in producing the evaluation knowledge; and the depth of peoples' participation in the process (Cousins et al., 2016).

3.5.1 What Can Practically Be Done to Incorporate Participatory Methods into Social Impact Measurement?

Research on international development indicates that evaluators use participatory evaluation approaches because the funder supports this – and so there is sufficient will, money, and time allocated to conducting a participatory evaluation (Cullen et al., 2011). The finding indicates the need for powerful actors (such as sponsors or funders) to recognise that their power and resources influence social impact measurement practice and how they use or share their power and resources is impactful (Bengo et al., 2016). Besides, Cullen et al. (2011) find that participatory evaluation is more likely to be used when the context and dynamics between people are conducive to a participatory approach – for example, stakeholders are on good terms, and there are no major conflicts.

Thus, whether participatory methods can support empowerment and positive social impact measurement outcomes depends partly on the existing distribution of power and resources and the will and capacity to transform these. For example, do the intended beneficiaries have the interest and capacity to participate in the evaluation? Does the funder or sponsor support this approach? Using participatory methods without adequately resourcing participants might mean beneficiaries are required to do unpaid labour, or the process is rushed because there is not enough time to engage and support people properly. A tokenistic or under-resourced participatory process can negatively affect both the participants and the evaluation or project goals (Cousins et al., 2016; Cullen et al., 2011; Munoz, 2013). Negative outcomes can include reinforcing existing power imbalances (Kingston et al., 2020), increased conflict between stakeholders, and exacerbation of local issues (Chouinard & Cousins, 2015).

The potential of participatory evaluation to facilitate positive outcomes, build capacity and empower people depends on:

- who and what the evaluation is ultimately designed for,
- who makes decisions and how they are made,
- the diversity of participants,
- how power dynamics between different actors are addressed, and
- the resources available to support meaningful participation (Cousins et al., 2016; Curran & Taylor-Barnett, 2019).

In practical terms, this requires the initiator of social impact measurement (the funder or other decision-makers) to consider their specific perspective and purpose in undertaking social impact measurement, what knowledge is valued, and whom this process is intended to benefit. For example, evaluation scholars have noted that the practice of evaluation itself draws on Western European traditions that value 'objective' evidence and 'expert' knowledge (Chouinard & Cousins, 2015). Further, the valuing of these forms of knowledge production over local and Indigenous ways of knowing has implications for distributing resources and reinforcing existing power relations (Andreotti et al., 2015).

Chouinard and Cousins (2015) argue that the primary purpose of social impact measurement is to demonstrate financial accountability to funders rather than to increase social value to intended beneficiaries. There may be little value or success in undertaking a participatory evaluation when the actual purpose of a social impact measurement is not to learn from others' perspectives, transform existing power dynamics or empower participants (Cullen et al., 2011). However, if social impact measurement goals are aligned with transformation and empowerment, several common elements of participatory methods can contribute to the process. These include:

- the value placed on learning to inform practice and influence change;
- providing training to support meaningful participation; acknowledgement of the evaluators' positionality in the process; and
- attending to multidimensional relational and contextual elements of participation and power (Chouinard & Cousins, 2015).

Chukwu (2017) acknowledges the identity and power differences at play in his evaluation of a hospital in Nigeria by "embedding self" – maintaining awareness of how his gender, age, culture, values, professional background, organisational role, and insider/outsider status influenced decisions and relationships. This process included the evaluator acknowledging that knowledge is co-created by people, all with their own subjective experiences. In another example, researchers commissioned to improve outcomes for young people experiencing family violence in Australia used the project's social justice aims to guide decisions about resource distribution, prioritising directing resources towards the young people participating (Curran & Taylor-Barnett, 2019).

Overall, where there is the willingness to enable meaningful participation of diverse people, learn from everyone, and facilitate equitable distribution of power, resources, and decision-making, participatory evaluation can add practical and transformative value and reshape power dynamics. However, the literature suggests that participation is often conceptualised and practised at the level of recognition (acknowledging the value of diverse perspectives) and representation (efforts to include diverse people, often as data sources), and not necessarily in terms of the redistribution of power, resources, or rights (Chouinard & Milley, 2018).

In this chapter, by using an anthropological analytic approach, which overcomes some of the more instrumental (management) conceptions of the role and nature of social impact measurement, and rendering visible its empowering and regressive effects, we have invited the reader to consider a people-centred approach in social impact measurement by integrating 'local voices', questioning assumed values, and attending to local contexts. We argue that despite the espoused empowerment goals of social impact measurement (IAIA, 1995), current social impact measurement practice involves limited participation of particular stakeholders, often only including intended beneficiaries as sources of data (Chouinard & Milley, 2018). Moving the participation and empowerment goals of social impact measurement from intent to action requires honest reflection and dialogue about existing power relations between the actors involved in a social impact project (from intended beneficiaries, to funders, to staff and volunteers), and openness to transforming the distribution of power and resources within and through social impact measurement practice. As we have highlighted, participatory evaluation methods have the potential to support the desired social impact measurement and SDG16 goals of facilitating responsive, inclusive, participatory and representative decision-making, and empowerment of people and communities. However, if participatory social impact measurement methods are attempted without equitable redistribution of power and resources, both the people participating and the social impact measurement outputs themselves are likely to be negatively affected by the reinforcement of existing inequities.

References

Andreotti, V. D. O., Stein, S., Ahenakew, C., & Hunt, D. (2015). Mapping Interpretations of Decolonisation in the Context of Higher Education. *Decolonization: Indigeneity, Education and Society, 4*(1), 21–40.

Baur, V. E., Abma, T. A., & Widdershoven, G. A. M. (2010). Participation of Marginalised Groups in Evaluation: Mission Impossible? *Evaluation and*

Program Planning, 33(3), 238–245. https://doi.org/10.1016/j.evalprogplan.2009.09.002

Bebbington, A., Lewis, D., Batterbury, S., Olson, E., & Siddiqi, M. S. (2007). Of Texts and Practices: Empowerment and Organisational Cultures in World Bank-Funded Rural Development Programmes. *The Journal of Development Studies, 43*(4), 597–621.

Bengo, I., Arena, M., Azzone, G., & Calderini, M. (2016). Indicators and Metrics for Social Business: A Review of Current Approaches. *Journal of Social Entrepreneurship, 7*(1), 1–24. https://doi.org/10.1080/19420676.2015.1049286

Bryson, J. M., Patton, M. Q., & Bowman, R. A. (2011). Working with Evaluation Stakeholders: A Rationale, Step-Wise Approach and Toolkit. *Evaluation and Program Planning, 34*(1), 1–12. https://doi.org/10.1016/j.evalprogplan.2010.07.001

Chouinard, J. A., & Cousins, J. B. (2015). The Journey from Rhetoric to Reality: Participatory Evaluation in a Development Context. *Educational Assessment, Evaluation and Accountability, 27*(1), 5–39. https://doi.org/10.1007/s11092-013-9184-8

Chouinard, J. A., & Milley, P. (2018). Uncovering the Mysteries of Inclusion: Empirical and Methodological Possibilities in Participatory Evaluation in an International Context. *Evaluation and Program Planning, 67*, 70–78. https://doi.org/10.1016/j.evalprogplan.2017.12.001

Chukwu, G. M. (2017). Giving 'Power to the People' in a Nigerian Hospital: From Evaluation over to Evaluation with Stakeholders. *Action Research, 16*(4), 361–375. https://doi.org/10.1177/1476750317691104

Cousins, J. B., Shulha, L. M., Whitmore, E., Hudib, H. A., & Gilbert, N. (2016). How Do Evaluators Differentiate Successful from Less-Than-Successful Experiences with Collaborative Approaches to Evaluation? *Evaluation Review, 40*(1), 3–28. https://doi.org/10.1177/0193841X16637950

Cullen, A. E., Coryn, C. L. S., & Rugh, J. (2011). The Politics and Consequences of Including Stakeholders in International Development Evaluation. *American Journal of Evaluation, 32*(3), 345–361. https://doi.org/10.1177/1098214010396076

Curran, L., & Taylor-Barnett, P. (2019). Evaluating Projects in Multifaceted and Marginalised Communities: The Need for Mixed Approaches. *Evaluation Journal of Australasia, 19*(1), 22–38. https://doi.org/10.1177/1035719X19832688

Dart, J., Curnow, M., Behrendt, R., Kabore, C., Oldham, C., Rose, I., & Thompson, A. (2011). The National Lifetimewool Project: A Journey in Evaluation. *Animal Production Science, 51*(9), 842–850.

Dart, J., & McGarry, P. (2006). *People-Centred Evaluation.* Paper Presented at the Proceedings of the AES 2006 International Conference. Darwin. (Australasian Evaluation Society: Canberra).

Dimaggio, P. (1988). Interest and Agency in Institutional Theory. *Institutional Patterns and Organizations Culture and Environment*, 3–21. Retrieved from https://ci.nii.ac.jp/naid/10030010621/en/

Eliadis, F. P., Furubo, J.-E., & Jacob, S. (2011). *Evaluation: Seeking Truth or Power* (Vol. 17). Transaction Publishers.

Erfani, G. (2020). Sense of Place as an Investigative Method for the Evaluation of Participatory Urban Redevelopment. *Cities, 99*, 102648.

Gaventa, J. (1982). *Power and Powerlessness: Quiescence and Rebellion in an Appalachian Valley*. University of Illinois Press.

Gibbon, J., & Dey, C. (2011). Developments in Social Impact Measurement in the Third Sector: Scaling up or Dumbing Down? *Social and Environmental Accountability Journal, 31*(1), 63–72.

Gibbon, R. J. (2010). *Enacting Social Accounting within a Community Enterprise: Actualising Hermeneutic Conversation*. University of St Andrews.

Giddens, A. (1982). Power, the Dialectic of Control and Class Structuration. In *Profiles and Critiques in Social Theory* (pp. 197–214). Springer.

Giddens, A. (2016). *Profiles and Critiques in Social Theory*. Macmillan International Higher Education.

Gilchrist, A. (2000). The Well-Connected Community: Networking to the 'Edge of Chaos'. *Community Development Journal, 35*(3), 264–275. Retrieved from http://www.jstor.org/stable/44257557

Gray, R. (2001). Thirty Years of Social Accounting, Reporting and Auditing: What (if Anything) Have We Learnt? *Business Ethics: A European Review, 10*(1), 9–15.

Greene, J. C. (2006). Evaluation, Democracy, and Social Change. In I. F. Shaw, J. C. Greene, & M. M. Mark (Eds.), *The SAGE Handbook of Evaluation*. https://doi.org/10.4135/9781848608078

Grieco, C. (2015). *Assessing Social Impact of Social Enterprises: Does One Size Really Fit All?* Springer.

Herbert, S. (2005). The Trapdoor of Community. *Annals of the Association of American Geographers, 95*(4), 850–865. https://doi.org/10.1111/j.1467-8306.2005.00490.x

Hoque, Z., & Kaplan, R. S. (2012). The Balanced Scorecard: Comments on Balanced Scorecard Commentaries. *Journal of Accounting and Organizational Change, 8*(4), 539–545.

IAIA. (1995). Guidelines and Principles for Social Impact Assessment. *Environmental Impact Assessment Review, 15*(1), 11–43.

Kah, S., & Akenroye, T. (2020). Evaluation of Social Impact Measurement Tools and Techniques: A Systematic Review of the Literature. *Social Enterprise Journal, 16*(4), 381–402. https://doi.org/10.1108/sej-05-2020-0027

Kay, A. (2011). *The New Guide to Social Accounting and Audit.* Social Audit Network.

King, J. A., Cousins, J. B., & Whitmore, E. (2007). Making Sense of Participatory Evaluation: Framing Participatory Evaluation. *New Directions for Evaluation, 2007*(114), 83–105.

Kingston, K. L., Furneaux, C., de Zwaan, L., & Alderman, L. (2020). Avoiding the Accountability 'Sham-Ritual': An Agonistic Approach to Beneficiaries' Participation in Evaluation Within Nonprofit Organisations. *Critical Perspectives on Accounting, 102261*. https://doi.org/10.1016/j.cpa.2020.102261

Maier, F., Schober, C., Simsa, R., & Millner, R. (2015). SROI as a Method for Evaluation Research: Understanding Merits and Limitations. *VOLUNTAS: International Journal of Voluntary and Nonprofit Organisations, 26*(5), 1805–1830. https://doi.org/10.1007/s11266-014-9490-x

McLoughlin, J., Kaminski, J., Sodagar, B., Khan, S., Harris, R., Arnaudo, G., & Mc Brearty, S. (2009). A Strategic Approach to Social Impact Measurement of Social Enterprises. *Social Enterprise Journal, 5*(2), 154–178. https://doi.org/10.1108/17508610910981734

Millar, R., & Hall, K. (2013). Social Return on Investment (SROI) and Performance Measurement. *Public Management Review, 15*(6), 923–941. https://doi.org/10.1080/14719037.2012.698857

Munoz, S. A. (2013). Co-Producing Care Services in Rural Areas. *Journal of Integrated Care, 21*(5), 276–287. https://doi.org/10.1108/JICA-05-2013-0014

Nicholls, A. (2009). 'We Do Good Things, Don't We?':'Blended Value Accounting' in Social Entrepreneurship. *Accounting, Organisations and Society, 34*(6–7), 755–769.

Nicholls, A. (2018). A General Theory of Social Impact Accounting: Materiality, Uncertainty and Empowerment. *Journal of Social Entrepreneurship, 9*(2), 132–153.

Nicholls, J., Lawlor, E., Neitzer, E., & Goodspeed, T. (2012). *A Guide to Social Return on Investment.* UK Cabinet Office.

Noya, A. (2015). Social Entrepreneurship-Social Impact Measurement for Social Enterprises, 10, 29. https://doi.org/10.1787/5jrtpbx7tw37-en

Olsen, S., & Galimidi, B. (2008). Catalog of Approaches to Impact Measurement: Assessing Social Impact in Private Ventures. *The Rockefeller Foundation*.
Ostrom, E. (1998). The Institutional Analysis and Development Approach. *Designing Institutions for Environmental and Resource Management, 6890*.
Pearce, J. (2001). *Social Audit and Accounting Manual*. CBS Network.
Pearce, J., & Kay, A. (2008). *Really Telling Accounts*. Retrieved from Spalding Lincs: https://citeseerx.ist.psu.edu/viewdoc/download?doi=10.1.1.459.2525&rep=rep1&type=pdf
Rawhouser, H., Cummings, M., & Newbert, S. L. (2019). Social Impact Measurement: Current Approaches and Future Directions for Social Entrepreneurship Research. *Entrepreneurship Theory and Practice, 43*(1), 82–115.
Somers, A. B. (2005). Shaping the Balanced Scorecard for Use in UK Social Enterprises. *Social Enterprise Journal, 1*(1), 43–56. https://doi.org/10.1108/17508610580000706
Vanclay, F. (2003). International Principles for Social Impact Assessment. *Impact Assessment and Project Appraisal, 21*(1), 5–12.
Vanclay, F., Esteves, A. M., Aucamp, I., & Franks, D. M. (2015). *Social Impact Assessment: Guidance for Assessing and Managing the Social Impacts of Projects*. International Association for Impact Assessment.
Zappalà, G., & Lyons, M. (2009). *Recent Approaches to Measuring Social Impact in the Third Sector: An Overview*. Centre for Social Impact Sydney.
Zucker, L. G. (1988). Where Do Institutional Patterns Come from? Organisations as Actors in Social Systems. *Institutional Patterns and Organisations: Culture and Environment, 20*(3), 23–49.

4

Why and What to Measure? The Justification for Social Impact Measurement

Jim Clifford and Katie Barnes

4.1 The Sustainable Development Goals and Impact Measurement

The UN's Sustainable Development Goals (SDGs) are ambitions that represent a better world – one in which 'no one is left behind'. They tell a story of a world beset by inequalities and entrenched social and environmental challenges but do so in the context of a vision that by 2030 the world will be different (United Nations, 2015; UN Sustainable Development Group, 2021). Visions have a purpose beyond the symbolic. The Goals are carefully constructed to show that these challenges are global and to achieve the Goals requires both commitment and an effective response. Our world is interconnected in such a way that we are all part of the problem – our choices and behaviours have effects that ripple out far beyond the limits of what we perceive to be our own

J. Clifford (✉) • K. Barnes
Sheffield Hallam University, Sheffield, UK
e-mail: j.clifford@sonnetimpact.co.uk; k.barnes@sonnetimpact.co.uk

R. Hazenberg, C. Paterson-Young (eds.), *Social Impact Measurement for a Sustainable Future*, https://doi.org/10.1007/978-3-030-83152-3_4

personal responsibility – and we must all be part of the solution (Capra & Luisi, 2014; Kania & Kramer, 2011; Klijn & Koppenjan, 2000).

Whether they can succeed in their ambition – and to what degree social impact measurement can help – depends largely on how we perceive the role of the SDGs. Here we recognise two main arguments:

1. That the SDGs set out globally agreed targets and indicators to which local improvement efforts and progress reporting, initiated by Governments, should align.
2. That the SDGs provide a globally agreed framework of urgently required action, to which local improvement efforts should contribute.

The first expects a governance and monitoring effort to evolve that is implicitly centralised with regard to both structure and accountability. From here it is easy to infer an assumption that the targets are the right ones (and will remain so) and that effort, aligned to them, can be expected to help in the delivery of positive social change. The second recognises the important role that the SDGs have in challenging existing structures of accountability, power and resource allocation. The Goals are a powerful re-evaluation of what matters at a global level and – purely by being so – act to legitimise, enable and model a different type of conversation about what matters locally. Next to these the targets and indicators should be viewed as being flexible, requiring local interpretation in the context of the right governance *environment* created by the SDGs.

We live in a world which is not only hierarchical, but also relational and intricately interconnected (Capra & Luisi, 2014; Luhmann, 2013). It has never been easier to gain insight and analysis into the causes and drivers of social challenges, but effective response is constrained by rigid structures that better serve centralised monitoring than system-wide learning (Klijn & Koppenjan, 2004). Whilst such structures have their place, they are not appropriate for governance of a programme of ambitious and complex social change. Success for the Goals relies instead on collective action which aligns and amplifies the impact delivered through States, communities and individuals. In its turn, collective action requires a shared focus, a sense of urgency, and engagement (UN Sustainable Development Group, 2021). Goal setting is important in inviting participants to the journey, but for change to be sustainable we need to know what's working over time – and that demands an effective measurement framework, concerned with the change that is experienced or recognisable as a result of our actions (Paterson-Young & Hazenberg, 2021). A change in the capacity of wider systems to adapt in pursuit of increasingly better outcomes is as important over the long term as achievement of the targets laid out in the Goals.

If this is true, then what purpose does measurement serve? Is social impact measurement relevant? How can it help? Social impact measurement (social impact being the effect on people and communities that happens as a result of an action or inaction, an activity, project, programme or policy) is an important and well-respected tool. Social impact measurement turns the attention away from activities, towards the outcomes or, causatively, the impact of those activities. Focussing on outcomes (changes arising in the lives of people) demands flexibility in the delivery approach and for visibility of progress in multiple timeframes. This is particularly important in long term programmes in which the context and assumptions morph and flex in ways we cannot preconceive. Social impact measurement places great emphasis on measuring what matters, not simply those things that are easy to measure. In so doing, it resists data for the sake of data and encourages data that is helpful in supporting ongoing decision-making (Clifford et al., 2014).

This chapter reflects on theoretical and research evidence in key fields related to system and societal change and its governance, drawing out those aspects which are critical for the realisation of the SDG ambitions. Our research comprised a literature review and interviews with specialists (listed at the end of this chapter) who bring a variety of perspectives on the subject, covering both the current environment and the present challenges for social impact measurement. Drawing on our interviews we have developed 'case study' examples in two areas of social challenge in the UK. In these we explore the extent to which life at the 'front line' is experiencing and benefitting from the global focus that the SDGs provide. We identify ways in which the SDGs are being hampered in their success and explore how social impact measurement can help to remedy that situation.

4.2 Systems Context for the Goals

The Goals must be understood in their proper context. They are not 17 self-contained areas for action – they are interrelated and are played out within systems. We live in a complex, interconnected world, in which actions and interventions have implications that can be remote in terms of both time and space, and a change in one area has consequences that ripple far and wide (Capra & Luisi, 2014). System behaviours are complex and often uncertain – reacting to multiple influences and feedback. Acceptance of this as a fundamental truth is central to our thinking and allows us to consider implications that would otherwise be ignored (Justesen & Mouritsen, 2011), for example, the fact that information whether presented verbally, in writing or visually, acts to change the recipient's understanding – and consequently their actions. Actor-Network theory considers the active role of a set of measures in a change programme, and how reporting against inappropriate measures can lead unwittingly to high levels of engagement, high levels of confidence that we are 'on track', and reporting that confirms existing strategies, yet ultimately fails to deliver the outcomes that are sought (Brown & Capdevila 1999; Latour, 2005; Law, 2007).

Understanding that systems work in three dimensions simultaneously can help us to grasp this, with Beckford (2021, pp. 24–50) describing the focus of improvement to be a 'trialogue':

1. Manage the present (do things better)
2. Create the future (do better things)
3. Nurture identify (define 'better').

Within this context, the 17 SDGs paint a clear picture of what matters to our collective global identity – what is needed and what is achievable if, collectively, we focus our efforts towards that end. Understanding how to focus those efforts is where social impact measurement comes into play – responding to the 'creating the future' sphere of attention in Beckford's (2021) trialogue. A well-constructed social impact measurement Framework, designed around assumptions or theories of change, set in a systems context, and adhering to the EU's GECES standards

(Clifford et al., 2014) should enable us to understand our change efforts in multiple dimensions:

- Whether they are working
- How and why they are working
- How quickly they are working
- What other effects they are having in the wider system.

Such a framework can also allow a feedback loop to inform the continual improvement of systems.

4.3 Making It All Possible: Vision, Mobilisation, Legitimisation

The SDGs provide a banner under which individual nations can mobilise in response to the challenge (United Nations, 2015; UN Sustainable Development Goals, 2021). They articulate a vision, but the framework does not provide templates or advice as to how organisations should respond. Responsibility for setting policy direction lies fairly and squarely with governments, and it is they who report back on progress and share details of good practice and successes. Governments are only part of the story and their contribution includes developing policy and regulatory changes that enable better outcomes.

To understand how best to enable change requires ongoing dialogue with those at the 'front line' of change delivery. The enormity of the task at hand and the interconnected nature of our world mean that all parts of society must get involved – local and regional authorities, businesses (from social enterprises through to international corporations), financial markets and investors, and grass roots neighbourhood, community and volunteer groups. This may be counter-intuitive in a country which has become used to governance led by New Public Management philosophies, under which Government sets the agenda, then delegates and distributes responsibility, resource and funding in support of it (Hood, 1991; Ferlie et al., 1996). In stark contrast is the need to mobilise

Table 4.1 Five conditions for collective impact (Kania & Kramer, 2011)

Effective collective impact **requires:**
1. A common agenda: All participants share a vision for social change that includes a common understanding of both the problem to be solved and the approach to be taken in solving it.
2. A shared measurement system: Agreement on the ways success will be measured and reported with key indicators by all participants.
3. Mutually reinforcing activities: The activities of all players, across multiple sectors should be coordinated and mutually reinforcing.
4. Continuous communication: Communication needs to be frequent and to happen across and between participants in order to build and strengthen trust, to encourage ongoing learning and improvement.
5. An independent backbone organisation: Ongoing support and leadership.

contributions, ideas and solutions from multiple contributors under a model of collective impact (Kania & Kramer, 2011). Kania and Kramer (2011) argue that five conditions need to be met in order to create collective impact (see Table 4.1).

The SDGs effectively provide the first of these – the common agenda – and perhaps a model for the second, but their contribution is limited in the other areas.

If collective impact is necessary, then who makes up that collective and who coordinates it? Figure 4.1 illustrates the process of centrally-led goal setting and delivery as it might be thought to work. The SDGs, agreed by participating governments, represent a clarity of vision that demands responses from individual country governments. They work with their citizens, businesses and communities to establish what can collectively be achieved (mission). That in turn enables a collective setting of priorities, a development of enablers – resources, supporting activities, research and similar – and funding lines appropriately focused from public sources, and private sector funds. Priorities, enablers and funding combine to support delivery against the goals and measurement and reporting flow back up. This reflects the flow of Needs to Measurement as anticipated in social impact measurement (Clifford et al., 2014).

Mintzberg (2015 pp. 23–46) exposes the error of relying on establishment and formal organisations to deliver or direct lasting social change. Pointing to the multiplicity of voluntary, community and informal groups that play pivotal roles in our society, Mintzberg (2015) demonstrates that,

Fig. 4.1 A centralised view of SDG delivery

for sustainable change, the wider population and businesses of all types must engage and not just rely on elected governments to solve problems on our behalf. Each needs to engage with impact in both mind and action, in all spheres of life, to understand our role and responsibility in delivering the desired outcomes. Above all, we need to want it to happen – sustainable change relies on a critical mass of public engagement.

Existence outside of traditional governance structures confers another important role on the SDGs – that of legitimising a social and environmental focus, ambitious goal-setting and alignment of activities to deliver them. This is important because existing activities – trusted and proven by those delivering or benefitting from them – often remain unrecognised by mainstream policy and commissioning structures. The SDGs offer an alternative legitimate framework with which to align, and around which to coordinate, collaborate and co-develop solutions. With systems working simultaneously on the three aspects of Beckford's (2021) trialogue, it follows that measurement systems should do the same. Social impact measurement must recognise different outcomes at different levels, time frames and geographies and benefit from multiple narratives. All three levels need a measurement framework, but not necessarily the same one. With respect to the SDGs, social impact measurement also needs to support effective communication – to provide information that will serve to retain (or regain) focus, to encourage continued participation and to share stories about what works and why.

4.4 Delivering Against the SDGs: What Are We Seeing?

In our research interviews we explored the experience of experts working in the field. Rather than action coalescing around a set of shared goals and a mindset of collective impact, those experts spoke about a disjointed system, fraught with uncertainty, broken links and miscommunication. Four areas of concern are fragmented governance models, non-aligned activities and resources, strategies and communication. We discuss each of these below.

4.4.1 Fragmented Governance Models

We might seek the smooth transfer of responsibility to actors in a position to create change, galvanised by missions and meaningful goals. Instead, we see well-intentioned activity compromised by outdated decision-making frameworks combined with poor communication that lacks a compelling narrative and effective feedback loops. There is a wide gap between local knowledge about what works and prescribed targets (top-down governance). Governments and local authorities have proudly 'signed up' to the Goals, but many have not yet started the journey of internal behaviour change to support that commitment.

Misunderstandings about the need to draw direct links between local and global targets have given rise to 'cottage industries' of data collection and aggregation that tell us little more than we already know. Targets like 'make cities and human settlements inclusive, safe, resilient and sustainable' (UN

Sustainable Development Goals 2021, Goal 11 – Sustainable cities and communities), encompass an ambition which is hard to challenge. They make sense to most people and reflect the kind of society that most of us want to see, but how will it help simply to cascade down a target?

Charities working with vulnerable people tell us that whether an individual's problem has been addressed depends very much on which measure is chosen to identify, categorise and address that problem, and measures are often aligned to Governmental budgets, so fail to tell the story of inequality or harm. Both governance and measurement of delivery are undermined by (i) a lack of common understanding of what we want to measure, and (ii) the fact that we are neither measuring nor governing systems change, which is required if we are to fully address the problem.

There are pockets of good practice, certainly. One local authority to which we spoke has accepted that to 'sign up' to the SDGs entails more than simply displaying logos and commitments on official websites and that commitment means change. SDG champions in that authority are updating the fundamental criteria involved in everyday decision-making. Cases for future investment require not just a business case, but also a climate case – a dual threshold that sets environmental capital on a level with economic concerns and over time will rightly shift the focus accountability.

4.4.2 Non-aligned Activities and Resources

Central governments are too remote from individual experience to understand the nuances of local or neighbourhood need. Yet they have direct influence primarily on infrastructure, funding and other enablers. Local groups – of all types – are often better placed to develop solutions that will work locally. Structural challenges can include procedures and frameworks that, being entrenched, are viewed as immutable – for example, a budget allocation or financing system may have become too inflexible to cope with innovative solutions to complex social challenges, but remain unchallenged. Mutually reinforcing actions at different scales and in different timescales build over time into collective impact, and communication is a vital ingredient if efforts are to align. Making change sustainable draws on principles from Nudge theory – the theory that people can be encouraged to make the 'best' choice by making that choice an easier one to take (Thaler & Sunstein, 2008) and collective impact – changed behaviour will only 'stick' if its supporting infrastructure – social, cultural, financial and physical – encourage that new behaviour more strongly than the old one (Raven, 1992).

4.4.3 Strategies for Change Tend Towards the Linear

Too often linear strategies are developed that are loaded with unspoken assumptions about cause and effect. Often, the easiest strategy is to change the structure – even when the required change is a behavioural one. Structural or process changes may be safe havens that are easy to recognise and monitor, whilst providing an illusion of meaningful change. Experts in the field point out that the smallest changes in behaviour can make a far bigger difference. We must properly understand the systemic causes of the effects witnessed. It is common to see measurement systems that track outputs (points of delivery of products or services designed to help) rather than monitoring social or environmental impact. In that sense our governance theory has failed to keep up with management science – it is stuck in the deterministic shadow of traditional analytical thinking which does not serve the problem well.

Case Study: Working with Survivors of Domestic Abuse and Violence

Charities supporting survivors of domestic abuse and working in the complex area of VAWG (violence against women and girls*) have a deep understanding of the needs of the people they support and how those are rooted in their social situation and helped or hindered by the wider systems context. Their support is built in a psychosocial framework, embracing the complexity of the needs and responses of the people with whom they work. Research interviewees tell us that these charities have developed measurement frameworks that embrace that complexity and emerge from their delivery landscape.*

Funded in part by philanthropy, they are nevertheless substantially reliant on income from government and other public agency contracts. Depending on the source of the funds, social impact measurement *requirements are shaped by government targets (often without local context), local priorities or those of the funder. Government ones tend to be cost- or output-based, rarely aligned to the systems context, the psychosocial reality, or indeed the*

(continued)

(continued)

better-informed measurement frameworks of the delivery organisations. Many of them focus on supposed efficiency of response (How much of the 'problem' do we address? How quickly are women moved on from refuge? How many are we turning away?). In practice, delivery organisations are forced to spend time on both sets of measures.

A further problem arises in the way services are commissioned by Government, with an apparent preference for large-scale contracts catering to groups assumed to have homogenous needs, while smaller, highly specialised organisations, struggle to compete for resources. From this perspective, the bid evaluation *criteria may be as poorly nuanced and inappropriate to local need as the preferred* social impact measurement *frameworks. We risk the wrong services being commissioned, leaving the real human targets missed (NAO* 2019*;* Blake & Villeneuve-Smith, 2016*). The identity of Criminal Justice agencies as the main commissioners also brings problems, tending towards a philosophy of dealing with perpetrators and reported incidents of abuse, rather than prevention, trauma-informed approaches and strengths-based recovery (*Home Office, 2020*).*

The related SDG targets (outlined below) are focused on prevalence of need – at headline level, reflecting the systemic and psychosocial experience of front-line delivery – but to delve more deeply reveals a disconnected picture. We encounter large-scale metrics that misrepresent the nature of the problem and its solution because the full range of views that are needed to paint the full picture are not effectively drawn together. Support charities know about the survivors; police know about reported incidents; schools and social workers know about children at risk. Each of these views is partial and isolated.

A government's focus, reflecting the SDGs, may be on demonstrating a fall in prevalence, but even this may lead to inappropriate resource allocation. Two SDG indicators that relate to VAWG demonstrate this (UN Sustainable Development Goals, 2021*):*

- *Indicator 5.2.1 (Proportion of ... women and girls ... subjected to ... violence by a current or former intimate partner in the previous 12 months...). The incentive implied here, to reduce the number of cases, can only provide a partial picture as many go unreported.*
- *Indicator 16.1.3 (Proportion of population subjected to (a) physical.., (b) psychological.. and (c) sexual violence..) makes no mention of coercive or economic control that are prominent factors in many cases of domestic abuse (*Women's Aid, 2019*;* Stark and Hester, 2019*; CPS, 2017;* Citizens Advice, 2014*).*

Successful reduction in prevalence under those targets does not necessarily mean that domestic abuse is reducing.

4.4.4 Insufficient Focus on Communication and Engagement

Mintzberg (2015) outlines the need for pluralistic, collaborative action, drawing together governments, business and society, and expresses a need for emergent and responsive strategies, enabling everyone to play their part in addressing problems in which all are complicit. Such thinking is gaining traction elsewhere, including in the work of the Future of the Corporation initiative, which defines the overall purpose of business as "Profitably solving the problems of people and planet, and not profiting from creating problems" (British Academy, 2019, p. 8). The threshold of public acceptance when it comes to commercial activity has, it seems, been reset at a level where that activity must not adversely impact people, society or the natural world and doing well in one sphere does not justify an abdication of responsibility elsewhere.

Indeed, the narrative is starting to change perceptions about what success looks like and this shared understanding of 'good' is helping funders in the form of the investment community to play their part in effecting social change. Armed with the emerging standards for 'ESG' (Environmental, Social and Governance) reporting, investors and consumers can be confident that they are actively supporting positive impact and not inadvertently condoning harm (van Niekerk, 2020).

Communication is an important element in the success of change programmes like SDGs, which required a narrative that is – and remains – compelling. The power of the visual presentation of the SDGs is notable, with the logos and symbols used as a form of communication – acting as indicators of engagement by whoever is using them, regardless of what is being said or reported. This semiotic use of symbols places the conversation in a recognisable sphere where the narrative is already known and acknowledged, and full attention can be paid to the question at hand or the progress being reported. It also confers on the narrative the stability and tangibility of a legitimate discussion framework that is orthogonal to the traditional governance hierarchy (Culler, 1975).

The symbols and Goal icons act as gateways to communication, but to manage progress we need to draw from a different toolkit – that of measurement and reporting. Measurement may jar with the human need for storytelling but done well it is a powerful agent for change in its own right and grounds the story in a basis of 'fact'. Actor-network theory (Justesen & Mouritsen, 2011; Latour, 2005) explains how the very act of measuring, recording and communicating measurement serves to change the narrative. It is simply not possible to read (or listen to) measurement-based progress reports without updating one's view of the situation. For this reason, it is critical that the measures being communicated are the right ones.

Figure 4.2 illustrates an alternative to the centrally-driven process of goal delivery in Fig. 4.1. This model is suggested by the networked delivery of social change (Klijn & Koppenjan, 2004; Justesen & Mouritsen, 2011; Kania & Kramer, 2011) and recognises the need for collective action to deliver social and environmental change within the broad arenas laid out in the SDGs. We see groups of key actors taking action,

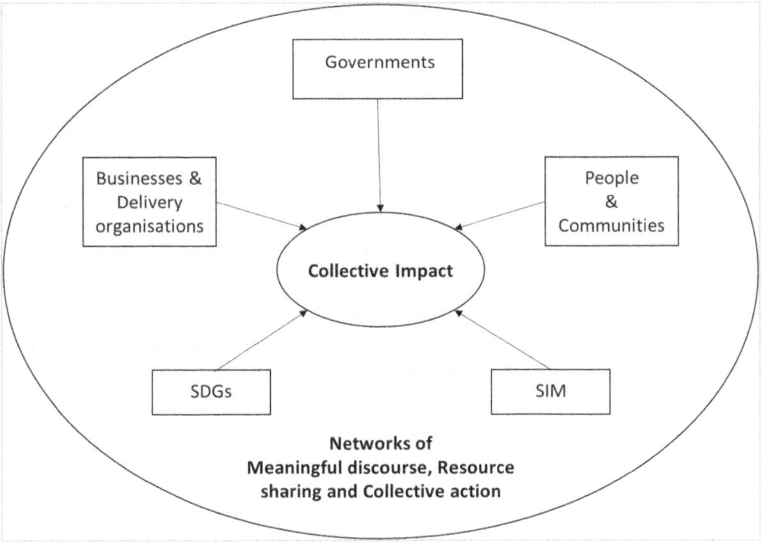

Fig. 4.2 A systems view of SDG delivery

bringing resources and insight, all focused on collective impact. This is a shared objective that is owned by all but with none taking priority over the others. The actors do not necessarily coordinate with others in their sector – they exist in a wider space of networks of meaningful discourse, resource sharing and collective action. Note that the actors include human and human organisations as well as the SDGs themselves, and social impact measurement working within those networks, communicating and influencing, stimulating and informing choices, and changing and developing activity within the networks towards (or away from) the desired collective impact.

With social impact measurement focused firmly on the collective impact and talking to many and various parties in the network it faces a challenge if it is to remain relevant and helpful (in accordance with the GECES requirements in Table 4.3) as outlined in Table 4.2 and be the "shared measurement system" needed (Table 4.1). It can no longer be simply a means of reporting back as confirmation of what has been delivered in a hierarchical relationship with government and funders as in Fig. 4.1.

Table 4.2 Requirements of a well-constructed social impact measurement framework

Aspect of change efforts to be tested	Requirements of measurement framework
Whether they are working	Reflect and work within systems context
	Be based in front-line metrics relevant to people's conditions
	Adapt and keep pace with outcome priorities
How and why they are working	Align funder and delivery organisation metrics
	Test assumptions surrounding cause and effect
	Measure alignment of understanding
How quickly they are working	Work within timeframes that can respond to changes in environment
	Measure changes in system flows, such as resources or commissioning behaviours
	Measure observable changes in real lives
What other effects they are having (wider system)	Understand and move with the system
	Establish a robust theory of change
	Monitor effects on critical success factors or enablers
	Enable a holistic narrative of change

Case Study: Homelessness and Affordable Housing

Another complex area of social inequality is that of housing – or more importantly the lack of suitable housing. Homelessness is a very visible problem even in affluent areas, but the sheer number of those who do not have homes, and the complexity underlying the issue is seldom grasped by policy and government targets (Fitzpatrick et al., 2019; Shelter, 2020, 2019). Local authorities understand the needs of their communities well and recognise the tangled web of cause and effect that leads to individuals losing their homes, but policies and funded approaches to address these contributory factors are often decided at regional or national level – and in part are aimed at reducing prevalence in those aspects of the homelessness phenomenon that can readily be counted.

The 'Everyone In' policy, which housed the UK's homeless in vacant hotel rooms at the start of the Covid-19 pandemic is one such example. Hailed as a success, it nevertheless masks systemic problems, not least that many homeless people are not on the streets – they are unsuitably and often dangerously housed in temporary accommodation (Davies, 2016; Rowland & McCoy, 2020; Boobis & Albanese, 2020). Many others are completely hidden from view, flitting from sofa to sofa (Coombs & Gray, 2020; Sanders et al., 2019; Clarke, 2016). To truly understand the impact of such a scheme in tackling homelessness, we would need to follow the lives of those people who were 'brought in' over the longer term. Where do they end up in 6 months' time...or after a year...or 5? The short-term 'fix' masks the complex and systemic nature of the underlying problem.

Government policy on housing is designed to address an underlying deficit in available housing, which is one key critical factor underpinning a reduction in homelessness. Actual provision and take-up of affordable homes measured alongside the homelessness prevalence figure would tell a more rounded story. What we are seeing instead is the supply of additional affordable homes – by local authorities working with housing associations, with even that definition of affordability not consistently reflecting whether people can afford to live there – being used as a measure of success.

Alongside that government focus, the social housing sector is coming together with institutional funders interested in both the social impact and the stable financial returns from housing. They are developing impact measurement from a collective delivery viewpoint, and using it not just to inform their alignment, but also their discourse with government. The social impact measurement underpinning this increasingly recognises the complexity of the problem, and the systemic nature of the solutions, whilst including the cost-based measurement which resonates with traditional HM Treasury views.

(continued)

(continued)

The SDG indicator (UN Sustainable Development Goals 2021, *11.1.1 – Proportion of urban population living in slums, informal settlements or inadequate housing) is a blunt instrument associated with homelessness. To be useful it needs to relate to the enabling infrastructure that allows that proportion to be reduced. Here we are not talking just about the physical infrastructure of affordable homes, but also the eligibility criteria, the processes of allocation,* definitions *of affordability, measures to identify and help families at risk of being made homeless, policies that would make private sector housing provision safer and more secure, and so on.*

Homelessness *is a particularly clear example of why action to achieve the Goal must be understood at a local system level, since every area has its own challenges according to demographic and social needs, availability of jobs and housing stock availability. Only by understanding what is making the difference locally can we measure and monitor the extent of that positive difference, to challenge the centralised assumptions about what measurements matter, and to channel funding and other resources to the right places.*

4.5 Closing the Gap: How Can Social Impact Measurement Help?

With so much relying on measurement it is evident that measurement should be good. Here, 'good' does not necessarily mean well-formed, complete or consolidated. All those things are desirable, but not essential. More important is the utility of the measurement as described in the GECES characteristics (see Table 4.3, from Clifford et al., 2014). It is worth considering, specifically, what measurement can do for the SDGs and to reflect on the four requirements of a well-constructed social impact measurement framework in Sect 4.1 above.

The SDGs imply a theory of change (a description of how desired outcomes can be delivered by planned activities), but do not overtly express it in a way that enables truly aligned collective impact. Assumptions lying behind the theory are not voiced, so not openly acknowledged or tested by those with alternative perspectives on the challenge. Creating a narrative of change that is *framed* by the Goals, but *formed* to resonate with what matters locally, would enable us both to recognise and celebrate when our actions have contributed to the improvement of people's lives and planetary wellbeing in some tangible way.

Table 4.3 Characteristics of good measurement (Clifford et al., 2014, p. 33)

A good social impact measure should be:
Relevant – related to and arising from the outcomes it is measuring
Helpful – in meeting the needs of the of the stakeholders, both internal and external
Simple – both in how the measurement is made and in how it is presented
Natural – arising from the normal flow of activity to outcome
Certain – both in how it is derived and how it is presented
Understood and accepted – by all relevant stakeholders
Transparent and well-explained – so that the method by which the measurement is made and how that relates to the services and outcomes concerned are clear
Founded on evidence – so that it can be tested, validated and form the grounds for continuous improvement.

On the question of system flows such as finance, social impact measurement can contribute to a more holistic understanding of progress. Funders at all levels are looking for clues to guide impactful investments and a number of frameworks are emerging:

- In some sectors (such as social housing), sophisticated market-based or thematic reporting standards are being developed from the bottom up
- In others, ESG reporting is embracing impact but is not aligned to core impact delivery
- International initiatives, such as the SDG Impact initiative (UNDP, 2021) or IRIS+ from the GIIN (2021) are formulating structured blueprints (or 'standards') to help investors recognise an SDG-aligned business.

A social impact measurement approach could add a more agile and timely glimpse into how impact is being delivered in close to real time.

Relevant and helpful measurement needs to derive from the stories of front-line delivery and be meaningful in support of that delivery. If efforts to deliver the Goals are not optimised, this is partly due to misplaced efforts to aggregate and align measures that cannot meaningfully be aggregated and are not helpful even when we do manage to do so. Consequences arising from this desire to draw linear relationships within a system-based approach include a duality of reporting requirements stemming simultaneously from 'top down' Goals cascading through policy and governance frameworks and local 'bottom up' or needs-based priorities existing alongside, but not meeting up with, global Goals. Furthermore, with many of the SDGs having a significant focus on developing world contexts, social impact measurement that does not recognise the actions of 'Tier 1' economies in promoting or disadvantaging progress in those countries falls short of what is required. Finally, in some sectors external funders or investors add yet a third measurement overhead, in direct contrast to the best practice outlined in the GECES social impact measurement standards (see Table 4.3).

In the SDG delivery landscape, measurement and progress reports tell a fragmented story. They are a patchwork of progress against a plan and trends in prevalence, but they do not yet reflect well whether the figures reported are what we expect and hope them to be, nor whether apparent success in one area is driving deficit elsewhere as systems flex and evolve. Neither do they make any assertion about what is possible within the time and resource constraints. Moving towards a social impact measurement framework that is co-produced can help to address this, providing both a more rounded view of the challenge itself and a common language to lubricate ongoing dialogue about how to address it. Measurement and reporting needs not only to reflect deterministic actions and progress towards predicted outcomes in the short term but must also provide a broader aggregated view of systems change. This could be helped by mission-oriented approaches towards coordinating and democratising contributions and enabling co-production of solutions that work. Whatever the approach it is clear that there is currently very little in the way of an independent coordinating 'backbone' as prescribed by collective impact theory (Kania & Kramer, 2011).

Mission-oriented approaches (MOISS, 2019) and well-constructed social impact measurement frameworks both point towards another weakness in current practice – the lack of good storytellers. Humans respond to stories – particularly stories that spark a degree of empathy or recognition. Stories told well are also remembered and serve as networks to connect diverse activities and actors. They:

- Render the task achievable by painting a compelling vision and path towards it

- Socialise stories of early adopters who show that change is possible
- Have emotional appeal, useful in emphasising proximity of the problem and urgency of the response.

Finally, we have seen that a coordinated response is necessary and that a platform to coordinate that response is key. Co-created measurement frameworks can motivate through reporting and celebrating success and can help steer ambitions into successful responses. Mintzberg (2015) goes further, insisting that coordination platforms must also allow us to collaborate – across sectoral, geographical and organisational boundaries. If change is to be sustainable, we should make use of co-created social impact measurement frameworks to help us communicate and to challenge governance structures and behavioural norms that may be working to actively exacerbate the problem, albeit unintentionally.

4.6 Is Measurement Key?

We started by seeing the SDGs as a set of ambitions that represent a better world, in which 'no one is left behind', – providing goals to be delivered by 2030. We considered two main arguments:

1. That the SDGs set out globally agreed targets and indicators to which local improvement efforts and progress reporting initiated by Governments should align.
2. That the SDGs provide a globally agreed framework of urgently required action, to which local improvement efforts should contribute.

Our conclusion is that they do both, and neither.

The SDGs certainly offer focus to Governments, bringing legitimacy to the pursuit of ambitious goals, unconstrained by traditional beliefs of what is possible or worthwhile. Their presentation as a collection of coloured blocks and symbols is at once engaging, and an over-simplification of what is needed to deliver them. They bring recognition to an agenda of topics, but risk downplaying those not explicitly included. Delivering these Goals is far from simple. They require tackling problems that are deeply rooted in complex human and social systems and environments, and that manifest themselves differently in different local contexts. They require collective action by all involved in those systems, demanding not just the common agenda that the SDGs offer, but translation of that agenda into local settings, the cohesion and communication of a well-led and properly resourced network, and a shared measurement system.

Social impact measurement is key and its influence is as complex as the settings and changes it describes. The act of planning and compiling measurement and sharing it with others in the collective impact space, draws together and further influences the views of change deliverers, funders, and all those involved. These effects arise, not just through what the measurement says, but from awareness of its existence, from the stories that underpin it, from the experience of measurement, and from the discourse –listening, exploring, challenging and learning – that it stimulates. Yet, social impact measurement cannot do this alone, particularly if it is undermined by governance, funding and public commissioning approaches that compromise both measurement and the delivery of change itself. It is compromised by:

1. Top-down objectives-setting and metrics trapped in cost- and output-measurement models
2. A lack of funding and wider resourcing of meaningful measurement
3. A lack of systemic understanding by funders and commissioners, and incomplete systems views of those at the delivery end
4. Funders and commissioners failing to listen to the wisdom from the front line.

If these can be addressed, social impact measurement can take its full place in driving collective effort towards the SDGs within multiple local contexts. In doing so it must:

- Focus not just on how we measure outcomes at delivery level, but also how we measure meaningfully the changes in systems that are needed
- Embrace the complexity and multiple viewpoints in its underpinning Theory of Change – it has to emerge from the front line of collective impact delivery
- Speak clearly to all those involved, embracing different viewpoints and ways of engaging

- Work positively and flexibly such that emergent strategies for delivery are reflected in emergent social impact measurement frameworks and metrics.

As to whether social impact measurement can deliver in time – perhaps it can if it is allowed to do so. Only time will tell.

List of Interviewees

Dr Charles Alessi	Chief Clinical Officer (International), Healthcare Information and Management Systems Society, Inc. (HIMSS), and Senior Advisor, Public Health England
Daniela Barone Soares	CEO, Snowball IM, and formerly CEO at Impetus Trust
Peter Denton	CEO, The Hyde Group
Joy Doal	CEO, Anawim Women Working Together
Philipp Essl	Senior Social Impact Director, Big Society Capital
Amanda Feldman	Engagement Lead, SDG Impact at the United Nations Development Programme, and formerly Co-Founder and Director at the Impact Management Project
Nick Grayson	Climate Change and Sustainability Manager, Birmingham City Council and Senior Research Fellow, University of Birmingham
Lois Guthrie	Director, Redefining Value at World Business Council for Sustainable Development, and Founding Director and Special Advisor to the Climate Disclosure Standards Board
Lucy Hadley	Head of Policy and Campaigns, Women's Aid Federation of England
Prof. Lisa Hehenberger	Assistant Professor, Department of Strategy and General Management, ESADE University, and Director ESADE Entrepreneurship Institute; Strategic Advisor to European Venture Philanthropy Association, and member of European Commission GECES
Susan Hickey	Chair, Sustainable Reporting Standards group for Social Housing, Group Investment Officer for Igloo Group, Former CFO, Peabody
Prof. Colin Mayer CBE	Professorial Fellow in Management Studies, Saïd Business School, University of Oxford, and leader of the British Academy's review of the Future of the Corporation
Polly Neate CBE	Chief Executive at Shelter, formerly Chief Executive at Women's Aid Federation of England
James Noble	Associate Director, Data and Learning, New Philanthropy Capital (NPC)
Laura Seebohm	Executive Director Innovation and Policy, Changing Lives
Anna Shiel	Head of Origination, Big Society Capital
Justin Travlos	Global Head of Responsible Investment, AXA Investment Managers

References

Beckford, J. (2021). *The Intelligent Nation. How to Organise a Country* (pp. 24–50). Routledge.

Blake, J., & Villeneuve-Smith, F. (2016). *The Art of the Possible in Public Procurement*. E3M Publications. Social Business International. https://e3m.org.uk/the-art-of-the-possible-in-public-procurement/. Accessed 21 Feb 2021.

Boobis, S., & Albanese, F. (2020). *The Impact of COVID-19 on People Facing Homelessness and Service Provision Across Great Britain*. Crisis.

Brown, S., & Capdevila, R. (1999). Actor Network Theory and After. In J. Law & J. Hassard (Eds.), *Perpetuum Mobile: Substance, Force, and the Sociology of Translation* (pp. 26–50). Blackwell.

Capra, F., & Luisi, P. (2014). *The Systems View of Life: A Unifying Vision*. CUP. Chapters 14 and 17 (pp. 297–321 and 362–393).

Citizens Advice. (2014). *Controlling Money, Controlling Lives: Financial Abuse in Britain*. Citizens Advice. https://www.citizensadvice.org.uk/Global/Migrated_Documents/corporate/controlling-money-controlling-lives%2D%2D1-.pdf. Accessed 21 Feb 2021.

Clarke, A. (2016). The Prevalence of Rough Sleeping and Sofa Surfing Amongst Young People in the UK. *Social Inclusion, 4*, 60–72.

Clifford, J., Hehenberger, L., & Fantini, M. (2014). *Proposed Approaches to Social Impact Measurement in European Commission Legislation and in Practice Relating to EuSEFs and the EaSI*. GECES (Groupe d'experts de la Commission sur l'entrepreneuriat social) Sub-Group on Impact Measurement. European Commission. Ref pbKE0414665.

Coombs, J., & Gray, T. (2020). *Lessons Learnt from Councils' Response to Rough Sleeping During eth COVID-19 Pandemic*. LGA. https://www.local.gov.uk/lessons-learnt-councils-response-rough-sleeping-during-covid-19-pandemic. Accessed 21 Feb 2021.

Crown Prosecution Service. (2017). *Controlling or Coercive Behaviour in an Intimate or Family Relationship: Legal Guidance*. Domestic Abuse. https://www.cps.gov.uk/legal-guidance/controlling-or-coercive-behaviour-intimate-or-family-relationship. Accessed 21 Feb 2021.

Culler, J. (1975). *Structuralist Poetics. Structuralism, Linguistics and the Study of Literature* (p. 131). Routledge/Kegan Paul.

Davies, B. (2016). In Filthy, Dangerous Accommodation, Britain's Hidden Homeless Are Suffering. *The Guardian*. https://www.theguardian.com/housing-network/2016/jan/20/britain-hidden-homeless-temporary-accommodation-ippr. Accessed 21 Feb 2021.

Ferlie, E., Ashburner, L., Fitzgerald, L., & Pettigrew, A. (1996). *The New Public Management in Action*. OUP. pp. 10ff.

Fitzpatrick, S., Pawson, H., Bramley, G., Wood, J., Watts, B., Stephens, M., & Blenkinsopp, J. (2019). *The Homelessness Monitor: England 2019*. Crisis.

GIIN. (2021). *IRIS+: An Impact Measurement and Management System*. https://iris.thegiin.org/. Accessed 21 Feb 2021.

Home Office. (2020). *Domestic Abuse Bill 2020: Overarching Factsheet*. https://www.gov.uk/government/publications/domestic-abuse-bill-2020-factsheets/domestic-abuse-bill-2020-overarching-factsheet. Accessed 21 Feb 2021.

Hood, C. (1991). A Public Management for All Seasons? *Public Administration, 69*(1), 3–19.

Justesen, L., & Mouritsen, J. (2011). Effects of Actor-Network Theory in Accounting Research. *Accounting, Auditing and Accountability Journal, 24*(2), 161–193.

Kania, J., & Kramer, M. (2011). Collective Impact. *Stanford Social Innovation Review*, (Winter), 36–41.

Klijn, E.-H., & Koppenjan, J. (2000). Public Management and Policy Networks: Foundations of a Network Approach to Governance. *Public Management, 2*(2), 135–158.

Klijn, E.-H., & Koppenjan, J. (2004). *Managing Uncertainties in Networks: A Network Approach to Problem Solving and Decision Making* (pp. 9, 160–239). Routledge.

Latour, B. (2005). *Reassembling the Social: An Introduction to Actor-Network Theory* (pp. 4ff and 106ff). OUP.

Law, J. (2007). *Actor Network Theory and Material Semiotics*. Version of 25th April 2007. Available online at: http://www.heterogeneities.net/publications/Law2007ANTandMaterialSemiotics.pdf. Accessed Sept 2020.

Luhmann, N. (2013). *Introduction to Systems Theory* (p. 28ff.). Trans. P. Gilgen & Ed. D. Baecker. Polity.

Mintzberg, H. (2015). *Rebalancing Society: Radical Renewal Beyond Left, Right and Center*. Berrett-Koehler Publishers Inc.

MOISS (Commission for Mission-Oriented Innovation and Industrial Strategy). (2019). *A Mission-Oriented UK Industrial Strategy*. UCL Institute for Innovation and Public Purpose.

National Audit Office. (2019). *Transforming Rehabilitation: Progress Review* (p. 10ff.). London.

Paterson-Young, C., & Hazenberg, R. (2021). Transformative Outcomes. In W. L. Filho, P. Gökçin Özuyar, A. M. Azul, L. L. Brandli, & W. Wall (Eds.), *Encyclopaedia of the UN Sustainable Development Goals: Justice, Peace and Strong Institutions*. Springer.

Raven, B. H. (1992). A Power/Interaction Model of Interpersonal Influence: French and Raven Thirty Years Later. *Journal of Social Behavior and Personality, 7*(2), 217–244.

Rowland, J., & McCoy, S. (2020). *Danger Zones and Stepping Stones: Phase Three.* Depaul UK. https://uk.depaulcharity.org/wp-content/uploads/2020/11/Exec-Summary-Danger-Zones-and-Stepping-Stones-Phase-Three.pdf. Accessed 21 Feb 2021.

Sanders, B., Boobis, S., & Albanese, F. (2019). *'It Was Like a Nightmare' The Reality of Sofa Surfing in Britain Today.* Crisis. https://www.crisis.org.uk/ending-homelessness/homelessness-knowledge-hub/types-of-homelessness/it-was-like-a-nightmare-the-reality-of-sofa-surfing-in-britain-today/. Accessed 21 Feb 2021.

Shelter. (2019). *Strategy 2019–2022.* Section 4. https://england.shelter.org.uk/what_we_do/strategy_2019-2022. Accessed 21 Feb 2021.

Shelter. (2020). *Homeless at School: 56% of Teachers Have Worked with Homeless Children.* https://england.shelter.org.uk/media/press_release/homeless_at_school_56_per_cent_of_teachers_have_worked_with_homeless_children. Accessed 21 Feb 2021.

Stark, E., & Hester, M. (2019). Coercive Control: Update and Review. *Violence Against Women, 25*(1), 81–104. https://doi.org/10.1177/1077801218816191

Thaler, R., & Sunstein, C. (2008). *Nudge: Improving Decisions About Health, Wealth, and Happiness.* Yale University Press.

The British Academy. (2019). *Principles for Purposeful Business. How to Deliver the Framework for the Future of the Corporation. An Agenda for Business in the 2020s and Beyond* (p. P8). The British Academy.

UN Sustainable Development Goals. (2021). *The 17 Goals.* Available online at: https://sdgs.un.org/goals. Accessed on: Jan 2021.

UN Sustainable Development Group. (2021). *Leave No-One Behind.* https://unsdg.un.org/2030-agenda/universal-values/leave-no-one-behind. Accessed Jan 2021.

UNDP. (2021). *SDG Impact: Investment Solutions for Global Impact*. https://sdgimpact.undp.org/. Accessed 21 Feb 2021.

United Nations. (2015). *Transforming Our World: The 2030 Agenda for Sustainable Development*. https://sustainabledevelopment.un.org/post2015/transformingourworld. Accessed 9 May 2020.

van Niekerk, A. (2020). Inclusive Economic Sustainability: SDGs and Global Inequality. *Sustainability Basel, Switzerland, 12*(13), 5427.

Women's Aid. (2019). *The Domestic Abuse Report 2019: The Economics of Abuse*. Women's Aid.

Section II

Agency, Expertise and Partnerships

5

Impact and Gender: Agency and Capability in Empowering Women in Kenya

Linda Odhiambo Hooper

5.1 Gender Equality

Gender equality is key for social change as outlined in the UN Sustainable Development Goals (SDGs) SDG5: Achieve gender equality and empower all women and girls. Without gender equality sustainable development is unrealisable (UN Women, 2018). Measuring the social impact of interventions is key to determining the impact of interventions that aim to contribute to SDGs (Fukuda-Parr & McNeill, 2019). There are toolkits that can be used for social impact measurement which vary depending on the sectors and nature of intervention. An example being the social sector network toolkit specifically designed for SDG impact measurement (Social Sector Network, 2020). Increasingly, evaluation and social impact discourse hinges on transformative outcomes with social issues addressed from the micro (individual), meso (organisational), and macro (societal) levels which both require and extend the

L. O. Hooper (✉)
Ulster University, Ulster, UK
e-mail: Hooper-L@ulster.ac.uk

R. Hazenberg, C. Paterson-Young (eds.), *Social Impact Measurement for a Sustainable Future*, https://doi.org/10.1007/978-3-030-83152-3_5

strengthening of institutions (Paterson-Young & Hazenberg, 2020). The growing complexities and global nature of social problems means that sectors increasingly collaborate with blurred distinctions and hybridity (Nicholls, 2008; Battilana & Dorado, 2010; Billis, 2010). Their global scope means that the SDGs have the power to alter power relations, affect the distribution of resources, create perverse incentives for performance, reorganise national and local priorities, and produce narratives that shape thinking and communication (Fisher & Fukuda-Parr, 2019). These effects were evident in the now superseded Millennium Development Goals (MDGs) where the complexities bred distortions resulting in policy priorities and the framing of discourses based on the power of numbers rather than the actual social implication of interventions. Social impact measurement seeks to demonstrate value, but at the same time, require inputs including resource, research, time and finance, and stakeholder commitments.

Given that social transformation and structural change were key in the departure from the MDGs to SDGs, coupled with the growing global interest in inequality and distribution within and between countries (Stiglitz, 2014; Aaberge & Brandolini, 2015; Atkinson, 2015; Piketty, 2015) gaps based on the use of goals and indicators and inequality begin to emerge. New data reveals that gender-based discrimination, existing across all goals, is pervasive, deeply rooted and present across all countries. Women and girls are still experiencing intersecting forms of discrimination resulting in their marginalisation and exclusion from development. The 2030 Agenda responds to the challenge to live humanely, justly, peacefully and sustainably in an increasingly interconnected globe, with the key vision to "transform the world" and to "leave no one behind" (United Nations, 2015). When it comes to gender, gender inequality data and the lack of trends in gender related data make it difficult to monitor and assess the pace and direction of equality for women and girls. Indeed, it is argued that data is only available for 10 out of 54 gender specific indicators, which would impact the realisation of the goal (Fisher & Fukuda-Parr, 2019) and that the purported data revolution requires acknowledgement of the 'unofficial statistics' to populate the gaps (Macfeely & Nastav, 2019).

Like the MDGs, the SDGs are likely to fail to meet targets unless factors that led to failings in achieving MDGs are taken into account for the success of SDGs (Clemens et al., 2007; Pogge & Sengupta, 2015). The answer lies in concrete efforts to create a bridge from rhetoric to reality on this development consensus by developing tools and frameworks for measuring and reporting impacts. To ascertain progress requires the urgent development of actionable ways to realise data that is useful and serves all sectors and actors, creating a nexus between social impact measurement and SDGs.

Acknowledging social impact as the enhancement of agency and capabilities, this chapter proposes a perspective derived from the analysis of both social innovation and social impact measurement literature, as well as empirical data collected by the author. The former outlines practitioners and scholars' efforts to establish social impact measurement, while the latter offers a path derived from Sen's and Nussbaum's Capability Approach (Sen, 1999; Nussbaum, 2000). The use of the Capability Approach. Capability Approach, with its emphasis on the evaluation of a person's achievements and freedoms rather than resources, is rooted in debates around inequality. This chapter locates gender equality within the developing country context where gender equality is lagging behind (UN Women, 2018).

Given the prevailing backdrop of the neoliberal market economy and the self-sustaining structural and systemic factors that have contributed to global poverty, like the MDGs, the SDGs are unlikely to be the 'best' instruments to address this problem. The SDGs are in tension with human development and the capability approach, the focus of which is delineating the aspects of wellbeing that are difficult to quantify, including, among others: equity, non-discrimination, human agency and participation (Fukuda-Parr & McNeill, 2015; Fukuda-Parr, 2016). The presence of these infer development and are explored in a study conducted on women in low-income areas in Kenya. Assessing the impact of interventions is rendered even more salient as the harmful effects of the Covid-19 pandemic will disproportionately impact women (Alon et al., 2020).

5.2 SDG 5 and the Challenge of Achieving Gender Equality and Empower All Women and Girls

Gender inequality manifests itself in society through socially constructed roles and responsibilities that societies ascribe for men and women (Okeyo, 1981; Butler & Trouble, 1990; Fraser, 1994). The pursuit of gender equality means women and men enjoy the same rights and opportunities across all sectors of society and that the different behaviours, aspirations and needs of women and men are equally valued and favoured. Gender equality is therefore a fundamental human right and the keystone to a prosperous modern economy that provides inclusive and sustainable growth (OECD, 2019). In Kenya for example, 96% of the rural working population are women but only 6% hold titles to land (Bennett, 2006; Oxfam International, 2020). Examples such as these reveal persistent gender inequality, despite the global consensus and efforts for more equity.

Since the UN's inception over 70 years ago, advancing gender equality has been a key goal demonstrated by the establishment of the Commission on the Status of Women. Among these are global bodies dedicated to the promotion of gender equality arising from landmark agreements, such as the Convention on the Elimination of all forms of Discrimination Against Women (CEDAW), the Beijing Declaration (Women, 1995), UN security council's resolution 1325 on Women Peace and Security and the recognition of these persistent inequalities, which led to the establishment of UN Women (UN Women, 2018). UN Women highlights the vital role women and girls play in society and their potential in realising sustainable development. The crucial role of gender equality as a driver of development and the recognition that the potential of women has not been fully realised owing to, inter alia, persistent social, economic and political inequalities, is evident (UN Women, 2018). In Kenya gender equality is a key agenda for Vision 2030, Kenya's key strategic document (Vision, 2., 2007; UN Women, 2018). SDG5 consists of 9 targets and 14 indicators. The case of SDG5 is rendered even more complex with its interrelations with other goals where direct links to goals 1, 3, 5, 8 and

16, while marginal links to goals 2, 10, 11, 13, and 17 with the rest of the goals being gender blind. Therefore, SDG5's interrelations with 10 of the other goals, gender equality accounts for 22% of the total indicators making SDG5 an important and crosscutting goal of agenda 2030 (UN Women, 2018; UNDP, 2018; Elson & Fontana, 2019).

The empowerment of women and girls, including fostering their voice and agency, is fundamental to social and economic development (Okeyo, 1981; Cooke & Kothari, 2001; Bradshaw, 2008). This includes establishing their sense of self-worth, decision-making power, access to opportunities and resources, capacity to exercise power and control over one's own life inside and outside the home as well as one's ability to effect change (Razavi & Miller, 1995; Nussbaum, 2000; Kabeer, 2005). According to UN Women, in Kenya as in many countries, women still suffer from the lack of decent work, occupational segregation and wage gaps. They are denied health care, education and are often the victims of violence and discrimination (Kimani, 2007; Ali, 2017). They lack voice and representation in political and economic decision making (COVAW, 2021). Kenya records high poverty levels with nearly 40% of the population in absolute poverty (World Bank, 2020). Kenya is also vastly unequal, with statistics revealing that 0.1% (8300) people own more wealth than the 99.9% (44 million) people. Economic growth registered by the World Bank in 2019 at 5.7% has been steady on average been, although steady since 2005, but the gains have failed to trickle down to the poorest (Oxfam, 2021; World Bank, 2021). This is coupled with the general global trends where there is an increase in deprivation for marginalised groups both in industrialised as well as developing countries, while on the other hand, the top end of the population exhibits growing affluence and advantage (Sen, 1999; Oxfam, 2021). Evidence shows that disempowering women has dire negative consequences (Hudson, 2020). Together with the financing and policies for gender, addressing these challenges requires the development of statistical data that can be used to monitor the attainment of equality. This must be coupled with robust ideas on what and how to measure, especially for data that is more challenging to access. With the proliferation of social innovation and the need to assess value and impact, social impact measurement encounters SDG5.

5.2.1 Challenges of Social Impact measurement on Gender Equality and Development

Complex societal problems lead to challenges in the measurement of interventions' impact resulting in data gaps (Millar & Hall, 2013; Hall et al., 2015). As a result, there has been the development of various approaches in social impact measurement that aim to provide a more comprehensive and applicable impact measurement approach. Among the issues encountered in social impact measurement are, on one hand, the conceptual differences and, on the other hand, the practice related challenges. Social impact measurement conceptualisation and terminology have led to an array of terms that are sometimes used interchangeably including social value (Lumpkin et al., 2013) social performance (Mair & Marti, 2006; Nicholls, 2008), social returns (Emerson, 2003), social return on investment (SROI) (Millar & Hall, 2013; Hall et al., 2015) or social accounting (Nicholls, 2010; Nicholls & Ziegler, 2019). The array of terminologies, although similar, possess distinctive constructs. For consistency in the chapter, the term 'social impact', impact or social impact measurement are used interchangeably. Social impact is defined as the beneficial outcomes resulting from prosocial interventions that are enjoyed by the intended targets of that intervention and/or by the broader community of individuals, organisations, and/or environments (Millar & Hall, 2013; Hall et al., 2015). This definition covers the diversity of approaches, the differences in social impact phenomena, differences in target populations and the current and/or future impact. Additionally, it resonates with and creates the space for Capabilities Approach.

On a practical level, social impact measurement is now contributing to SDGs goals and indicators. Among the challenges are data collection and analysis which are disproportionately controlled by rich countries with the exercise of production and role of official statistics carried out with deep seated biases (Merry, 2019; Eden & Wagstaff, 2020) resulting in data gaps (Bartling et al., 2015). Social impact measurement therefore risks being used as a tool that legitimises actions undertaken on behalf of vulnerable people without their involvement or consent. Secondly, difficult to measure indicators are sidestepped by measuring proxies instead or rely on secondary data which results in skewed realities that create confusion and take time to remedy (Rawhouser et al., 2019). Based on FAO (2018) directives on property ownership proxies, it is evident that property ownership has a direct influence on violence against women - a misleading proxy reading would contradict this theory with significant implication for development policy (Agarwal & Bina, 1994; Merry, 2016). Thirdly, social impact measurement focuses a great deal on quantitative methods where gender-based statistics, despite the underlying limitations, are the most common empirical method to assess gender differences for key organisations (Hausmann et al., 2012; Permanyer, 2013). The challenges with the discrepancies in outcomes, which results from differences in the choice of indices, results in a lack of capacity and cumulative insights. Consequently, it will be some years before the various indexes build and share their time series datasets (Eden & Wagstaff, 2020). Quantitative methods are criticised for taking a 'counterfactual' approach therefore a reliance on this hinders aspects such as planning and tackling systematic challenges (Schaffer, 2014). Furthermore, the current data revolution holds the potential to satisfy the need for disaggregated data and would ensure that no one is invisible, important in informing decision makers, but which has not been realised (United Nations, 2015). Measuring impact of interventions requires the implementation of broad crosscutting quantitative approaches in combination with approaches that delineate and disaggregate marginalisation, to provide useful data for better policy making and the realisation of SDGs.

Despite the SDGs more dynamic genesis compared to MDGs, the translations of their broader and aspirational goals into indicators have reduced their transformative significance (Fukuda-Parr Fukuda, 2016). Merry (2019) argues that the turn to indicators in effect defines development narrowly in terms of specific accomplishments rather than as structural change thus restricting the vision of development. Indexes therefore do not capture SDG5 as they fail to capture disempowerment indicators particularly of marginalised groups; it is with these challenges in mind that the Capabilities Approach is applicable.

5.3 Social Innovation and the Capability Approach

Both social innovation (SI) and the Capabilities Approach are progressive approaches to social change hold the view that intentional effort leads to social transformation. Globally there has been a proliferation of social innovation, a situation that is attributed to the growing complexities in depth and interrelations of societal problems (Nicholls & Ziegler, 2019) . Previous sector-based solutions are increasingly blurred through hybridity in their efforts to realise transformative change and alleviate suffering, especially for marginalised groups. Despite the diversity of social innovation definitions, both scholars and practitioners agree on the basic principles and characteristics of social innovation, particularly with regard to its fluidity and diversity - similar to third sector organisations (Nicholls et al., 2015). Parallel to these developments, economists and philosophers led by Nussbaum (2000) and Sen (1999) called for a view from development as merely economic growth, in favour of a focus on human development based on the Capabilities Approach.

Social innovation is defined as the development and delivery of new ideas and solutions (products, services, models, markets, processes) targeted at different socio-structural levels that intentionally seek to change power relations and improve human capabilities, as well as the processes by which these solutions are executed (CRESSI, 2018; Baglioni & Sinclair, 2014). Social innovation delivered through social enterprises have been particularly encouraged, as they have the potential to be responsive, efficient and cost-effective with double or triple 'bottom-lines'. They combine environmental and social aims with trading thus promising innovative service delivery (Dart, 2004; Teasdale, 2012; Ayob et al., 2016). The multitude of approaches to service delivery means that social impact needs to be demonstrated to ensure access to resources, legitimacy and organisational development (Nicholls & Murdock, 2012; Clifford et al., 2013). All these aspects must be considered, whilst retaining underlying frameworks and principles of the organisation and interventions.

Behind the Capabilities Approach is the move from the focus on economics, goods and services to the focus on what one actually does with the goods and services, meaning a move away from 'commodity fetishism' (Ziegler, 2018). With contributions from Sen (1999) and Nussbaum (2000), as well as a growing multidisciplinary research community, an approach that focusses on opportunities and freedoms that people can access and enjoy forms the core of Capabilities Approach (Sen, 1999; Nussbaum, 2000; Robeyns, 2003; Alkire & Deneulin, 2009). The Capabilities Approach takes into account and attempts to accomodate the ends rather than the means and reveals a diversity of people and a diversity of goals. Each person is treated as an end and not as an aggregate. With a focus on functioning, the beings and doings of a person, capability is seen as the freedom of a person to enjoy various functionings that they value and have a reason to value. This relies on the conversion factors which is their capacity to convert resources into functioning. A focus on agency, which is the ability of a person to pursue the goals they value and have reason to value, calls for involvement so that people are not just passive recipients. Capabilities and functionings are best thought of as plurals, as the reduction of a single measure of welfare has implications on the ends and diversity. Diversity also means that treating people as equal and as ends does not mean treating them the same. Their personal differences and social contexts need to be considered. The Capabilities Approach promotes an increase in focus on functionings such as schooling or life expectancy as the basis for policy in a country, policy or project. The Capabilities Approach has played a great role in conceptualising and influencing the measurement of poverty and inequality including the human development index (Sen, 1992a, 1992b; Unterhalter, 2005), synthesising data on education, health and standards of living. This data contributes to the evaluation and improvement of policy. Functionings are the common metrics to measure, as capability freedom is more complex requiring a multidisciplinary effort.

The Capabilities Approach provides a framework that enables an analysis of problematic areas of social impact measurement such as measuring gender inequality. To illustrate the use of Capabilities Approach in social impact measurement, the next section uses findings based on results from interviews and focus groups with female participants living in low-income areas in Kenya who have been beneficiaries of social innovation. In establishing social innovation, the potential for the realisation of UN SDG5 by improving capabilities of all women and girls, provides insights into how Capabilities Approach contributes to social impact measurement. Providing a greater understanding of inequality, the Capabilities Approach exposes disadvantage as opposed to the traditional concern with poverty (Milanovic, 2011; Bourguignon, 2017; Burchardt & Hick, 2018). The nature of poverty is gendered as outlined in previous sections thus targeted approaches are needed to enable the push out of the poverty trap especially for women and girls (Orloff, 1993; Kabeer et al., 2013; Muhibbu-Din, 2017; Patel, 2019). This is illustrated later in the chapter in a study which evaluates interventions in slum areas in Kenya, which sought to establish the impact of social innovation in areas where (i) welfare provision was non-existent, (ii) the extent to which social innovation transformed their lives and (iii) their perceptions of social innovation interventions. The Capabilities Approach is put forward not as alternative to social impact measurement but as a practical solution to implementing social impact measurement in areas with data scarcity due to invisibility.

5.3.1 Capabilities Approach and Social innovation in Kenya

In Kenya, welfare provision is influenced by global, international, national, grassroots down to the family/household level factors (Gough, 2013). Over 50% of Kenyans are living below the poverty line (Ojiambo et al., 2015; Wamuchiru, 2015; World Bank, 2018). Neoliberal policies introduced as Structural Adjustment Programmes in the 1980's decimated any emergent welfare programmes (Stiglitz & Ocampo, 2008; Amaeshi & Idemudia, 2015). The result is a weak state that Wood and Gough's (2006) welfare regime analysis locates as an 'informal security regime', consistent with having poor outcomes in socio-cultural conditions, institutional performance and welfare provision (Wood & Gough, 2006). Social policy in the development context has been inhibited due to a focus on welfare state models and past historical development agendas for developing countries (Mkandawire, 2011; Stiglitz, 2014; Midgley et al., 2019). The uncertainty in the global economy and a withdrawal from neoliberalism frames debates, resulting in concepts such as social investment and inclusive growth that encourage inclusion and cohesion (Deeming & Smyth, 2017). The idea of development is problematic leading some scholars to suggest alternative socio-political ideas (Harvey, 2007; Lewis, 2014; Emas, 2015; Ncube, 2015; Deeming & Smyth, 2017; Hemerijck, 2018), shun exogenous participatory processes, and advocate for indigenous innovation and local intelligence (Matthews, 2017; Gumede, 2018). Africa possesses context specific issues including lack of credible data, heterogeneity, fragmented ecosystems, talent, infrastructure and financing, all of which affect the implementation and impact of social innovation (Nwuneli, 2016). This affects costs and distribution thus impacting on the scaling and diffusion of social innovation which brings back the argument for public goods and how to best deliver (Ravallion & Chen, 2003; Mkandawire, 2005; Rawls, 2009; Nwuneli, 2016). Gender equality is still an unrealised goal (Chant, 2008; Sepúlveda Carmona & Donald, 2014; Cornwall & Rivas, 2015). Kenyan women are more likely to be in poverty (in comparison to men), lag in decision-making power, are susceptible to domestic violence, provide unrecognised and unpaid labour, have unfavourable enrolment and attainment in education and earn less income than men (Geda et al., 2001; UN Women, 2018; Jagoe et al., 2020). It is under this backdrop that social innovation is gaining popularity. The rise in poverty and inequality requires that social innovation be critically analysed to ensure that welfare provision results in well-being and capabilities, especially as the inclusivity of women is at the core of development strategies and policies.

Using data collected from 42 interviews of beneficiaries of social innovation initiatives in slum areas as well as four focus group data, this section demonstrates an alternative impact measurement concept, suitable for the purposes of delineation, disaggregation and thorough scrutiny, which is required especially for disadvantaged groups at the cusp of being left behind. The Capabilities Approach considers the differences in starting points for the individual women, with a common starting point being disadvantage. Their capacity to translate the support provided by social innovation into the impact anticipated by the intervention or goals that they value is varied. Their various human resource endowments, rather than their initial material conditions, determine their levels of success. A key factor that reflects this is the variations in health, skills, experience, education and initiative; in Capabilities Approach terms their *capability set*. Education levels were varied but, in general, low attainment and illiteracy was common. The women were all engaged in various occupations, with small business as the most common occupation.

The study asked the participants to recollect their past. Their lives had been characterised by hunger, inability to educate their families, large debts, humiliation, dependency and insecurity. A broad and quick overview of the data reveals themes which include valued functioning. In a focus group session Achieng explains:

> I was suffering so much that I had to make papyrus mats to get some money. Making these mats is the lowliest work here. In these marshes, one has to get into the water to harvest the papyrus, there are chances of being bitten by poisonous snakes and the water gets right up to the waist.

Among the valued functionings realised is the improved capacity to tap into inter and intra household relationships, including aspects such as better collaboration with their spouses and assistance from the extended family. Jemima says:

> If you find the man doing part of the work and then the woman doing some other work it makes life a lot easier. It matters because a woman has to be sharp and has to use what she can to do and think about tomorrow.

Despite some participants meeting resistance from their spouses in the early days, their partners began, and continue, to support their efforts now given the positive outcomes and this is also coupled with the increased exercise of the voices of women within the household. Most intra family collaborations were supported within households but there were limits as male dominance was reported when it came to access and spending microcredit loans. At this level, the participants often expressed fear and insecurity. The threat of violence dissipated in some cases, with improvement shown over time as the livelihoods of the family improved.

Improved social networks is the second acquired functioning that the participants are able to tap into and that influenced their progress. Finding new ways of tapping into old and new social networks including extended family and local authority as well as broad recognition of women as social and economic agents and knowledge expansion all contributed to this achievement. Christine says:

> the ability to borrow is not dependent on your level of education but by being part of a group. It has enabled women to learn ways to borrow as well as get business ideas.

A third achievement is the ability to save and borrow. The social innovation allowed women, who had no previous experience in saving and were barely subsisting, to, now save and keep records of these savings. The ability to feed the family and to pay for school fees were the most cited improvement especially as nutrition and education streams of saving and borrowing was offered. Francesca's experience:

> I think what has contributed to the success is us women coming together, otherwise it would be difficult to save. When you are saving your own money, it is easy to dip into it when there is a crisis, but with the savings groups you get your lumpsum you do something with it and then you are left with the task of repaying it. You work hard because you know you are in debt.

The fourth is the diversification of livelihood options, with the strengthening and diversification of the household earnings. Diversification of livelihoods can be undetected if indicators failed to locate the possibilities as participant experience learning, partnerships and developed networks over and beyond the programme walls. The considerations of the intersection of factors including religion, tribe, gender also emerge and explicitly inform change as systematic rather than random in the heterogeneity of impacts recorded. For instance, those with previous experience, older and higher education show more success than those with less experience. Self Help Groups (SHG) plays a key role in the empowerment as it enabled loans that enabled investment. Florence says:

> when the fish dries out I try to do other things. As my other business, I am buying party chairs (plastic event chairs) which I rent out for funerals. I will buy 200 of them. I would also like a small motorbike to offer transport to earn extra income.

A fifth set of valued functioning is cognitive change, that women claim to have gained from the advice, training and information built into the project. The women developed new ideas and a way of thinking. The knowledge gained underpins and runs through all the livelihood achievements. Wamboi's account:

> When I was in kikuyu, Lillian the manager and trainer was really nice, she taught us sales tricks and how to proudly display the products and we felt she was very nice she encouraged us to go far. We can use this skill everywhere.

Finally, participants spoke of the personal changes as beneficiaries of the social innovation. Many referred to gaining courage and mental strength, while others cited improved self-confidence. They were more confident in their ability to tackle new activities, to think beyond survival. They are now able to plan for the future and to participate in social life in way that they had not previously though possible. For Shiru:

> The group has been very helpful, now I plan to get a loan for 50,000 shillings which I will put into business. I will get stocked so that by the time my girl goes to college I will have the money.

Despite the generally positive response from the women about the social innovation, this analysis must consider the contextual background and how the various aspects that impact wellbeing is incorporated by the social innovation initiatives. The interventions targeting the socio-structural levels of the slum social innovation impact in the development and delivery of new ideas and solutions is evident from the beneficiaries' responses. In SIs favour, further empirical evidence demonstrates that human capabilities are improved, in terms of functioning, agency and participation. The social innovations, although offering alternative solutions to welfare and livelihoods, were not necessarily realised after a democratic discursive process that would establish that this process was undertaken for the validity of interventions. Although policy prescriptions both local and global, including the SDG5, are in favour of the empowerment of women and girls. The prevailing economic system that disproportionately impact women, in a country characterised by weak laws power relations, are difficult to shift requiring a bigger concerted effort to this end. High and growing poverty levels, the increase in cost of living, informality and with the government cutting welfare spending is enabling social innovation proliferation. There are limitations to the extents to which beneficiaries of the social innovation can realise capabilities both in the long and short term. Nancy's statement summarises this:

> My future plans are not clear, I cannot plan anything as you can see the money that I make and the way it goes. There is not much left to put aside and to save or anything. If you save a little the school fees takes it all, uniforms, health, you name it. One cannot have savings when they have children.

5.4 The Capabilities Approach as a Means for Gender Inclusion

Similar to the MDGs, the SDGs are likely to fail to meet targets unless scholars and practitioners can contribute to the realisation of SDGs by engaging in concrete efforts to create a bridge from rhetoric to reality on this development consensus by developing tools and frameworks for measuring and reporting impacts. This chapter focused on poverty and marginalisation, bringing the voices of women to the forefront. An interrogation of a progressive concept is necessary to ascertain its use in progress. This requires the urgent development of actionable ways to realise data that is useful and serves all sectors and actors creating the nexus between social impact measurement and SDGs. Gender equality is key for social change, as outlined in the literature, and without it equality and therefore sustainable development is unrealisable (UN Women, 2018).

Developing countries under the prevailing backdrop of the neoliberal market economy has allowed gender inequality to manifest itself in society. Despite over 70 years advancing gender equality, inequality continues to persist and with it far-reaching consequences given the interlinkages between SDG goals. The increasing complexity of societal problems have culminated in challenges in both interventions and their measurements. The global interest in inequality, the growing popularity of social innovation in a country with high poverty levels, weak institutions and high levels of informality when it comes to livelihoods means that the challenges in getting data suitable for policy making must seek to be more inclusive and offer opportunities for delineation and disaggregation. This will enable better policy and interventions. The areas that social innovation impact as welfare and livelihood support of effective are established in the experiences and the methods and the increasing applications of Capabilities Approach.

The growing complexities and global nature of social problems means sectors increasingly collaborate with blurred distinctions and hybridity in their means and ends. Areas that require further innovation and input are recognised from the experience of the participants and the omission of what is considered salient and necessary for a valuable life. For this, aspects such as thresholds, basic minimum lists and the democratic discursive ends of the Capabilities Approach can be employed. Despite the SDG's more dynamic genesis, as compared to the MDGs, the translations of their broader and aspirational goals into indicators have reduced their transformative significance. That is why especially for marginalised groups, both social innovation and the Capabilities Approach as progressive approaches to social change hold the view that intentional effort leads to social transformation.

References

Aaberge, R. and Brandolini, A. (2015). Multidimensional Poverty and Inequality. *In:* Anon. Handbook of Income Distribution, 141–216.

Agarwal, B., & Bina, A. (1994). *A Field of one's Own: Gender and Land Rights in South Asia*. Cambridge University Press.

Ali, F. A. (2017). Women's Agency and Violence against Women: The Case of the Coalition on Violence against Women in Kenya. *African Conflict and Peacebuilding Review, 7*(1), 51–65.

Alkire, S., & Deneulin, S. (2009). Introducing the Human Development and Capability Approach. In *An Introduction to the Human Development and Capability Approach*. Earthscan.

Alon, T. M., Doepke, M., Olmstead-Rumsey, J., & Tertilt, M. (2020). *The impact of COVID-19 on gender equality*.

Amaeshi, K., & Idemudia, U. (2015). Africapitalism: A Management Idea for Business in Africa? *Africa Journal of Management, 1*(2), 210.

Atkinson, A. B. (2015). *Inequality: What Can Be Done?* Harvard University Press.

Ayob, N., Teasdale, S., & Fagan, K. (2016). How Social Innovation 'Came to Be': Tracing the Evolution of a Contested Concept. *Journal of Social Policy, 45*(4), 635–653.

Baglioni, S., & Sinclair, S. (2014). Introduction: Social Innovation and Social Policy. *Social Policy and Society, 13*(3), 409–410.

Bartling, B., Weber, R. A., & Yao, L. (2015). Do Markets Erode Social Responsibility? *The Quarterly Journal of Economics, 130*(1), 219–266.

Battilana, J., & Dorado, S. (2010). Building Sustainable Hybrid Organisations: The Case of Commercial Microfinance Organisations. *Academy of Management Journal, 53*(6), 1419–1440.

Bennett, S. (2006). Widening Participation for Women Returners to Learning–Meeting the Challenge through eLearning. In Creighton, Colin and Yieke Felicia (eds.) *Gender Inequalities in Kenya* (p. 61).

Billis, D. (2010). *Hybrid Organisations and the Third Sector: Challenges for Practice, Theory and Policy*. Palgrave Macmillan.

Bourguignon, F. (2017). *The Globalization of Inequality*. Princeton University Press.

Bradshaw, S. (2008). From Structural Adjustment to Social Adjustment: A Gendered Analysis of Conditional Cash Transfer Programmes in Mexico and Nicaragua. *Global Social Policy, 8*(2), 188–207.

Burchardt, T., & Hick, R. (2018). Inequality, advantage and the capability approach. *Journal of Human Development and Capabilities, 19*(1), 38–52.
Butler, J., & Trouble, G. (1990). *Feminism and the Subversion of Identity.* Routledge.
Chant, S. (2008). The 'Feminisation of Poverty' and the 'Feminisation' of Anti-Poverty Programmes: Room for Revision? *The Journal of Development Studies, 44*(2), 165–197.
Clemens, M. A., Kenny, C. J., & Moss, T. J. (2007). The Trouble with the MDGs: Confronting Expectations of Aid and Development Success. *World Development, 35*(5), 735–751.
Clifford, J., Markey, K., & Malpani, N. (2013). Measuring Social Impact in Social Enterprise: The State of Thought and Practice in the UK. *London, E3M*, 1–10.
Cooke, B., & Kothari, U. (2001). *Participation: The New Tyranny?* Zed books.
Cornwall, A., & Rivas, A. (2015). From 'Gender Equality and 'women's Empowerment' to Global Justice: Reclaiming a Transformative Agenda for Gender and Development. *Third World Quarterly, 36*(2), 396–415.
COVAW. (2021). *The Coalition on Violence against Women in Kenya.* Available online at: https://covaw.or.ke/. Accessed 5 Mar 2021.
CRESSI. (2018). *Creating Economic Space for Social Innovation.* CRESSI. Available online at: https://www.sbs.ox.ac.uk/faculty-research/research-projects/creating-economic-space-social-innovation-cressi. Accessed 15 June 2018.
Dart, R. (2004). The Legitimacy of Social Enterprise. *Nonprofit Management & Leadership, 14*(4), 411–424.
Deeming, C., & Smyth, P. (2017). *Reframing Global Social Policy: Social Investment for Sustainable and Inclusive Growth.* Policy Press.
Eden, L., & Wagstaff, M. F. (2020). Evidence-Based Policymaking and the Wicked Problem of SDG 5 Gender Equality. *Journal of International Business Policy,* 1–30. https://doi.org/10.1057/s42214-020-00054-w [Epub ahead of print].
Elson, D., & Fontana, M. (2019). Conceptualizing Gender-Equitable Inclusive Growth. In Anon (ed.) *Gender Equality and Inclusive Growth.* New York: United Nations, 20–45.
Emas, R. (2015). *The Concept of Sustainable Development: Definition and Defining Principles.* Florida International University.
Emerson, J. (2003). The Blended Value Proposition: Integrating Social and Financial Returns. *California Management Review, 45*(4), 35–51.
FAO. (2018). *Realizing Women's Rights to Land in the Law.* United Nations.

Fisher, A., & Fukuda-Parr, S. (2019). Introduction—Data, Knowledge, Politics and Localizing the SDGs. *Journal of Human Development and Capabilities, 20*(4), 375–385.
Fraser, N. (1994). After the Family Wage: Gender Equity and the Welfare State. *Political Theory, 22*(4), 591–618.
Fukuda-Parr, S. (2016). From the Millennium Development Goals to the Sustainable Development Goals: Shifts in Purpose, Concept, and Politics of Global Goal Setting for Development. *Gender and Development, 24*(1), 43–52.
Fukuda-Parr, S., & McNeill, D. (2015). Post 2015: A New Era of Accountability? *Journal of Global Ethics, 11*(1), 10–17.
Fukuda-Parr, S., & McNeill, D. (2019). Knowledge and Politics in Setting and Measuring the SDG S: Introduction to Special Issue. *Global Policy, 10*, 5–15.
Geda, A., De Jong, N., Mwabu, G., & Kimenyi, M. (2001). Determinants of Poverty in Kenya: A Household Level Analysis. *ISS Working Paper Series/ General Series, 347*, 1–20.
Gough, I. (2013). Social Policy Regimes in the Developing World. In Anon (ed.) *A Handbook of Comparative Social Policy*, 2nd ed. (p. 205–224). Cheltenham UK: Edward Elgar Publishing.
Gumede, V. (2018). Social policy for inclusive development in Africa. *Third World Quarterly, 39*(1), 122–139.
Hall, M., Millo, Y., & Barman, E. (2015). Who and What Really Counts? Stakeholder Prioritization and Accounting for Social Value. *Journal of Management Studies, 52*(7), 907–934.
Harvey, D. (2007). *A Brief History of Neoliberalism*. Oxford University Press.
Hausmann, R., Tyson, L. D., Bekhouche, Y., & Zahidi, S. (2012). The Global Gender Gap Index 2012. *The Global Gender Gap Report, 2012*, 3–27.
Hemerijck, A. (2018). Taking Social Investment Seriously in Developed Economies. *In:* Anon. *Reframing Global Social Policy.* 1st Ed. , 45–76.
Hudson, V. M. (2020). *The First Political Order: How Sex Shapes Governance and National Security Worldwide*. Columbia University Press.
Jagoe, K., Rossanese, M., Charron, D., Rouse, J., Waweru, F., Waruguru, M., Delapena, S., Piedrahita, R., Livingston, K., & Ipe, J. (2020). Sharing the Burden: Shifts in Family Time Use, Agency and Gender Dynamics after Introduction of New Cookstoves in Rural Kenya. *Energy Research and Social Science, 64*, 101413.
Kabeer, N. (2005). Gender Equality and Women's Empowerment: A Critical Analysis of the Third Millennium Development Goal 1. *Gender and Development, 13*(1), 13–24.

Kabeer, N., Milward, K., & Sudarshan, R. (2013). *Organizing Women Workers in the Informal Economy: Beyond the Weapons of the Weak*. Zed Books Ltd..
Kimani, M. (2007). Taking on Violence against Women in Africa. *Africa Renewal, 21*(2), 4–7.
Lewis, D. (2014). *Non-governmental Organisations, Management and Development*. Routledge.
Lumpkin, G. T., Moss, T. W., Gras, D. M., Kato, S., & Amezcua, A. S. (2013). Entrepreneurial Processes in Social Contexts: How Are They Different, If At All? *Small Business Economics, 40*(3), 761–783.
MacFeely, S., & Nastav, B. (2019). "You say you want a [data] revolution": A proposal to use unofficial statistics for the SDG Global Indicator Framework. *Statistical Journal of the IAOS, 35*(3), 309–327.
Mair, J., & Marti, I. (2006). Social Entrepreneurship Research: A Source of Explanation, Prediction, and Delight. *Journal of World Business, 41*(1), 36–44.
Matthews, J. R. (2017). Understanding Indigenous Innovation in Rural West Africa: Challenges to Diffusion of Innovations Theory and Current Social Innovation Practice. *Journal of Human Development and Capabilities, 18*(2), 223–238.
Merry, S. E. (2016). *The Seductions of Quantification: Measuring Human Rights, Gender Violence, and Sex Trafficking*. University of Chicago Press.
Merry, S. E. (2019). The Sustainable Development Goals Confront the Infrastructure of Measurement. *Global Policy, 10*, 146–148.
Midgley, J., Surender, R. and Alfers, L. (2019). Introduction to the Handbook of Social Policy and Development. In*:* Anon. *Handbook of Social Policy and Development.* ,
Milanovic, B. (2011). *Worlds Apart: Measuring International and Global Inequality*. Princeton University Press.
Millar, R., & Hall, K. (2013). Social Return on Investment (SROI) and Performance Measurement: The Opportunities and Barriers for Social Enterprises in Health and Social Care. *Public Management Review, 15*(6), 923–941.
Mkandawire, T. (2005). Targeting and Universalism in Poverty Reduction. .
Mkandawire, T. (2011). Running while Others Walk: Knowledge and the Challenge of Africa's Development. *African Development, 36*(2), 1–36.
Muhibbu-Din, M. O. (2017). Gender Justice and Women Empowerment in Africa: A Critical Perspective of Post MDGs. *Journal of Gender, Information and Development in Africa, 6*(1/2), 95–116.

Ncube, M. (2015). Inclusive Growth in Africa. In Monga, Célestin and Lin, Justin Yifu (eds.) *The Oxford Handbook of Africa and Economics: Volume 1: Context and Concepts* (p. 831). Oxford: OUP Oxford.

Nicholls, A. (2008). Social Entrepreneurship: New Models of Sustainable Social Change. .

Nicholls, A. (2010). The Legitimacy of Social Entrepreneurship: Reflexive Isomorphism in a Pre-Paradigmatic Field. *Entrepreneurship Theory and Practice, 34*(4), 611–633.

Nicholls, A. and Murdock, A. (2012). The Nature of Social Innovation. Anon. *Social Innovation.* Springer, 1–30.

Nicholls, A., et al. (2015). *New frontiers in social innovation research.* Springer.

Nicholls, A., & Ziegler, R. (2019). *Creating Economic Space for Social Innovation.* Oxford University Press.

Nussbaum, M. (2000). *Women and Human Development: The Capabilities Approach.* Cambridge University Press.

Nwuneli, N. O. (2016). *Social Innovation in Africa: A Practical Guide for Scaling Impact.* Routledge.

OECD. (2019). *OECD Yearbook 2017.* Available online at: https://www.oecd-ilibrary.org/content/publication/g2g7e25f-en

Ojiambo, E., Oduor, J., Mburu, T., & Wawire, N. (2015). *Aid Unpredictability and Economic Growth in Kenya* (African Development Bank, Working Paper, (226)).

Okeyo, A. P. (1981). Reflections on Development Myths. *Africa Report, 26*(2), 7.

Orloff, A. S. (1993). Gender and the Social Rights of Citizenship: The Comparative Analysis of Gender Relations and Welfare States. *American Sociological Review, 58*(3), 303.

Oxfam. (2021). *Kenya: Extreme Inequality in Numbers.* Available online at: https://www.oxfam.org/en/kenya-extreme-inequality-numbers. Accessed 5 Mar 2020.

Oxfam International. (2020). *Time to Care: Unpaid and Underpaid Care Work and the Global Inequality Crisis.* Oxfam International. Available online at: https://search.informit.org/documentSummary;res=APO;dn=273436

Patel, L. (2019). Gender: Toward Gender Equality and Poverty Reduction. *:* Anon. *Handbook of Social Policy and Development.*

Paterson-Young, C. and Hazenberg, R. (2020). Transformative Outcomes: The Use of Social Impact Measurement. In*:* Anon. *Encyclopaedia of the UN Sustainable Development Goals. Peace, Justice and Strong Institutions.*

Permanyer, I. (2013). A Critical Assessment of the UNDP's Gender Inequality Index. *Feminist Economics, 19*(2), 1–32.

Piketty, T. (2015). About Capital in the Twenty-First Century. *American Economic Review, 105*(5), 48–53.

Pogge, T., & Sengupta, M. (2015). The Sustainable Development Goals: A Plan for Building a Better World? *Journal of Global Ethics, 11*(1), 56–64.

Ravallion, M., & Chen, S. (2003). Measuring pro-Poor Growth. *Economics Letters, 78*(1), 93–99.

Rawhouser, H., Cummings, M., & Newbert, S. L. (2019). Social Impact Measurement: Current Approaches and Future Directions for Social Entrepreneurship Research. *Entrepreneurship Theory and Practice, 43*(1), 82–115.

Rawls, J. (2009). *A Theory of Justice: Revised Edition.* Harvard university press.

Razavi, S. and Miller, C. (1995). From WID to GAD: Conceptual Shifts in the Women and Development Discourse. .

Robeyns, I. (2003). Sen's Capability Approach and Gender Inequality: Selecting Relevant Capabilities. *Feminist Economics, 9*(2–3), 61–92.

Sen, A. (1992a). *Inequality Re-Examined.* Oxford University Press.

Sen, A. (1992b). Missing Women. *BMJ* (Clinical Research ed.), *304* (6827), 587–588.

Sen, A. (1999). *Development as Freedom.* Oxford University Press.

Sepúlveda Carmona, M., & Donald, K. (2014). What Does Care Have to Do with Human Rights? Analysing the Impact on women's Rights and Gender Equality. *Gender and Development, 22*(3), 441–457.

Social Sector Network. (2020). *SDG Impact Measurement and Reporting.* Available from: https://socialsectornetwork.com/sdg-impact-measurement-and-reporting/. Accessed 5 Mar 2021.

Stiglitz, J. E. (2014). *Inequality Is Holding Back the Recovery.* Columbia University. Available from: https://explore.openaire.eu/search/publication?articleId=datacite____::330ef1ed8c4c1b709ee2ea9d3e92e992

Stiglitz, J. E., & Ocampo, J. A. (2008). *Capital Market Liberalization and Development.* Oxford University Press on Demand.

Teasdale, S. (2012). What's in a Name? Making Sense of Social Enterprise Discourses. *Public Policy and Administration, 27*(2), 99–119.

UN Women. (2018). Turning Promises into Action. *Gender equality in the, 2030*

UNDP. (2018). *UNPD Kenya Country Programme Document (CPD) 2018 to 2022.* UNDP.

United Nations. (2015). Global Sustainable Development Report.

Unterhalter, E. (2005). Global Inequality, Capabilities, Social Justice: The Millennium Development Goal for Gender Equality in Education. *International Journal of Educational Development, 25*(2), 111–122.

Vision, 2. (2007). Vision 2030 . *A Globally Competitive and Prosperous Kenya.* https://www.opendatagoke/download/jih3-amby/application/pdf.

Wamuchiru, E. (2015). Social Innovation: The Bio-Centre Approach to Water and Sanitation Infrastructure Provision in Nairobi's Informal Settlement, Kenya. In *RC21 International Conference on "the Ideal City: Between Myth and Reality. Representations, Policies, Contradictions and Challenges for tomorrow's Urban Life" Urbino.* Italy.

Wood, & Gough, I. (2006). *A Comparative Welfare Regime Approach to Global Social Policy.* Available from: http://www.sciencedirect.com/science/article/pii/S0305750X06001124

Women, U.N. (1995). Beijing Declaration and Platform for Action-Beijing 5 Political Declaration and Outcome.

World Bank. (2018). *World Development Report 2000/2001: Attacking Poverty.* World Bank. Available Online at: http://documents.worldbank.org/curated/en/230351468332946759/World-development-report-2000-2001-attacking-poverty. Accessed 8 Aug 2018.

World Bank. (2020). Kenya Economic Update: COVID-19 Erodes Progress in Poverty Reduction in Kenya. *Increases Number of Poor Citizens.* Available online at: https://www.worldbank.org/en/country/kenya/publication/kenya-economic-update-covid-19-erodes-progress-in-poverty-reduction-in-kenya-increases-number-of-poor-citizens. Accessed 5 Mar 2021.

World Bank. (2021). *The World Bank in Kenya.* Available Online at: https://www.worldbank.org/en/country/kenya/overview. Accessed 5 Mar 2021.

Ziegler, R. (2018). Social Innovation and the Capability Approach. *Atlas of Social Innovation: New Practices for a better Future.* TU Dortmund University, 37–40.

6

Competing Discourses of Impact Measurement: Insights from the Field of Impact Investment

Jarrod Ormiston

6.1 Impact and Investors

Impact investors define and differentiate themselves by their focus on achieving measurable social impact (Höchstädter & Scheck, 2015; Ormiston et al., 2015). Indeed, impact measurement has been pushed by impact investors as a core part of their identity and essential to how they make their investment decisions (Hazenberg et al., 2014; Hehenberger et al., 2019). However, most research on impact measurement is focused on how investees organisations such as social enterprises and non-profit organisations enact impact measurement (often in response to the demands of funders and investors) (Ormiston, 2019; Rawhouser et al., 2019). To overcome this focus on investees, this chapter explores how and why impact investors engage in impact measurement practices. In doing so, the chapter responds to calls to focus on the ways in which investors report and measure impact (Ebrahim & Rangan, 2014).

J. Ormiston (✉)
Maastricht University, Maastricht, The Netherlands
e-mail: j.ormiston@maastrichtuniversity.nl

R. Hazenberg, C. Paterson-Young (eds.), *Social Impact Measurement for a Sustainable Future*, https://doi.org/10.1007/978-3-030-83152-3_6

Prior reviews of impact measurement highlight a wide range of purposes and rationales for engaging in the practice including accounting, marketing, strategising, decision-making, and learning (Maas & Liket, 2011; Ormiston, 2019; Ormiston & Castellas, 2019; Rawhouser et al., 2019; Kah & Akenroye, 2020). There is limited research however on the interaction between these multiple, potentially conflicting, rationales, and how they coexist in practice (see for exception André et al., 2018; Jäger & Rothe, 2013; and Liket et al., 2014). This chapter aims to explore the extent to which impact investors draw on these diverse rationales in framing their impact measurement practices. It uses discourse analysis to understand how and why do impact investors measure social impact. Discourse analysis focuses on the ways in which text and language shape the social world (Fairclough, 2013). Through the lens of discourse analysis, the chapter examines the ways in which impact investment funds explain the rationale for their impact measurement practices on their websites, in the description of the impact measurement frameworks, and in their annual reports and impact reports. It zooms in on 50 impact investment funds in the United Kingdom. The analysis examines the different ways in which the impact investment funds spoke about measuring: (i) their own impact internally, (ii) measuring their impact on their investees, and (iii) measuring the impact of their investees on the wider community. The seven main discourses on impact measurement as: (i) legitimacy, (ii) decision-making, (iii) identity; (iv) reflection; (v) learning, (vi) dialogue; and (vii) a response to grand challenges. These diverse discourses highlight the need for organisations to appreciate the multidisciplinary nature of impact measurement as they strive to create social, environmental, cultural and economic impact.

6.2 Diverse Rationales of Impact Measurement

Prior reviews of impact measurement practice highlight a wide range of purposes and rationales for engaging in the practice (Maas & Liket, 2011; Ormiston, 2019; Ormiston & Castellas, 2019; Rawhouser et al., 2019;

Kah & Akenroye, 2020). These reviews suggest that impact measurement is simultaneously used as a tool for a range of organisational activities such as accounting, marketing, strategising, decision-making, and learning (Ormiston, 2019). The following sub-sections briefly review these diverse purposes and rationales of impact measurement, paying particular attention to prior research on the how funders and investors enact impact measurement and reporting practices.

6.2.1 Impact Measurement, Accountability, and Legitimacy

One of the main drivers of impact measurement practices is the desire for funders and investors to hold their investees accountable (Molecke & Pinkse, 2017). Studies exploring impact measurement in relationships between funders and social sector organisations have predominantly focused on the role of philanthropists, foundations, government, and impact investors in driving the measurement of outcomes and impact to ensure accountability (Hwang & Powell, 2009; Grimes, 2010; Nicholls, 2010; Thomson, 2010; Benjamin, 2012; Liket et al., 2014; Lee & Nowell, 2015). These studies highlight the role of impact measurement as a practice for ensuring transparency to funders and as a means for funders and investors to exert control over investee organisations. Through the lens of accountability and control, funders and investors often impose a mix of uniform and bespoke approaches being employed across funder portfolios (Grimes, 2010; Thomson, 2010; Ruff & Olsen, 2018). Hayes and Westrup (2012) have highlighted the dangers of these top-down approaches to impact measurement, suggesting that they may compromise possibilities for social innovation by focusing on a narrow set of funder-determined metrics.

Viewing impact measurement as a tool for accountability highlights its role in legitimising organisational actions. Nicholls (2009) highlights how through this lens, impact measurement acts as a boundary object to provide legitimacy for organisations. For example, Garcia-Meca and Martinez-Ferrero (2021) have found that many organisations engage in SDG reporting as symbolic practice that aims to achieve legitimacy by responding to stakeholder pressure. Similarly, Jäger and Rothe (2013) explored the importance of strategic accountability in ensuring public trust and legitimacy for their organisational actions. Sareen and Haarstad (2020) eloquently capture this relationship between accountability and legitimacy by explaining how holding an organisation to account serves to validate the actions of that organisation, which in turn lends legitimacy to those actions.

6.2.2 Impact Measurement, Strategising and Decision-Making

Impact measurement is increasingly viewed as a management tool for purpose driven organisations to enhance their impact (Nicholls, 2009). The role of impact measurement as a method for strategising and decision-making alongside accountability is highlighted by the Impact Management Project (IMP) in their definition of impact measurement: *"Measuring and managing the process of creating social and environmental impact in order to maximize and optimize it."* Ormiston and Castellas (2019) provide a review of the wide range of ways in which impact is used as a measurement, highlighting the ways in which organisations utilise impact measurement to: develop strategy (Nicholls, 2009; Mouchamps, 2014); enhance their impact (Benjamin & Misra, 2006; Campbell et al., 2012; Ebrahim & Rangan, 2014; Liket et al., 2014); and make decisions (Bagnoli & Megali, 2009; Nicholls, 2010; Antadze & Westley, 2012; Liket et al., 2014; Willems et al., 2014). In the context of funding and investment, Benjamin and Misra (2006) studied how impact measurement shaped the management practices of a set of US funders, including foundations and intermediary funders. They found that impact measurement was predominantly used as a strategic tool that created a space for a strategic conversation around collective goals with grantees, thereby ensuring the refinement of program direction for both funders and grantees.

6.2.3 Impact Measurement and Organisational Learning

One of the cited benefits of impact measurement is organisational learning (Barraket & Yousefpour, 2013; Newcomer et al., 2013; Arvidson & Lyon, 2014; Liket et al., 2014). For example, Sawhill and Williamson (2001) in their study of 30 US nonprofits, revealed that impact measurement was perceived as useful for learning and improving outcomes when measures were mission-aligned, simple and communicable. However, many studies of impact measurement have questioned the potential contribution of impact measurement to organisational learning. Barraket and Yousefpour (2013) found no evidence that organisational learning was used to pursue mission-related goals, finding rather that impact measurement was predominantly employed to appease funders and attract external funding support. Gasper (2000) drew a similar conclusion in a review of logical frameworks, noting that the overt focus on intentional actions and effects encouraged a problematic prioritisation of audit over learning, in which unintended benefits were not valued or incorporated into future decision-making. Mayhew (2012) neatly captured the conflict between enhancing impact and promoting accountability, showing that failure was discouraged in the latter, which, when excluded, detracted from the potential for learning and program improvement. To overcome these challenges, Newcomer et al. (2013) explored the challenges of ensuring organisational learning as an outcome of impact measurement for Non-Government Organisations in the development context, suggesting the importance of "reverse accountability" whereby funders should design impact assessment approaches that strategically and intentionally affect the learning behaviours of grantees.

6.2.4 Impact Measurement and Stakeholder Dialogue

The impact measurement literature has also highlighted the importance of impact measurement in creating a space for dialogue with a wide range of organisational stakeholders. Engaging a broad range of stakeholders in impact measurement has been shown to deliver benefits for designing appropriate actions (Liket et al., 2014), minimising required resources and time (Smith & Stevens, 2010), and avoiding mission drift (Ramus & Vaccaro, 2017). Jäger and Rothe (2013) highlight the importance of beneficiary voice in impact measurement, arguing that despite the dominant focus on accountability to donors, increased beneficiary-focused data leads to better negotiations around accountability with donors. The importance of genuinely engaging clients and beneficiaries in impact measurement has been consistently underscored in the nonprofit literature (Benjamin, 2012). The nonprofit literature has also voiced frontline employees' dissatisfaction with impact measurement, particularly frustration with the heavy focus on monitoring how staff implement programs rather than how programs benefit the community (Carman, 2007; Hwang & Powell, 2009; Benjamin, 2012). This short review highlights the diversity of rationales and benefits for engaging in impact measurement. To examine the rationale for impact measurement forwarded by impact investors, the chapter now outlines the critical discourse analysis methodology.

6.3 Critical Discourse Analysis

This study utilises discourse analysis to explore the diverse rationales of impact investors engaging in impact measurement. Discourse analysis focuses on the way's language is used to frame organisational activities and how this reproduces power dynamics (Fairclough, 2013). The focus on power and language is relevant to our focus on impact investors considering prior research which suggests that investors shape and impose impact measurement practices on investee organisations (GIIN 2020; Ormiston, 2019). For example, the growing practice of investors reporting against the SDGs, and requiring SDG reporting from investees, can be viewed as an example of the top-down imposition of metrics. The aim of the discourse analysis was to explore the differing ways that individual impact investment funds explained their rationale for impact measurement and how this differed between different funds.

6.3.1 Case Selection

The United Kingdom was chosen as the site for this research as it has been identified as one of the global leaders in impact investment (Calderini et al., 2018). A decision was made to focus on impact investment funds (the asset managers) rather than the underlying investors (asset owners), as these intermediary funds are directly engaged with investees and are the main site of impact measurement practice in impact investment relationships. The Good Finance database[1] was used to identify the impact investment funds. Good Finance's mission is to assist social enterprises and charities in understanding and accessing information on impact investment in United Kingdom. It provides the most comprehensive listing of impact investors in the United Kingdom, with a list of 50 impact investment funds. All 50 impact investment funds were included in the study. Table 6.1 shows the name of each impact investment fund, the date it was founded, the impact measurement practices stated on their websites or in their reports, and the documents accessed for the analysis.

6.3.2 Data Collection and Analysis

As highlighted in Table 6.1, the following documents were analysed for each of the 50 impact investment funds: (i) website pages related to mission, values, investment approach impact, outcomes, portfolio; (ii) annual reports; (iii) impact reports; (iv) impact measurement frameworks; (v) case studies on investees (both written and video). Data analysis focused on critically exploring the ways in which the impact investment funds were justifying and explaining their use of impact measurement practices in the websites and reports. The analysis also paid attention to the subject of the impact measurement, attempting to explore the different ways in which the impact investment funds spoke about measuring: (i) their own impact internally, (ii) measuring the impact of their investees, and (iii) measuring the impact of the investees on the wider community. The documents were inductively coded to identify the

[1] https://www.goodfinance.org.uk/investors-advisors

Table 6.1 Impact investment funds, measurement approaches, documents analysed

Fund	Date founded	Stated impact measurement approaches	Documents analysed
Allia C&C	1999	Qualitative case studies on investees, bespoke metrics (e.g. dollars lent, enterprises supported, jobs created)	Website, case studies of investees
ART Business Loans	1997	Qualitative case studies on investees, bespoke metrics (e.g. dollars lent, enterprises supported, jobs created)	Website, case studies of investees, 2020 annual report
Bank Workers Charity	1883	Qualitative case studies on investees, bespoke metrics (e.g. dollars lent, enterprises supported, jobs created)	Website, case studies of investees
BCRS Business Loans	2002	Qualitative case studies on investees, bespoke metrics (e.g. dollars lent, enterprises supported, jobs created)	Website, case studies of investees
Bethnal Green Ventures	2012	Impact management Project (IMP), SDGS, certified B Corp (B impact assessment), qualitative case studies on investees, bespoke metrics (e.g. dollars lent, enterprises supported, jobs created)	Website, 2019 impact report, 2018 impact report, 2017 impact report
Big Issue Invest	2005	Theory of change, investee survey, DEI survey, SDGs, big Society capital outcomes, qualitative case studies on investees, bespoke metrics (e.g. dollars lent, enterprises supported, jobs created)	Website, case studies of investees, 2020 impact report
Bridges Fund Management	2002	SDGs, qualitative case studies on investees, bespoke metrics (e.g. dollars lent, enterprises supported, jobs created)	Website, case studies of investees, 2019/2020 annual report

(continued)

Table 6.1 (continued)

Fund	Date founded	Stated impact measurement approaches	Documents analysed
Bristol City Funds	2019	Theory of change, SGDS, one City framework, post-drawdown surveys, bespoke KPIs, qualitative case studies on investees, bespoke metrics (e.g. dollars lent, enterprises supported, jobs created)	Website, case studies of investees, theory of change documents, 2020 impact report
Business Enterprise Fund	2004	SDGs, qualitative case studies on investees, bespoke metrics (e.g. dollars lent, enterprises supported, jobs created)	Website, case studies of investees, 2019/2020 impact report
CAF Venturesome	2002	SDGs, qualitative case studies on investees, bespoke metrics (e.g. dollars lent, enterprises supported, jobs created)	Website, case studies of investees, 2018 impact report
CAN Invest	1998	Theory of change, muesli tool, qualitative case studies on investees, bespoke metrics (e.g. dollars lent, enterprises supported, jobs created)	Website, case studies of investees, Impact approach
Charity Bank	2002	SDGs, BSC metrics, certified B Corp (B Impact assessment), qualitative case studies on investees, bespoke metrics (e.g. dollars lent, enterprises supported, jobs created)	Website, case studies of investees, 2020 impact report
City Bridge Trust	1995	Better reporting initiative, qualitative case studies on investees, dollars lent, enterprises supported	Website, case studies of investees, Impact and learning strategy
Co-op Foundation	2015	Qualitative case studies on investees, bespoke metrics (e.g. dollars lent, enterprises supported, jobs created)	Website, case studies of investees, 2020 impact report

(*continued*)

Table 6.1 (continued)

Fund	Date founded	Stated impact measurement approaches	Documents analysed
Community Impact **Partnership CIC**	2018	No information on impact on website as rethinking approach	Website
Community Shares Scotland	2014	Qualitative case studies on investees, bespoke metrics (e.g. dollars lent, enterprises supported, jobs created)	Website, case studies of investees
Devon Community Foundation	1996	Qualitative case studies on investees, bespoke metrics (e.g. dollars lent, enterprises supported, jobs created)	Website, case studies of investees, 2017 annual review,
Ecology Building Society	1981	SDGs, carbon footprint, global greenhouse gas accounting and reporting standard, qualitative case studies on investees, bespoke metrics (e.g. dollars lent, enterprises supported, jobs created)	Website, case studies of investees, 2020 annual report, 2019 annual report
Esmee Fairbairn Foundation	1961	Qualitative case studies on investees, bespoke metrics (e.g. dollars lent, enterprises supported, jobs created)	Website, case studies of investees, 2019 annual report, 2018 insight report
Ethex	2013	Qualitative case studies on investees, bespoke metrics (e.g. dollars lent, enterprises supported, jobs created)	Website, case studies of investees
Fair by Design	2018	Bespoke commissioned research, qualitative case studies on investees, bespoke metrics (e.g. dollars lent, enterprises supported, jobs created)	Website, case studies of investees
Finance for Enterprise	1985	Qualitative case studies on investees, bespoke metrics (e.g. dollars lent, enterprises supported, jobs created)	Website, case studies of investees, 2020 impact report

(continued)

Table 6.1 (continued)

Fund	Date founded	Stated impact measurement approaches	Documents analysed
First Enterprise	1989	Qualitative case studies on investees, bespoke metrics (e.g. dollars lent, enterprises supported, jobs created)	Website, case studies of investees
Loans for Enlightened Agriculture Programme ("LEAP")	2019	Bespoke impact toolkit, qualitative case studies on investees, dollars lent, enterprises supported	Website, case studies of investees, Impact toolkit report
Impact **Ventures** UK	2013	Bespoke metrics (e.g. dollars lent, enterprises supported, jobs created)	Website
Joseph Rowntree Foundation	2015	Bespoke metrics (e.g. dollars lent, enterprises supported, jobs created)	Website
Kent Community Foundation	2001	Impact videos, qualitative case studies on investees, bespoke metrics (e.g. dollars lent, enterprises supported, jobs created)	Website, case studies of investees, 2018/2019 impact report
Key Fund	1999	IMD (index of multiple deprivation), impact videos, qualitative case studies on investees, bespoke metrics (e.g. dollars lent, enterprises supported, jobs created)	Website, case studies of investees, 2019 social impact report
Livv Investment	2016	Qualitative case studies on investees, bespoke metrics (e.g. dollars lent, enterprises supported, jobs created)	Website, case studies of investees
Mustard Seed	2015	Impact management Project (IMP), qualitative case studies on investees, bespoke metrics (e.g. dollars lent, enterprises supported, jobs created)	Website, case studies of investees, 2019 impact report
Natwest Social and Community Capital	1968	IRIS metrics, big Society Capital's outcomes matrix, impact videos, qualitative case studies on investees, bespoke metrics (e.g. dollars lent, enterprises supported, jobs created)	Website, case studies of investees, 2020 impact report

(continued)

Table 6.1 (continued)

Fund	Date founded	Stated impact measurement approaches	Documents analysed
Nesta Impact **Investments**	2012	Theory of change, standards of evidence, bespoke impact framework, qualitative case studies on investees, bespoke metrics (e.g. dollars lent, enterprises supported, jobs created)	Website, Case studies of investees, 2017 Annual Report, 2018 Impact strategy audit
Northstar Ventures	2004	Qualitative case studies on investees, bespoke metrics (e.g. dollars lent, enterprises supported, jobs created)	Website, case studies of investees
Postcode Innovation Trust	2016	Qualitative case studies on investees, bespoke metrics (e.g. dollars lent, enterprises supported, jobs created)	Website, case studies of investees, 2019 annual report
Resilient Scotland	2012	Bespoke metrics, impact videos, qualitative case studies on investees, bespoke metrics (e.g. dollars lent, enterprises supported, jobs created)	Website, case studies of investees, 2020 directors report
Resonance	2002	Bespoke metrics, B Impact assessment, SDGs, qualitative case studies on investees, bespoke metrics (e.g. dollars lent, enterprises supported, jobs created)	Website, case studies of investees, 2020 annual report
Royal Bank of Scotland Social and Community Capital	1999	IRIS metrics, big Society Capital's outcomes matrix, impact videos, qualitative case studies on investees, bespoke metrics (e.g. dollars lent, enterprises supported, jobs created)	Website, case studies of investees, 2019/2020 impact report
Social and Sustainable Capital (SASC)	2012	Impact management Project (IMP), SDGs, qualitative case studies on investees, bespoke metrics (e.g. dollars lent, enterprises supported, jobs created)	Website, case studies of investees, 2020 impact report

(continued)

Table 6.1 (continued)

Fund	Date founded	Stated impact measurement approaches	Documents analysed
Social Finance	2007	Qualitative case studies on investees, bespoke metrics (e.g. dollars lent, enterprises supported, jobs created)	Website, case studies of investees, 2018 impact report
Social Investment Business	2002	Impact videos, qualitative case studies on investees, bespoke metrics (e.g. dollars lent, enterprises supported, jobs created)	Website, case studies of investees, 2019/2020 impact report
Social Investment Cymru	2011	Bespoke metrics, qualitative case studies on investees, bespoke metrics (e.g. dollars lent, enterprises supported, jobs created)	Website, case studies of investees, 2019/2020 annual report
Social Investment Scotland	2001	Impact videos, qualitative case studies on investees, bespoke metrics (e.g. dollars lent, enterprises supported, jobs created)	Website, case studies of investees, 2020 impact report
Social Tech Trust	2008	Impact management Project (IMP), qualitative case studies on investees, bespoke metrics (e.g. dollars lent, enterprises supported, jobs created)	Website, case studies of investees, 2020 impact report
Somerset Community Foundation	2002	Qualitative case studies on investees, bespoke metrics (e.g. dollars lent, enterprises supported, jobs created)	Website, case studies of investees, 2019/2020 annual report
Sporting Capital	2019	Impact videos, qualitative case studies on investees, bespoke metrics (e.g. dollars lent, enterprises supported, jobs created)	Website, case studies of investees
The Architectural Heritage Fund	1976	Qualitative case studies on investees, bespoke metrics (e.g. dollars lent, enterprises supported, jobs created)	Website, case studies of investees, 2018 impact report

(continued)

Table 6.1 (continued)

Fund	Date founded	Stated impact measurement approaches	Documents analysed
Triodos Bank Corporate Finance	1995	Impact videos, qualitative case studies on investees, bespoke metrics (e.g. dollars lent, enterprises supported, jobs created)	Website, case studies of investees
Trust for London	2010	Qualitative case studies on investees, bespoke metrics (e.g. dollars lent, enterprises supported, jobs created)	Website, case studies of investees
Unity Trust Bank	1984	Qualitative case studies on investees, bespoke metrics (e.g. dollars lent, enterprises supported, jobs created)	Website, case studies of investees
UnLtd	2000	Qualitative case studies on investees, bespoke metrics (e.g. dollars lent, enterprises supported, jobs created)	Website, case studies of investees, 2019 impact report

diverse discourses on impact measurement forwarded by the impact investment funds. This inductive coding revealed seven main discourses on impact measurement. The findings sections provide examples of each of these main discourses.

Please note that the author had conducted interviews with fourteen of these impact investment funds as part of an earlier study (Ormiston, 2019). Whilst these interviews were not used in the analysis for this study, the insights from those discussions shaped the interpretation of the documents.

6.4 Discourses on Impact Measurement

There are seven main discourses on impact measurement: (i) legitimacy, (ii) decision-making, (iii) identity; (iv) reflection; (v) learning, (vi) dialogue; and (vii) a response to grand challenges. The following sub-sections unpack the ways in which impact investment funds forward these discourses on their websites and in the impact reports and annual reports.

6.4.1 Impact Measurement as Legitimacy

The most common discourse revealed in the analysis is impact measurement as a tool for legitimacy. Impact investors frame their engagement impact measurement as the 'proper and appropriate way' of doing impact investment (Suddaby et al., 2017). Impact investment funds tend to highlight the way their impact measurement and reporting practices are aligned with standardised approaches as means to gain legitimacy. For example, about a quarter of the impact investment funds analysed are explicitly aligning their impact measurement and reporting practice with the SDGs. The icons of the specific SDGs were commonly used as a visualisation tool attached to case studies in the impact reports. The following quotes highlight the ways in which these funds describe their alignment with the SDGs as a form of legitimacy.

> We have continued to align all our business activities to the United Nations Sustainable Development Goals, and re-energised our Environmental, Social and Governance structure to further embed the principles throughout 2021. (Unity Trust Bank—2020 Impact Report)

> In 2018 we announced our commitment to adopt a long-term plan to support the United Nations Sustainable Development Goals (SDGs). Using our Responsible Finance model, we continually contribute to these goals. We measure success by the volume of lending attributable to each goal. We are proud that over the past year we have seen a significant increase in lending that supports No Poverty, Zero Hunger, Good Health and Well Being, Quality Education and Gender Equality. (Business Enterprise Fund—2019/2020 Impact Report)

From a critical perspective, some reports seem limited in the extent to which they authentically engaged with the specific actions related to the SDGs, using them as a tool for categorising existing initiatives rather than redirecting action.

The Impact Management Project (IMP) norms, B Impact Assessment, and Big Society Capital Outcomes Matrix were also forwarded as standards that provided legitimacy. Aligning with a range of standardised impact measurement and reporting tools was utilised as justification of the sophistication of their practices, and their legitimacy as an impact investor.

> To assess our impact as an investor, we use 'Impact Management Project's 'Impact Class Matrix', which categorises investors based on the impact of their underlying assets and level of contribution. (Bethnal Green Ventures—2019 Impact Report)

> We use the standardised social impact monitoring categories widely adopted by UK social investors and promoted by Big Society Capital and follow accounting methodology where each part of a loan is attributed to the year that it was drawn by the borrower. (Charity Bank 2019—Social Impact Report)

Beyond standardised metrics, other impact investors highlighted their engagement with universities as a means of legitimising their impact measurement approach. Engaging in collaborative research projects with universities served to legitimise bespoke impact measurement practices and provide more trustworthy evidence of impact.

> In order to manage and reduce our carbon emissions, we want to make the most accurate assessment possible of our carbon footprint. So, for several years, we've been working with Small World Consulting, a team based at Lancaster University and led by footprinting expert Mike Berners-Lee, to develop our approach to measuring our emissions. (Ecology Building Society—website)

> Since 2015 we have been developing an impact toolkit to help us to begin to measure the impact of the enterprises that we work with. This work has been led by Coventry University's Centre for Agroecology, Water and Resilience (CAWR) and was developed in a participatory process with seven enterprises, many of them recipients of funding through the Just Growth programme. (LEAP—website)

6.4.2 Impact Measurement as Decision-Making

Many impact investment funds reflected on the role of impact measurement as a management tool for making decisions about investments. For these funds, impact measurement is presented as part of the due diligence process and for managing their portfolio enterprises after the investment decision is made. The investors utilise impact measurement as a tool to guide investment committee meetings and to guide their engagement with their portfolio. The following quotes highlight how impact investors that use the Impact Management Project (IMP) framework are more engaged with the discourse around impact measurement as a management decision-making tool.

> We start by categorising each fund and investment according to how they address one or more of the UN Sustainable Development Goals. In addition, we evaluate the impact of each investment using the five impact dimensions of the Impact Management Project framework (IMP): what; who; how much; contribution; and risk .... We use the framework during our due diligence process and in our ongoing portfolio management. It allows us to analyse and summarise the impact of each of our investees in a concise and consistent manner. (Social and Sustainable Capital (SASC)—2020 impact report)

> Impact management is about understanding what's working well, and what isn't. It brings together both impact measurement (collecting data) and impact practice (using data to inform decisions). Understanding the difference our support makes has always been important. The impact management field has evolved in recent years, and we, like others, are seeing how measurement can be a much more powerful tool when rooted in a mindset of continual improvement. We're developing our approach in line with the Impact Management Project Norms – a global consensus on measuring and reporting on social impact. (Social Tech Trust—2020 Impact Report)

Previous studies on impact measurement and impact investment (Ormiston, 2019) suggest that utilising impact measurement as a decision-making tool is common practice. However, given that this chapter focuses on publicly available document there was limited discussion relatively limited discussion by the impact investment funds about their decision—making processes.

6.4.3 Impact Measurement as Identity

Impact investors often differentiate themselves from traditional/commercially focused investors by their focus on attaining measurable impact (Ormiston et al., 2015). In these ways, many impact investment funds in the United Kingdom frame impact measurement as part of their identity. They discuss their engagement with impact investment practices as part of who they are as impact investors, and as a tool that allows them to be an authentic impact investor. Given that impact investors encourage and request impact metrics and reporting from their investors, the notion of practicing what you preach regarding impact measurement was a constant trope observed in the data.

> Resonance has been working with social enterprises since 2002 and we believe one of the best ways to demonstrate our track record, and the impact of the organisations we have helped, is to practice what we preach and record our own impact in "words and numbers". Look at what we achieved during our financial year 2019/20. (Resonance—Website)

> We also worked on better defining BGV's direct impact and developing our impact methodology, including aligning ourselves with the Impact Management Project and undertaking a BGV team diversity and inclusion survey – all of which we hope you enjoy finding out about in this report! (Bethnal Green Ventures—2019 Impact Report)

As highlighted by Bethnal Green Ventures, authentically engaging in impact measurement practice ensures that impact investors avoid potential criticisms of 'impact washing'. The following quote highlights the concern of many of the early proponents—that as impact investment grows in popularity, the focus on measurable impact will be diluted.

> the amount of money classified as impact investment is doubling year on year. 2020 may well see it surpass the trillion dollar mark. However not all types of impact investment are created equal. At their worst some 'impact' funds are simply existing funds that have been rebadged and rebranded. As large financial service companies recognise rapidly increasing customer

> demand for 'values-aligned' investment opportunities, the risk of 'impact washing' rises – buyer beware. (Bethnal Green Ventures—2019 Impact Report)

6.4.4 Impact Measurement as Reflection

The analysis suggests that majority of the discourse around impact measurement is focused on the impact of the portfolio of investees. This focus on social enterprises and social sector organisations in the portfolio results in impact reports emphasising investees and their impact as a proxy for the impact of the impact investment funds. There were a few novel examples of impact investors utilising impact measurement as a tool to reflect on their own internal practices as organisations. These funds are utilising impact measurement as a tool to reflect on their diversity and inclusion practices:

> One of our core principles is that diverse teams perform better. This belief extends beyond our portfolio ventures. We actively implement measures to ensure that BGV itself supports people from all backgrounds and 2020 marks the first year when we started reporting on diversity and inclusion metrics within our team. (Bethnal Green Ventures—2019 Impact Report)

These processes of reflection allowed these funds to show humility around where they can improve their own social impact, as reflected in the following quotes on improving work-life balance and diversity:

> The results also showed us where we can improve. Opportunities and resources was a particularly notable area, where only 67% of our team believe that BGV enables them to balance their work and personal life. This result was 10 points below Culture Amp's benchmark. (Bethnal Green Ventures—2019 Impact Report)

> I have been working at this for the last two years and, while we have made some progress, there is still a way to go. I've reformed and increased our maternity pay, checked and adjusted pay where needed, I've formed a working group internally, supported the wider women's group across the

organisation, gender word checked our job adverts, pushed hard for short-listing women and even forced recruitment panels to go back and recheck and review their hiring decisions. While we are diverse in many ways, we are not on gender. This is one of the reasons we are delivering our Diversity, Equalities and Inclusion strategy at Big Issue Invest. We welcome others to share their experiences, recommendations and lessons to help Big Issue Invest and the sector improve our approach our gender and wider equality aims. (Big Issue Invest—2020 impact report)

6.4.5 Impact Measurement as Learning

Related to the discourses on reflection, impact investment funds often framed impact measurement as a tool for organisational learning. As highlighted in the following quotes, these investors view impact measurement as core to enhancing their impact in the future through figuring out which enterprises to support and how to support them.

> We are working to become a learning organisation, to improve our impact and learn from our funded partners. This is part of our commitment to be led by our values and to adopt an equitable approach in everything we do… City Bridge Trust uses evidence and learning strategically and flexibly to drive its work to reduce inequality and grow stronger, more resilient and thriving community in London and Beyond (City Bridge trust—website)

> We continue to collect and analyse information from our work across different funds and programmes, looking back, looking at now (current practice) and looking ahead to where we need to improve or do more. We also continue to be open about ourselves and our internal impact: sharing information about our pay, our team, and our spend (Social Investment Business—2019 report)

The Esmee Fairburn foundation highlights how the learning insights offered form impact measurement are more important than the broader claims they might make about the impact of their work:

> Impact measurement is a challenge. For organisations working on complex issues, success is not defined by houses built, job numbers or exam results. And social investment often plays a small part in a wide range of support

> individuals receive. Attempting to define the total impact of Esmée's social investment fund would not be helpful to us or others. It is more important that we learn from each investment and use that learning to refine our approach as we go, increasing the strength of support for each organisation we fund (Esmee Fairburn Foundation—2018 Insights Report)

6.4.6 Impact Measurement as Dialogue

An underlying discourse in the impact investment reports is the role of impact measurement in opening up dialogue with investees and beneficiaries. The most dominant form of impact reporting was through qualitative case studies of social enterprises or communities supported (either written or videos). These case studies highlight the value of impact measurement for opening a dialogue between investors and investees, as well as with broader stakeholders who ultimately benefit from the investment. The following quotes highlight this focus on dialogue for impact investors:

> As part of the impact measurement, we may request updates on the project's progress and from time to time will also be in touch to schedule a visit with you. We love to see projects in action and we always make sure visits are arranged at a convenient time for all parties involved. (Devon Community Foundation—website)

> Improving our approach to impact management to track impact against our mission. This includes setting clear goals, targets and indicators and continuing to listen to our investees. (Big Issue Invest—2020 impact report)

From a more critical perspective, one must question how authentic this dialogue is, and how the power relationship between investors and investees shapes the nature of those conversations.

6.4.7 Impact Measurement as a Response to Grand Challenges

Finally, given that most of the impact reports and annual reports were written in 2020 during the Covid-19 crisis, the role of impact investment and impact measurement as a tool to 'build back better' after the epidemic was a consistent trope within the analysis. This could be viewed as impact measurement being framed as a tool to address grand societal challenges. This discourse around future impact in response to the epidemic was particularly observed within the forewords to the reports. This discourse aims to emphasise the role of impact investment and measurable impact as necessary elements of the recovery from the Covid-19 crisis. This discourse could be viewed as speaking directly to asset owners (e.g. government, philanthropists, foundations, institutional investors), whose investment is viewed as essential in the recovery:

> 2020 was a tough year for all, with Covid-19 hitting hard from March onwards. As an impact investor, we've seen how the ongoing pandemic has disproportionately affected many of the communities that we have a mission to fund—and particularly those living in the context of long-term economic, social, and environmental inequality. This has highlighted more clearly than ever the need for a local and democratic approach to finance that is targeted and effective. We know that to 'Build Back Better', we need to invest in projects that tackle the root causes of inequality in our communities. (Bristol City Funds—2020 Impact Report)

6.5 Impact Measurement as Performative and Multi-Disciplinary

This chapter has offered a discourse analysis of the diverse ways in which impact investment funds frame their rationale for engaging in impact measurement practices. Most of the main discourses outlined in the findings echo prior research on the diverse rationales for impact measurement (Maas & Liket, 2011; Ormiston, 2019; Ormiston & Castellas, 2019; Rawhouser et al., 2019; Kah & Akenroye, 2020). The wide range of impact measurement discourses observed in the analysis highlight the value in considering impact measurement as a multi-disciplinary practice (Ormiston, 2019).

The findings on impact measurement as identity provide a novel contribution to the extant research. By focusing on impact investors, who define themselves by their focus on impact investment (Hazenberg et al., 2014; Hehenberger et al., 2019), the chapter sheds like on the ways in which impact measurement is forwarded as a practice that is core to organisational identity. Future research should engage with the theoretical lens of organisational identity (Scott & Lane, 2000; Hatch & Schultz, 2002) to examine how impact measurement and reporting practices shape, and are shaped by, organisational identity of impact investors and social enterprises.

This chapter makes two key contributions to research on impact measurement. First, by highlighting how language and power shape perceptions of impact measurement, the chapter reveals the performative roles of texts such as website materials and impact reports in producing the meaning of impact measurement (Wodak & Meyer, 2009; Balogun et al., 2014). In particularly, the chapter highlights how standardised impact measurement approaches such as the SDGs, the Impact Measurement Project, and IRIS metrics allow powerful actors to shape the meaning of impact measurement at the field-level. Second, the paper contributes to the growing literature on the multidisciplinary nature of impact measurement as an organisational practice that support accountability, legitimacy, decision-making, learning, reflection and dialogue (Jäger & Rothe, 2013; Liket et al., 2014; André et al., 2018; Ormiston, 2019).

6.6 Researching Impact Measurement

The findings presented in this chapter provide multiple opportunities for future research on impact measurement discourses. In order to overcome the reliance on publicly available data, future research using either interviews or participant observation in combination with public documents could investigate the extent to which impact measurement discourses forwarded by impact investment funds in external documents reflect those they enact in practice. Future studies could also explore bottom-up perspectives on impact measurement. The analysis highlighted that the impact generated by the impact investment funds is directly derived from the impact creating activities of the investee social enterprises and social sector organisations. Future research could explore the ways in which social enterprises experience the impact measurement practices of their funders, and their perceptions of the varying discourses on impact measurement of which they are recipients.

Future research could also explore comparisons between impact investors operating in diverse geographies. For example, future studies could explore the discourses forwarded by members of the GIIN, the European Venture Philanthropy Network (EVPN) or the Asian Venture Philanthropy Network (AVPN). Another fecund avenue for future research would be to explore other stakeholders' discourses on impact measurement. For example, industry bodies such as the GIIN, Social Enterprise UK, asset owners rather that asset managers, governments, social enterprises, or impact analysts. One additional avenue of future research could build on the growing practice of producing 'impact videos'. The analysis revealed that many impact investment funds are utilising videos to showcase their impact. Future research could utilise video-based research methods (Ormiston & Thompson, 2021), to explore the ways in which impact investors and social enterprises utilise audiovisual methods to communicate their impact.

References

André, K., Cho, C. H., & Laine, M. (2018). Reference Points for Measuring Social Performance: Case Study of a Social Business Venture. *Journal of Business Venturing, 33*(5), 660–678.

Antadze, N., & Westley, F. R. (2012). Impact Metrics for Social Innovation: Barriers or Bridges to Radical Change? *Journal of Social Entrepreneurship, 3*(2), 133–150.

Arvidson, M., & Lyon, F. (2014). Social Impact Measurement and Non-profit Organisations: Compliance, Resistance, and Promotion. *VOLUNTAS: International Journal of Voluntary and Nonprofit Organizations, 25*(4), 869–886.

Bagnoli, L., & Megali, C. (2009). Measuring Performance in Nonprofit Organizations. *Nonprofit and Voluntary Sector Quarterly, 40*(1), 149–165.

Balogun, J., Jacobs, C., Jarzabkowski, P., Mantere, S., & Vaara, E. (2014). Placing Strategy Discourse in Context: Sociomateriality, Sensemaking, and Power. *Journal of Management Studies, 51*(2), 175–201.

Barraket, J., & Yousefpour, N. (2013). Evaluation and Social Impact Measurement Amongst Small to Medium Social Enterprises: Process, Purpose and Value. *Australian Journal of Public Administration, 72*(4), 447–458.

Benjamin, L. M. (2012). Nonprofit Organisations and Outcome Measurement: From Tracking Program Activities to Focusing on Frontline Work. *American Journal of Evaluation, 33*(3), 431–447.

Benjamin, L. M., & Misra, K. (2006). Doing Good Work: Implications of Performance Accountability for Practice in the Nonprofit Sector. *International Journal of Rural Management, 2*(2), 147–162.

Calderini, M., Chiodo, V., & Michelucci, F. V. (2018). The Social Impact Investment Race: Toward an Interpretative Framework. *European Business Review, 30*(1), 66–81.

Campbell, D., Lambright, K., & Bronstein, L. (2012). In the Eyes of the Beholders: Feedback Motivations and Practices Among Nonprofit Providers and Their Funders. *Public Performance and Management Review, 36*(1), 7–30.

Carman, J. G. (2007). Evaluation Practice Among Community-Based Organisations: Research into the Reality. *American Journal of Evaluation, 28*(1), 60–75.

Ebrahim, A., & Rangan, V. K. (2014). What Impact? *California Management Review, 56*(3), 118–141.

Fairclough, N. (2013). *Critical Discourse Analysis: The Critical Study of Language.* Routledge.

Garcia-Meca, E., & Martinez-Ferrero, J. (2021). Is SDG Reporting Substantial or Symbolic? An Examination of Controversial and Environmentally Sensitive Industries. *Journal of Cleaner Production, 298,* Online First. https://www.sciencedirect.com/science/article/abs/pii/S0959652621010003

Gasper, D. (2000). Evaluating the 'Logical Framework Approach' Towards Learning-Oriented Development Evaluation. *Public Administration and Development, 20*(1), 17–28.

Global Impact Investing Network (2020). The State of Impact Measurement and Management Practice, Second Edition. https://thegiin.org/research/publication/imm-survey-second-edition.

Grimes, M. (2010). Strategic Sensemaking Within Funding Relationships: The Effects of Performance Measurement on Organisational Identity in the Social Sector. *Entrepreneurship: Theory and Practice, 34*(4), 763–783.

Hatch, M. J., & Schultz, M. (2002). The Dynamics of Organisational Identity. *Human Relations, 55*(8), 989–1018.

Hayes, N., & Westrup, C. (2012). Power/knowledge and Impact Assessment: Creating New Spaces for Expertise in International Development. *New Technology, Work and Employment, 27*(1), 9–22.

Hazenberg, R., Seddon, F., & Denny, S. (2014). Intermediary Perceptions of Investment Readiness in the UK Social Investment Market. *VOLUNTAS: International Journal of Voluntary and Nonprofit Organizations, 26*(3), 846–871.

Hehenberger, L., Mair, J., and Metz, A. (2019). The Assembly of a Field Ideology: An Idea-centric Perspective on Systemic Power in Impact Investing. *Academy of Management Journal, 62*(6), 1672–1704.

Höchstädter, A. K., & Scheck, B. (2015). What's in a Name: An Analysis of Impact Investing Understandings by Academics and Practitioners. *Journal of Business Ethics, 132*(2), 449–475.

Hwang, H., & Powell, W. W. (2009). The Rationalization of Charity: The Influences of Professionalism in the Nonprofit Sector. *Administrative Science Quarterly, 54*(2), 268–298.

Jäger, U. P., & Rothe, M. D. (2013). Multidimensional Assessment of Poverty Alleviation in a Developing Country: A Case Study on Economic Interventions. *Nonprofit Management and Leadership, 23*(4), 511–528.

Kah, S., & Akenroye, T. (2020). Evaluation of Social Impact Measurement Tools And Techniques: A Systematic Review of the Literature. *Social Enterprise Journal, 16*(4), 381–402.

Lee, C., & Nowell, B. (2015). A Framework for Assessing the Performance of Nonprofit Organisations. *American Journal of Evaluation, 36*(3), 299–319.

Liket, K. C., Rey-Garcia, M., & Maas, K. E. H. (2014). Why Aren't Evaluations Working and What to Do About It: A Framework for Negotiating Meaningful Evaluation in Nonprofits. *American Journal of Evaluation, 35*(2), 171–188.

Maas, K., & Liket, K. (2011). Social Impact Measurement: Classification of Methods. In *Environmental Management Accounting and Supply Chain Management* (pp. 171–202). Springer.

Mayhew, F. (2012). Aligning for Impact: The Influence of the Funder–fundee Relationship on Evaluation Utilization. *Nonprofit Management and Leadership, 23*(2), 193–217.

Molecke, G., & Pinkse, J. (2017). Accountability for Social Impact: A Bricolage Perspective on Impact Measurement in Social Enterprises. *Journal of Business Venturing, 32*(5), 550–568.

Mouchamps, H. (2014). Weighing Elephants with Kitchen Scales: The Relevance Of Traditional Performance Measurement Tools for Social

Enterprises. *International Journal of Productivity and Performance Management, 63*(6), 727–745.

Newcomer, K., Baradei, L. E., & Garcia, S. (2013). Expectations and capacity of performance measurement in NGOs in the development context. *Public Administration and Development, 33*(1), 62–79.

Nicholls, A. (2009). 'We do good things, don't we?': 'Blended Value Accounting' in Social Entrepreneurship. *Accounting, Organizations and Society, 34*(6–7), 755–769.

Nicholls, A. (2010). The Institutionalization of Social Investment: The Interplay of Investment Logics and Investor Rationalities. *Journal of Social Entrepreneurship, 1*(1), 70–100.

Ormiston, J. (2019). Blending Practice Worlds: Impact Assessment as a Transdisciplinary Practice. *Business Ethics: A European Review, 28*(4), 423–440.

Ormiston, J., & Castellas, E. (2019). Measuring Impact in Social Entrepreneurship: Developing a Research Agenda for the 'practice turn' in Impact Assessment. In *A Research Agenda for Social Entrepreneurship*. Edward Elgar Publishing.

Ormiston, J., Charlton, K., Donald, M. S., & Seymour, R. G. (2015). Overcoming the Challenges of Impact Investing: Insights from Leading Investors. *Journal of Social Entrepreneurship, 6*(3), 352–378.

Ormiston, J., & Thompson, N. A. (2021). Viewing Entrepreneurship "in motion": Exploring Current Uses and Future Possibilities of Video-based Entrepreneurship Research. *Journal of Small Business Management, 59*(5), 976–1011.

Ramus, T., & Vaccaro, A. (2017). Stakeholders Matter: How Social Enterprises Address Mission Drift. *Journal of Business Ethics, 143*(2), 307–322.

Rawhouser, H., Cummings, M., & Newbert, S. L. (2019). Social Impact Measurement: Current Approaches and Future Directions for Social Entrepreneurship Research. *Entrepreneurship Theory and Practice, 43*(1), 82–115.

Ruff, K., & Olsen, S. (2018). The Need for Analysts in Social Impact Measurement: How Evaluators Can Help. *American Journal of Evaluation, 39*(3), 402–407.

Sareen, S., & Haarstad, H. (2020). Legitimacy and Accountability in the Governance of Sustainable Energy Transitions. *Global Transitions, 2*, 47–50.

Sawhill, J. C., & Williamson, D. (2001). Mission Impossible?: Measuring Success in Nonprofit Organisations. *Nonprofit Management and Leadership, 11*(3), 371–386.

Scott, S. G., & Lane, V. R. (2000). A Stakeholder Approach to Organisational Identity. *Academy of Management Review, 25*(1), 43–62.

Smith, B. R., & Stevens, C. E. (2010). Different Types of Social Entrepreneurship: The Role of Geography and Embeddedness on the Measurement and Scaling of Social Value. *Entrepreneurship and Regional Development, 22*(6), 575–598.

Suddaby, R., Bitektine, A., & Haack, P. (2017). Legitimacy. *Academy of Management Annals, 11*(1), 451–478.

Thomson, D. E. (2010). Exploring the Role of Funders' Performance Reporting Mandates in Nonprofit Performance Measurement. *Nonprofit and Voluntary Sector Quarterly, 39*(4), 611–629.

Willems, J., Boenigk, S., & Jegers, M. (2014). Seven Trade-offs in Measuring Nonprofit Performance and Effectiveness. *VOLUNTAS: International Journal of Voluntary and Nonprofit Organizations, 25*(6), 1648–1670.

Wodak, R., & Meyer, M. (Eds.). (2009). *Methods for Critical Discourse Analysis*. Sage.

7

Putting Stakeholders at the Centre: Multi-Stakeholder Approaches to Social Impact Measurement

Ericka Costa and Caterina Pesci

7.1 Economic, Social and Financial Accounting

Social impact measurement has been the subject of academic and professional debate over the last ten years (Ebrahim & Rangan, 2010; Costa & Pesci, 2016; GECES, 2014; OECD, 2015). To date, it has mainly focused on social enterprises and hybrid organisations (Grossi et al., 2017; Avance et al., 2020; Gibbon & Day, 2011), which have become key players in the provision of public services at both the European and global levels (Defourny & Nyssens, 2010; Santos, 2012). Prior studies support the idea that organisations have a variety of impacts on the society and environments in which we live (Clark et al., 2004; Grossi et al., 2017; Bebbington & Unerman, 2018).

E. Costa (✉) • C. Pesci
University of Trento, Trento, Italy
e-mail: ericka.costa@unitn.it; caterina.pesci@unitn.it

R. Hazenberg, C. Paterson-Young (eds.), *Social Impact Measurement for a Sustainable Future*, https://doi.org/10.1007/978-3-030-83152-3_7

Within this emergent field, financial accounting and measurement systems have been shown to be overly focused on economic and financial returns on investment, providing no understanding of the social impacts of funding (Emerson, 2003; Epstein & McFarlan, 2011). As highlighted by Maddocks (2011), financial measurements present an incomplete picture of the organisation because information regarding success, performance and impact is often missing or underdeveloped. Therefore, it is today relevant to expand the approaches to social impact measurement developed for non-profit and hybrid organisations to other organisational types. Moreover, as many different organisations have to consider their social and environmental impact on society, the practice of social impact measurement must gain relevance beyond the non-profit sector (Molecke & Pinkse, 2017).

Similarly, national and international regulators and governing bodies are moving toward more extensive societal measurement of organisations' impact on society (European Commission, 2014; Korca & Costa, 2021). Recently, both the European Commission (EC, 2014) and the United Nations (UN 2016) endorsed a directive for mandatory non-financial disclosure (Directive 2014/95/EU, Korca & Costa, 2021) and the so-called 2030 Agenda for Sustainable Development Goals (SDGs, Bebbington & Unerman, 2018). The SDGs have been rapidly adopted as a global framework for understanding and achieving environmental and human development ambitions until the year 2030 (Bebbington & Unerman, 2018). This framework has the merit of integrating social, economic and environmental dimensions within each of the 17 proposed goals, while bringing attention to the long-term impact of organisational actions. The 2030 Agenda calls for an ambitious sustainable development strategy that overcomes the challenge of achieving social impact in addition to financial returns (OECD, 2019). Within this context, it has become critical to define and measure social impact and to better investigate the role of the multi-stakeholder approach in order to develop innovative micro-frameworks (Costa, 2021).

To date, proposed new forms of social impact measurement have often adopted formal methodologies based on the performance measurement and reporting practices of the fields of accounting and finance, which have limitations, ambiguities and frictions that remain in the new forms of measurement (Molecke & Pinkse, 2017). One of the main challenges recognised in the context of social (and environmental) impact measurement is accountability to multiple stakeholders and for multiple purposes (Ebrahim et al., 2014; Costa & Pesci, 2016). While social impact measurement remains dominated by different approaches and methodologies, in all such methodologies, stakeholders have a key role in assessment of the social environmental impact of different organisations in order to implement more complex, multi-directional and multi-stakeholder performance measurement systems (Christensen & Ebrahim, 2006; Costa & Pesci, 2016; Grossi et al., 2017).

The aims of this chapter are (i) to promote a multiple-stakeholder approach to social impact measurement and (ii) to investigate how this approach can contribute to fostering the SDGs by developing specific process frameworks that start at the micro-organisational level. It examines whether such frameworks can help to shape tailored impact measurement tools based on co-development with various stakeholders involved at both the micro and macro levels. The remainder of the chapter is structured as follows. The next section discusses the notion of social impact measurements and their advantages and disadvantages. Section three presents the multi-stakeholder approach to social impact measurement, and section four discusses the contribution of the multiple-stakeholder approach to social impact measurement to the 2030 Agenda for Sustainable Development. Finally, in section five, some concluding comments are drawn. The chapter supports a micro approach to social impact measurement and sustainable development, in which idiosyncratic metrics should be designed with the active participation of multiple stakeholders.

7.2 Social Impact Measurement and the Control Over Output and Outcome/Impact

As discussed in Chap. 2 of this book, social impact measurement is a burgeoning field that includes different concepts with many complexities and controversies (Ebrahim & Rangan, 2014; Bengo et al., 2016). What is central to social impact and social impact measurement is the conceptualisation of a *changing* status for people and communities as a result of the organisation's initiatives and activities. In this sense, change involves modifications to people's lives in terms of their norms, values, aspirations and beliefs as well as the community in terms of its political systems, environment, health or well-being (Costa, 2021).

In order to better investigate how organisations can impact the changing living conditions of people and society, the value chain approach (Clark et al., 2004) sees social impact as a 'logic chain of results' in which organisational inputs (the resources provided to the initiative) are used to support activities and services which result in the delivery of *outputs* to a target population (i.e., results that an organisation can measure or assess directly). The identified output can lead to different effects and changes in stakeholder' attitudes, behaviours, knowledge, skills and/or status (i.e., the *outcome* of the organisation's activity), which can then foster a societal *impact* on the broader society in the long term (Clark et al., 2004; Ebrahim & Rangan, 2010; Epstein & McFarlan, 2011; Ebrahim et al., 2014; Costa & Pesci, 2016). This approach (Clark et al., 2004) enables differentiation of two main concepts with different organisational perspectives:

I. *Outputs* assess performance measurement because they are countable and defined by the organisation itself (Kolodinsky et al., 2006). 'Output' refers to the products or services a social intervention generates and the immediate effect they have (Rawhouser et al., 2019)
II. *Outcome* and *impact* reflect the stakeholder/user perspective and broader societal changes. These changes and their benefits are reflected not only among users but also the public system more broadly.

Therefore, outcomes and impacts are considered to have 'multi-level' effects (Rawhouser et al., 2019)

While each organisation is able to internally control and measure the input-activity-output of the of the value chain, both outcomes and impacts require the adoption of a multiple-stakeholder perspective in order to include external perspectives and perceptions about the impact (Costa & Pesci, 2016; Costa, 2021), consistent with Theory of Change (Taplin & Clark, 2012). Indeed, practitioners with experience implementing the impact value chain approach often stress the ambiguity of this chain and express concerns regarding the difficulty of calculating and measuring outcomes and impacts (Ebrahim & Rangan, 2014; Molecke & Pinkse, 2017). Indeed, external and exogenous factors outside of the organisation's control may neutralise or counteract the intended effect of an intervention. Each organisation operates within an ecosystem that includes other for-profit, public and non-profit organisations, each of which may contribute to or interact with each other's impacts. Thus, attributing impact to a specific actor can be very difficult (Roche, 1999; Ebrahim & Rangan, 2014; Molecke & Pinkse, 2017; Costa, 2021).

7.3 The Role of Stakeholders in Social Impact Measurement

The role of stakeholders and stakeholder-engagement processes is well known in the accountability stream of literature (Najam, 1996; Gray, 2002; Emerson, 2003; Christensen & Ebrahim, 2006; Gibbon & Day, 2011; Costa & Pesci, 2016), and it has been engaged and adopted in the social impact measurement debate. One of the major topics about accountability that has been investigated is the 'to whom' question (Najam, 1996; Ebrahim, 2005; Christensen & Ebrahim, 2006; Williams & Taylor, 2013), or the multiple stakeholders to whom organisations are accountable. It has been broadly investigated with reference to non-profit organisations' accountability, and recently, it has been considered in the social impact measurement debate.

The stakeholder-based approach is interrelated with the interplay between output and outcome/impact, which can be evaluated and counted by organisations in different ways. Indeed, as Kolodinsky et al. (2006) clearly support, outputs could be countable from an internal organisation perspective, while outcome and impact could be countable from an external receiver perspective. As recently highlighted by Costa (2021), while input-activity-output could be measured internally by organisations through the consultation and involvement of different stakeholders, in order to measure the outcome/impact, it is urgent to adopt an external, multiple-stakeholder perspective and consider external perspectives and perceptions regarding the impact on stakeholders. Therefore, two different dimensions of stakeholders' role in social impact measurement will be investigated in this chapter: (i) the *process* according to which stakeholders and stakeholder engagement should be involved in social impact measurement and (ii) the different *metrics* that could be implemented from a stakeholder perspective.

In terms of process, recognition and identification of different stakeholders on whom an organisation could have an impact is not enough (Bengo et al., 2016). As suggested by Costa and Pesci (2016), when a stakeholder-based approach is adopted for social impact measurement, it needs to be based on stakeholder engagement, which differs from simply acknowledging the existence of many stakeholder viewpoints. Stakeholder engagement should be based on many different consultative forums with stakeholders, with the aim of extending beyond a multi-stakeholder, consensus-seeking approach to produce metrics that appropriately respond to stakeholders' needs (Maas & Liket, 2011). The stakeholder-based approach to social impact measurement should be designed and performed from the receiver's perspective, taking into account the expected change and impact. In other words, the organisation should act as an empathetic actor that is able to lead stakeholders to identify any effects and changes that may occur.

In terms of metrics, the socially constructed nature of social impact measurement calls for a more tailored and customised view of measurement in which there are no universal, golden metrics that can satisfy the needs of all stakeholders. The debate about social impact metrics ranges from two extremes. On one side, there are those in favour of defining standardised universal measurement units that facilitate comparison between organisations and over time (Arvidson et al., 2013). On the other side, there are those in favour of developing idiosyncratic measurement units that tailor social impact measurements to stakeholders' needs (Nicholls, 2009; Mook et al., 2015; Costa & Pesci, 2016).

The 'standardised universal measurement approach involves indiscriminate application of a golden standard for social impact measurement to all organisations' activities and interventions (Arvidson et al., 2013). This approach is traditionally adopted in the conventional financial accounting framework, and it mainly reflects the owners' and investors' perspectives. Similarly, some scholars and organisations (Clark et al., 2004; Thornley & Dailey, 2010; Best & Harji, 2013) are in favour of a more standardised impact measurement to enhance comparability across organisations in different sectors and integrate the investor perspective (Clark et al., 2004). This approach is preferred by lenders and public investors, who are mainly interested in justifying the allocation of public money as well as attracting other sources of public and private financing (European Commission, 2014). One of the most commonly adopted metrics within this approach is the Social Return on Investment Measurement (SROI), which is a modified version of the conventional return on investment business tool (Arvidson et al., 2013; Molecke & Pinkse, 2017; Rawhouser et al., 2019).

In essence, the SROI calculates the value of social impact in monetary terms as a ratio of outcomes over inputs. As such, the return on investment is based upon not only economic items that are exchanged on the market but also social items for which a market proxy is established, such as those used by economists in cost–benefit analyses (Mook et al., 2015). Thus, SROI is based on the (positivist) assumption of identifying a monetary proxy to measure social and societal impact, which are not normally exchanged on the market (Mook et al., 2015). This approach has received several critiques from those who argue that social value and social change have non-straightforward market value. It is therefore complicated, or maybe even impossible, to meaningfully adopt conventional accounting methods (Gray, 2002; Maas & Liket, 2011). Therefore, a second approach emerged that supports the definition of tailored and idiosyncratic metrics in order to better highlight the different impacts of organisations by identifying specific metrics that are able to capture stakeholders' perceptions of change (Nicholls, 2009; Costa & Pesci, 2016) (see Chaps. 3 and 11 for further information on SROI).

Recently, Mook et al. (2015) proposed the 'Stakeholder Impact Statement', which is rooted in interpretivism and evaluates the impact of organisations from a multiple-stakeholder perspective. The stakeholder impact statement includes and combines different types of value creation: economic, socioeconomic and social value. Economic value refers to inputs that are transformed into output with a greater market value. Socioeconomic value reflects both economic and social dimensions, and it is created when the organisation's value-adding activities imply different revenues and costs to the public sector, for instance through additional taxes, or decreased costs in social assistance transfers (Mook et al., 2015). Finally, social value refers to expected change and improvement in the lives of individuals or society.

Beyond specific social impact measures, recent contributions to the debate have considered which lessons could be learnt from the literature on social impact measurement to help foster the development of SDGs frameworks and measurement approaches (Costa, 2021). The link between social impact, its measurement and the sustainability debate are addressed in the next section.

7.4 Social Impact Measurement to Foster Sustainable Development

Discussions about sustainability and sustainable development may be considered to include everything and nothing at the same time, since these words seem to have become trends used in every context with different meanings (Pearce, 1988). Nevertheless, the terms draw upon debates in multiple disciplines that date back to the 1980s'. Since the 1980's academic debate and policy debate on sustainability increased and gained visibility in the United Nation Conference on Environment and Development (UNCED) held in Rio in 1992 (Scoones, 2007). Moreover, sustainable development is currently considered a key issue for the survival of our planet, and it has been at the core of numerous initiatives and studies. Driven by an awareness that humans are currently exploiting natural resources, efforts to promote sustainable development have adopted an anthropocentric approach (Bebbington & Larrinaga, 2014; Bebbington et al., 2019). The current epoch, defined as the Anthropocene (Williams et al., 2019), is a stage of human existence and co-existence with Earth that is deeply different from prior epochs because humans' actions are able to deeply alter the ecosystem. The United Nations (1987) recognised that it is almost impossible to separate the economic development issues from environmental issues because there are many forms of development that erode the environmental resources upon which they must be based, and this phenomenon is increasing. Furthermore, the same environmental degradation makes economic development undetermined by exploiting its foundations.

In sum, sustainable development is at the core of humanity's future, and the SDGs proposed by the United Nation must be considered key issues for ensuring future generations can live on the Earth. The Chap. 2 of this book has covered the 17 SDGs' content, targets and indicators, but here what is considered particularly worth of attention is that despite the work done they have been considered ambiguous (Hák et al., 2016) and their achievement still presents serious difficulties in terms of quantification, implementation and monitoring (Baker, 2002; Costanza et al., 2016; Swain, 2018). In addition, another relevant issue for the purpose of this Chapter is that due to their broad aim, analysis of difficulties in their operationalisation has been initially considered at the macro level (Turner, 2005), but operationalisation at the micro level is a key issue due to the importance of each actor involved in achieving these goals.

Definition of metrics for effective achievement of the SDGs in practice plays a paramount role in the operationalisation of SDGs at both the macro and micro levels. Among the possible approaches, studies on social impact measurements can shed light on how to design tailored measurement processes and how to operationalise tools that can implement the SDGs at the micro level.

Social impact measurements operate at the micro (i.e. organisational) level and go beyond financial measurement because they do not merely maximise the profit paradigm but also aim to produce evidence that social impacts satisfy the needs of different stakeholders connected to different goals. Studies on social impact measurement, put stakeholders at the core, and they drive the disclosure process intended to satisfy their informational needs (Costa & Pesci, 2016). Nevertheless, to fulfil the SDGs, it is necessary to also disclose information connected to the preservation and promotion of diverse societal constituencies across the world. In other words, multiple constituencies' needs must be always satisfied within the boundaries of the Earth equilibrium.

In the realm of social impact measurements, it has been established that a single, standardised approach to social impact measurement presents several issues (OECD, 2015) due to the difficulties of satisfying different constituencies' informational needs related to specific organisational goals. The same is true for achieving different SDGs and satisfying the multiple constituencies involved in achieving those goals. The aim of measurement determines its features and usefulness. In other words, for example, a desire to measure how to reduce inequalities or how much inequalities have been reduced can lead to the development of measurement tools that are quite different from those used to measure how and to what extent affordable and clean energy have grown. Thus, the goal to be achieved and the multiple constituencies involved in goals are key issues to consider when developing measurements.

In sum, to produce meaningful impacts that meet various stakeholders' needs, it is necessary to try to produce processes, systems and tools of measurement that align with the different interests of societal constituencies and the many efforts to develop new forms of measurement. In the accounting field, Bebbington and Unerman (2018) reviewed many studies on SDGs and tried to link them with the many streams of accounting research that offer insights into measurement systems and their engagement with the professional world. What has not yet been explored is the potential role of frameworks based on processes related to specific aims and constituencies. This is what social impact measurement studies can bring to the field of SDG implementation (Costa & Pesci, 2016; Costa, 2021). The ideas developed by social impact studies for operationalising social impact measurements at the micro level are based on frameworks used to design processes that centre stakeholders' informative needs regarding organisational activities. Instead of proposing pre-packaged standardised measures, the exigencies of multiple constituencies drive the development of the measurement toolkit. The same approach can be adopted at the micro level for setting SDG indicators. Multiple constituencies' needs and equilibrium with environmental issues should be at the core of a process framework developed at the micro level with consideration of the specific informative exigences at stake and the involved development goals.

Finally, the complex issue of integrating the macro and micro level must be considered when dealing with developing SDG measurement frameworks (Le Blanc, 2015; Stafford-Smith et al., 2017). Future efforts must complement and integrate social impact measurement ideas into the SDG arena in order to design a process framework to be applied at the micro level without forgetting its reverberations at the macro level.

7.5 Sustainable Change at the Micro and Macro Levels

The chapter has discussed the interplay between social impact measurement, stakeholder engagement and sustainable development. In detail, the aim of this contribution is to highlight how a stakeholder-based approach to social impact measurement could help foster the implementation of the SDGs. Prior studies have elucidated the complexities and ambiguities of social impact and social impact measurement (Ebrahim & Rangan, 2014; Bengo et al., 2016). To date, the notion of social impact has been mainly investigated at the micro level in non-profit and hybrid contexts (Gibbon & Day, 2011; Grossi et al., 2017; Avance et al., 2020), which have become relevant players at the European and global levels with an important role in providing public and social services (Defourny & Nyssens, 2010; Santos, 2012).

However, the lessons learnt from social impact measurement in this field could be extended to the current debate of sustainability and SDGs because of its interconnectedness with the basic assumption of *change*. Although various terms are used to refer to social impact measurement, the idea of change is common to all of them. In this context, change refers to lasting variations in people's and communities' lives as a result of an organisation's initiatives and activities. Such changes may be positive (Santos, 2012), or they may at least limit the negative long-term effect (Bartling et al., 2015).

Social impact measurement has been often discussed in terms of the value chain (Clark et al., 2004), which enables differentiation of two main concepts with different organisational perspectives: (i) output, which refers to performance measurement assessment, and (ii) outcome/impact, which reflects the stakeholder/user perspective and broader societal change. Both outcomes and impacts require the adoption of a multiple-stakeholder perspective to assess the changing status of people's lives and society (Costa & Pesci, 2016; Costa, 2021).

The multiple-stakeholder perspective makes evident how social impact studies can contribute to SDGs. In turn, sustainability requires us to think about the effect of human actions on different fields related to different constituencies. The most important contribution that social impact studies can bring to the realm of SDGs is a focus on micro-level constituencies, on their sustainable informational needs and on how constituencies' needs can drive the process of development of tailored measurements.

The SDGs were developed mainly at the macro level. A set of indicators was created for them, but its implementation has been criticised (Swain, 2018). The exigency of developing a framework in this arena has been discussed (Hák et al., 2016). The authors of this chapter argue that a process framework beginning at the micro level of stakeholders' informative needs, as proposed in social impact measurement studies (Costa & Pesci, 2016), can help to solve issues related to the achievement of the SDGs. The process should put stakeholders' information needs at the centre, consider organisational goals and propose proper measurement tools. In addition, his process needs to take into consideration the interplay among different sustainable issues at the micro and macro levels. In essence, the notion of social impact measurement and experiences with developing tailored sets of measurements are a potential source of inspiration for the development of SDG measures.

References

Arvidson, M., Lyon, F., McKay, S., & Moro, D. (2013). Valuing the Social? The Nature and Controversies of Measuring Social Return on Investment (SROI). *Voluntary Sector Review, 4*(1), 3–18.

Avance, Social Enterprise NL and Impact Centre Erasmus. (2020). Available online at https://impactpad.nl/wp-content/uploads/Het_Impactpad_EN_2020.pdf. Accessed April 2020.

Baker, S. (2002). The Evolution of European Union Environmental Policy. From Growth to Sustainable Development? In S. Baker et al. (Eds.), *The Politics of Sustainable Development. Theory, Policy and Practice Within the European Union* (pp. 91–106). London.

Bartling, B., Weber, R. A., & Yao, L. (2015). Do Markets Erode Social Responsibility? *Quarterly Journal of Economics, 130*(1), 219–266.

Bebbington, J., & Larrinaga, C. (2014). Accounting and Sustainable Development: An Exploration. *Accounting, Organizations and Society, 39*(6), 395–413.

Bebbington, J., Österblom, H., Crona, B., Jouffray, J. B., Larrinaga, C., Russell, S., & Scholtens, B. (2019). Accounting and Accountability in the Anthropocene. *Accounting, Auditing & Accountability Journal, 33*(1), 152–177.

Bebbington, J., & Unerman, J. (2018). Achieving the United Nations Sustainable Development Goals: An Enabling Role for Accounting Research. *Accounting, Auditing & Accountability Journal, 31*(1), 2–24.

Bengo, I., Arena, M., Azzone, G., & Calderini, M. (2016). Indicators and Metrics for Social Business: A Review of Current Approaches. *Journal of Social Entrepreneurship, 1*(2), 1–24.

Best, H., & Harji, K. (2013). *Social Impact Measurement Use Among Canadian Impact Investors*. Purpose Capital.

Christensen, R. A., & Ebrahim, A. (2006). How Does Accountability Affect Mission? *Nonprofit Management & Leadership, 17*(2), 195–209.

Clark, C., Rosenzweig, W., Long, D., & Olsen, S. (2004). *Double Bottom Line Project Report: Assessing Social Impact in Double Bottom Line Ventures*. Berkeley, Capabilities Approach. http://www.riseproject.org/DBL_Methods_Catalog.pdf

Costa, E. (2021). *Challenges for Social Impact Measurement in the Non-profit Sector*. In O. Lehner (Ed.), *A Research Agenda for Social Finance* (pp. 119–144). Edward Elgar Publishing.

Costa, E., & Pesci, C. (2016). Social Impact Measurement: Why Do Stakeholders Matter? *Sustainability Accounting, Management and Policy Journal, 7*(1), 99–124.

Costanza, R., Daly, L., Fioramonti, L., Giovannini, G., Kubiszewski, I., Mortensen, L. F., Pickett, K. E., Ragnarsdottir, K. V., De Vogli, R., & Wilkinson, R. (2016). Modelling and Measuring Sustainable Wellbeing in Connection with the UN Sustainable Development Goals. *Ecological Economics, 130*, 350–355.

Defourny, J., & Nyssens, M. (2010). Conceptions of Social Enterprise and Social Entrepreneurship in Europe and the United States: Convergences and Divergences. *Journal of Social Entrepreneurship, 1*(1), 32–53.

Ebrahim, A. (2005). Accountability Myopia: Losing Sight of Organisational Learning. *Nonprofit and Voluntary Sector Quarterly, 34*(1), 56–87.

Ebrahim, A., Battilana, J., & Mair, J. (2014). The Governance of Social Enterprises: Mission Drift and Accountability Challenges in Hybrid Organisations. *Research in Organizational Behavior, 34*, 81–100.

Ebrahim, A., & Rangan, V. K. (2010). The Limits of Nonprofit Impact: A Contingency Framework for Measuring Social Performance. *Harvard Business School Working Paper, 10–099*, 1–53.

Ebrahim, A., & Rangan, V. K. (2014). What Impact? A Framework for Measuring the Scale and Scope of Social Performance. *California Management Review, 56*(3), 118–141.

Emerson, J. (2003). The Blended Value Proposition: Integrating Social and Financial Returns. *California Management Review, 45*(4), 35–51.

Epstein, M. J., & McFarlan, F. W. (2011). Measuring the Efficiency and Effectiveness of a Nonprofit's Performance. *Strategic Finance, 93*(4), 27–34.

European Commission. (2014). *Social Innovation: A Decade of Changes. Luxemburg*. Retrieved from: https://espas.secure.europarl.europa.eu/orbis/document/social-innovation-decade-changes

GECES-Sub-group on Impact Measurement. (2014). Proposed Approaches to Social Impact Measurement in European Commission Legislation and in Practice Relating to: EuSEFs and the EaSI. Retrieved from: http://ec.europa.eu/internal_market/social_business/docs/expert-group/social_impact/140605-sub-group-report_en.pdf

Gibbon, J., & Day, C. (2011). Developments in Social Impact Measurement in the Third Sector: Scaling up or Dumbing Down? *Social and Environmental Accountability Journal, 31*(1), 63–72.

Gray, R. (2002). The Social Accounting Project and Accounting Organizations and Society Privileging Engagement, Imaginings, New Accountings and Pragmatism Over Critique? *Accounting, Organizations and Society, 27*(7), 687–708.

Grossi, G., Reichard, C., Thomasson, A., & Vakkuri, J. (2017). Theme: Performance Measurement of Hybrid Organisations – Emerging Issues and Future Research Perspectives. *Public Money and Management, 37*(6), 379–386.

Hák, T., Janoušková, S., & Moldan, B. (2016). Sustainable Development Goals: A Need for Relevant Indicators. *Ecological Indicators, 60*, 565–573.

Kolodinsky, J., Stewart, C., & Bullard, A. (2006). Measuring Economic and Social Impacts of Membership in a Community Development Financial Institution. *Journal of Family and Economic Issues, 27*(1), 27–47.

Korca, B., & Costa, E. (2021). Directive 2014/95/EU: building a research agenda. *Journal of Applied Accounting Research, 22*(3), 401–422. https://doi.org/10.1108/JAAR-05-2020-0085

Le Blanc, D. (2015). Towards Integration at Last? The Sustainable Development Goals as a Network of Targets. *Sustainable Development, 23*(3), 176–187.

Maas, K., & Liket, K. (2011). Talk the Walk: Measuring the Impact of Strategic Philanthropy. *Journal of Business Ethics, 100*(3), 445–464.

Maddocks, J. (2011). Debate: Sustainability Reporting: A Missing Piece of the Charity-Reporting Jigsaw. *Public Money and Management, 31*(3), 157–158.

Molecke, G., & Pinkse, J. (2017). Accountability for Social Impact: A Bricolage Perspective on Impact Measurement in Social Enterprises. *Journal of Business Venturing, 32*(5), 550–568.

Mook, L., Maiorano, J., Ryan, S., Armstrong, A., & Quarter, J. (2015). Social Return on Investment on Its Head. *The Stakeholder Impact Statement, Nonprofit Management and Leadership, 26*(2), 229–246.

Najam, A. (1996). Non-Government Organisation Accountability: A Conceptual Framework. *Development and Policy Review, 46*, 339–353.

Nicholls, A. (2009). 'We do good things, don't we?': 'Blended value accounting' in Social Entrepreneurship. *Accounting, Organizations and Society, 34*, 755–769.

OECD. (2015). Policy Brief on Social Impact Measurement for Social Enterprises. Policies for Social Entrepreneurship. Available online at: https://www.oecd.org/social/PB-SIM-Web_FINAL.pdf

OECD. (2019). *Social Impact Investment 2019: The Impact Imperative for Sustainable Development*. OECD Publishing.

Pearce, D. (1988). Economics, Equity and Sustainable Development. *Futures, 20*(6), 598–605.

Rawhouser, H., Cummings, M., & Newbert, S. L. (2019). Social Impact Measurement: Current Approaches and Future Directions for Social Entrepreneurship Research. *Entrepreneurship Theory and Practice, 43*(1), 82–115.

Roche, C. J. (1999). *Impact Assessment for Development Agencies: Learning to Value Change.* Oxfam.

Santos, F. M. (2012). A Positive Theory of Social Entrepreneurship. *Journal of Business Ethics, 111*(3), 335–351.

Scoones, I. (2007). Sustainability. *Development in Practice, 17*(4–5), 589–596.

Stafford-Smith, M., Griggs, D., Gaffney, O., Ullah, F., Reyers, B., Kanie, N., Stigson, B., Shrivastava, P., Leach, M., & O'Connell, D. (2017). Integration: The Key to Implementing the Sustainable Development Goals. *Sustainability Science, 12*, 911–919.

Swain, R. B. (2018). A Critical Analysis of the Sustainable Development Goals. In F. W. Leal (Ed.), *Handbook of Sustainability Science and Research* (World Sustainability Series). Springer.

Taplin D. H., & Clark H. (2012). *Theory of Change, Basics. A Primer on Theory of Change.* Retrieved from: https://www.theoryofchange.org/wp-content/uploads/toco_library/pdf/ToCBasics.pdf

Thornley, B., & Dailey, C. (2010). *Building Scale in Community Impact Investing through Nonfinancial Performance Measurement, Community Development Investment Review, Federal Reserve Bank of San Francisco.* Retrieved from: https://www.pacificcommunityventures.org/wp-content/uploads/sites/6/2015/07/Thornley_Dailey.pdf

Turner. (2005). Sustainability: Principles and Practices. In M. Redcliff (Ed.), *Sustainability Critical Concepts in the Social Sciences.* Routledge.

United Nations. (1987). *Our Common Future* (pp. 1–11). Oxford University press.

United Nations. (2016). The Sustainable Development Goals Report 2016, Department of Economic and Social Affairs, ISBN (PDF): 9789210582599, https://doi.org/10.18356/3405d09f-en

Williams, A. P., & Taylor, J. A. (2013). Resolving Accountability Ambiguity in Nonprofit Organizations. *Voluntas: International Journal of Voluntary and Nonprofit Organizations, 24*, 559–580.

Williams, G. J., Graham, N. A. J., Jouffray, J., Norström, A. V., Nyström, M., Gove, J. M., & Heenan, A. (2019). Coral Reef Ecology in the Anthropocene. *Functional Ecology, 33*(6), 1014–1022.

Section III

Politics and Public Good

8

The Politics of Social Impact Measurement in Indonesia

Ari Margiono, Tirta Nugraha Mursitama, and Roosalina Wulandari

8.1 'Just' Impact Measurement

Measurement is political, involving the inclusion and exclusion of parameters and indicators. It dictates what is relevant and irrelevant in determining the progress of a society. This chapter aims to critically unpack the contestation surrounding the politics of social impact measurement in Indonesia. Social impact measurement in this chapter is broadly defined as the effort to measure social value creation (Kroeger & Weber, 2014). Thus, social impact measurement may include the measurement of social value creation activities conducted by different institutional actors in capitalist economies, such as government, charities, private sector, activism, and social entrepreneurship (Santos, 2012).

Using a Rawlsian perspective (1971) in developing just measurement principles, this chapter will start with a brief historical survey of the

A. Margiono (✉) • T. N. Mursitama • R. Wulandari
Binus University, Jakarta, Indonesia
e-mail: mmargiono@binus.edu; tmursitama@binus.edu; rwulandari@binus.edu

R. Hazenberg, C. Paterson-Young (eds.), *Social Impact Measurement for a Sustainable Future*, https://doi.org/10.1007/978-3-030-83152-3_8

existing approaches to social impact measurement in Indonesia (for example, government-driven initiatives during the Suharto period and the private sector and third sector initiatives that emerged during the Reformation and Post-Reformation periods). This review will show that despite the shift from a government to private and social sector focus on social impact measurement (including the third sector and social entrepreneurship, as well as impact investment), the involvement of beneficiaries in social impact measurement is often tokenistic, if not neglected. These obscures the intention of many social initiatives as efforts to help marginalised and disadvantaged beneficiaries in Indonesia.

This chapter argues that there is a need to revisit strategies and policies regarding social impact measurement in Indonesia by demonstrating the importance of embracing the community context in applying the just measurement principles. Context in this chapter is defined not merely as external environments where particular locations (i.e. 'where') may affect particular outcomes, but also as historical and temporal factors (i.e. 'when') that affect and influence outcomes (Whetten, 1989; Welter, 2011); and, this means that agents that conduct measurement activities also 'do' contexts throughout history and time, in the sense that their interactions with these external environments construct and may also change the context they operate in (Welter & Baker, 2020). This chapter will close with recommendations for the government, the private sector and the third sector on participatory and community focused social impact measurement, and how the Sustainable Development Goals (SDGs) can support participatory and community focused recommendations.

8.2 The Politics of Social Impact Measurement

Political science scholars have long paid attention to the ways social impact measurement and evaluation are conducted. While scholars from psychology and other disciplines tend to look at the ways in which impact measurement and evaluation initiatives are delivered and conducted (i.e., the accuracy of a measure) (e.g., Maas & Liket, 2011), impact measurement can be viewed as a political endeavour, due to the fact that social programmes often happen within a particular political context (Weiss, 1973). Scholars argue that the accuracy of social impact measurement is essential, however, considering the political nature of social impact measurement is equally important (Weiss, 1973; Lewis, 2015). This is because the political nature of social impact measurement and evaluation affects what and how we see the beneficiaries and how resources are distributed as a result of this. Historical measurement (Kula, 2014) literature has highlighted that while it appears neutral, measurement activities may benefit certain group of people in the society over others. Thus, just measurement practice becomes essential to ensure fairness.

From a Rawlsian (Rawls, 1971) point of view, the political nature of social impact measurement and evaluation represents the ways in which societies develop their basic structures that serve as a 'background justice' affecting the lives of the people living in a society (Stein, 2016). As a basic structure of society, measurement and evaluation activities determine the conditions and the lives of each member of a society. Rawls (1971) asserts that a just society needs to follow two important principles: (a) persons in a society should have the same indefeasible claim to equal liberties; (b) social and economic inequalities need to follow two requirements—first, these inequalities must be coming from the offices and positions open to all with the fair equality of opportunity principles; second, they must be for the benefit of those who are the least advantaged in the society (Rawls, 2001). In other words, when inequality happens at the very least it must be fair and to follow these principles.

The Rawlsian perspective (Rawls, 1971) provides an opportunity to understand social impact measurement as an endeavour to achieve just and fair societies that involve different parties in different sectors (for example, state, civil society, and the private sector). Thus, social impact measurement processes should be seen as an effort to implement the Rawlsian principle in seeking a just society. It should serve to ensure that everyone has the same rights; and it should serve as a site where inequalities are justified via offices and positions that follow the fair equality of opportunity principle and are aimed at the least advantaged in society.

This is particularly true for social initiatives that aim to offer sustainable solutions to neglected areas and show broad support to Rawls' two principles. Much research on the measurement of social impact in the entrepreneurship sector asserts that measurement is essential for entrepreneurs to check whether social objectives have been achieved (Rawhouser et al., 2019; Beisland et al., 2020). For example, Kroeger and Weber (2014) argue that impact measurement is necessary because organisations working in the social sector need to know whether they are making progress and maximising social impact. Further, Stein (2016)—extending Rawlsian principles—proposes two rights that specifically related to the measurement context: (a) the right to objective measurement; and (b) the right to be objectively measured. The first highlights the right of citizens to have measurement practices that are founded on objective standards (Stein, 2016). Objective, according to Stein (2016), is a condition when things tend to be changeless; they tend to be less affected by context, content, and user bias. The second involves the right to participate in determining what measures are relevant to the beneficiaries, as well as the right to benefit from measurement practices that involves the beneficiaries (Stein, 2016).

This perspective allows the authors to construct a yardstick or criteria of just measurement principles in order to evaluate the practice of social impact measurement in Indonesia. The following section will explore the politics of social measurement in Indonesia using the discussed criteria of just measurement. It will show that despite the shift of focus from the government-driven to the private realm (including the third sector), measurement initiatives in Indonesia are yet to fully implement the right to objective measurement and the right to be objectively measured.

8.3 Social Impact in Indonesia

The landscape of social impact measurement in Indonesia can be characterised by three broad periods. First, is the government-driven period; the measurement of social initiatives in Indonesia began to receive serious attention during President Suharto's—Indonesia's second president—administration (1966–1998). During this period, social impact measurement was very much a government-driven initiative. Second, the period of involvement of the private and third sector. Following the collapse of Suharto's authoritarian regime in 1998, and with the rise of democracy in Indonesia, the private sector started to join the bandwagon of social impact measurement through the promotion of Corporate Social Responsibility. During this period, Non-Governmental Organisations also began to flourish as the civil society sector started to rapidly grow following the democratisation of Indonesia. Local Non-Government Organisations partnered or received support from foreign Non-Government Organisations, which allowed local Non-Government Organisations to learn the best measurement practices—including participatory assessment and evaluation. Third, the period of the emergence of social enterprises and impact investment institutions. The popularity of social entrepreneurship and impact investment in the last decade has further popularised social impact measurement. This includes the development and introduction of several metrics, such as Social Return on Investment (SROI) and sector-specific measurement metrics (Maas & Liket, 2011; Beisland et al., 2020) (see Chaps. 3 and 11 for further information on SROI).

Table 8.1 summarises the measurement practices in each period. The following section is by no means an exhaustive list of practices in each identified period but aims to serve as a preliminary sketch of how each period exercises just measurement practices. Thus, it should be seen as an illustration rather than a thorough description or elaboration of the periods.

8.4 Government-Driven Social Impact Measurement Initiatives

Suharto's administration inherited the post-independence chaotic economy. In 1966, the per capita income of the country was far below other similar countries (US$535 compared to US$650 in India) and the majority of Indonesians were experiencing disadvantage and inequality (Booth, 2000). The focus of the administration was to restore the economy and

Table 8.1 Social impact/social measurement in Indonesia

Just Measurement Principles	Government-Sector (Suharto's administration)	Private-Sector and Third Sector	Social Entrepreneurship and Impact Investment Sector
The right to objective measurement	The discussions and debates around how to measure poverty indicated effort to fulfil the right to objective measurement.	Scattered efforts to ensure objective measurement took place in several sectors, such as palm-oil and mining. Yet, in general, corporate social Responsibility measurement is vague and often reduced to publicities. The third sector in Indonesia is quite diverse. Those who were doing robust measurement were usually Non-Government Organisations receiving funding from foreign agencies. These Non-Government Organisations used participatory monitoring principles to develop objective measurement.	Many social enterprises have yet to conduct appropriate social innovation impact measurement. This is primarily because many of them are self-proclaimed social enterprises. However, the increasing popularity of impact investment has led to the introduction of a number of measurement tools (for example theory of change, SROI etc.).
The right to be objectively measured	Most of the discussions of poverty measures were conducted among experts and academics. There was very little involvement of the beneficiaries (disadvantaged and vulnerable groups) in determining the measures.	In some sectors, such as palm-oil and mining, efforts were made to ensure that beneficiaries were involved. This was evident in participatory processes involving beneficiaries in monitoring and evaluation efforts. Donor-funded Non-Government Organisations implemented participatory monitoring activities, involving beneficiaries in the development of measures and the processes of social innovation impact measurement.	The involvement of beneficiaries remains limited. A number of social enterprises, for example in the environmental sector, has implemented participatory measurement due to certification requirement.

Assessment	Partial fulfilment of just measurement principles; resulted in the continuing marginalisation of the poor from the measurement of poverty	Some sectors, such as palm-oil and mining, had developed just measurement practices. However, many other sectors still yet to include the beneficiaries in the process. Most foreign funded third sector Non-Government Organisations fulfiled both rights as part for the funding requirement.	Social enterprise and the impact investment sector have attempted to partially fulfil the just measurement principles. However, this is still scattered and not yet a widely accepted practice.

to lift Indonesians out of poverty. Social innovation and social initiatives, during Suharto's administration, were directed towards reducing poverty in Indonesia, with the most important measure of success revolving around the question of how many people were lifted out from poverty. The centrality and the importance of this question has sparked discussions and debates among experts and scholars on how poverty should be measured and what indicators are required in determining poverty level (for example, determining the poverty line) as many studies on Indonesia, including the government's Central Bureau of Statistics, have been using different methods of poverty measurement since 1965 (Booth, 1993). This resulted in different outcomes that affect how subsequent government policies are drawn.

For example, the most popular poverty measure in the 1990s was the so-called "Sajogyo Poverty Line" that was named after Professor Sajogyo of Bogor Agricultural Institute (Booth, 1993). Sajogyo introduced Milled Rice Equivalent (MRE) as a basis to determine the level of poverty in Indonesia. This definition determined poverty levels ('very poor' to 'poor') for people in Indonesia and served as a basis determining the government's poverty policies. They defined 'poor' households as those which had an annual consumption expenditure equivalent to 240–320 kg of rice, while those which had an annual consumption expenditure below 240 kg of rice were considered 'very poor' (Sajogyo & Wiradi, 1985). The milled rice equivalent was used to determine poverty primarily in rural Indonesia—particularly in Java, the most populated island—as rice was a standard to measure the wealth of a family (Booth, 1993). The debates and discussions on poverty measurement in Indonesia illustrate efforts to ensure that there was objective measurement in measuring social innovation activities, conducted, or funded by the government, to reduce poverty in 'New Order' era Indonesia.[1] Stein (2016) argued that the rights to objective measurement often refer to the reliability of measures, for

[1] President Suharto's (the second Indonesian president) government between 1966–1998 was characterized as the 'New Order' by the administration. This was to show a break from the 'Old Order' of President Sukarno's administration (1945–1966). The New Order departed from the expensive high-profile international projects that were central to the 'Old Order', for example, the Non-Aligned Movement (NAM), as well as the Games of Emerging Forces (GANEFO). The New Order focused more on poverty reduction initiatives and the improvement of the country's economy.

example, to what extent are poverty measures reliable when used in different context.

Yet, the debates and discussions on poverty measurement mostly occurred in academic and consultation meetings or in development journals; this is reflected for example in Pradhan et al. (2000) which revealed that methods of measurement of poverty in Indonesia were mostly based on statistical indicators and determined a priori. There was limited involvement of beneficiaries experiencing inequality and disadvantage in determining the measurement indicators. Most of the data used in the construction of poverty lines were from the government's economic and social surveys. It was not until the enforcement of Law No. 25 in 2000, which mandated the participatory policy processes through Musyawarah Rencana Pembangunan *(Musrenbang)*, that beneficiaries were included in determining the measurement indicators. Thus, the discussions and debates regarding poverty lines among academics and experts reflected efforts to ensure the rights to objective measurement of poverty in Indonesia. Yet, there seemed to be very limited—if not a complete lack of—participation from the beneficiaries in determining the measurement indicators. This reduces the validity of the measures that were introduced during this period (Stein, 2016).

8.5 Social Impact Measurement in the Private Sector and in the Third Sector

The popularity of Corporate Social Responsibility in the late 1990s and early 2000s in Indonesia encouraged many companies to join the bandwagon in social impact measurement. Waagstein (2011) reported that many companies had shown a commitment to beneficiary involvement, partly because it is mandated by the law. The most comprehensive measurement of Corporate Social Responsibility initiatives seems to be those activities that are conducted in the agriculture and plantation (such as palm oil) sector, or in the mining sector (Paoli et al., 2010; Mursitama et al., 2011). This is influenced by two external reasons. First, these sectors often face resistance from communities due to the scale of their operation; therefore, they need to get a 'license to operate' from the community.

The importance of obtaining a 'license to operate' in the plantation and mining industries have been well documented in the Corporate Social Responsibility literature (Demuijnck & Fasterling, 2016). Second, there has been a lot of pressure from foreign countries for sustainable mining and agriculture operations in Indonesia and the expectation to align Corporate Social Responsibility with the business side of the palm-oil industries (Maier-Knapp 2020).

This results in requirements for robust social impact measurement. For example, the Roundtable for Sustainable Palm Oil (RSPO) requires palm-oil companies to embrace the "Free, Prior, and Informed Consent" (FPIC) principle. The FPIC principle requires certified palm oil companies to ensure that beneficiaries and stakeholders are consulted and involved in the whole plantation processes. This includes the requirement to conduct participatory monitoring and periodic multi-stakeholder evaluation of agreement implementation (RSPO 2015). Despite the requirements in some sectors, Corporate Social Responsibility activities in other sectors tend to be haphazard, with many of them reduced to marketing and sales strategies. In one case, Corporate Social Responsibility was used as a way to circumvent strict regulation from the government. One of the largest tobacco companies in Indonesia had been using sport Corporate Social Responsibility as a way to overcome the advertisement limitation imposed on tobacco industries (Siahaya & Smits, 2021). Siahaya and Smits (2021) reported that because of this the company was able to circumvent regulations that prohibit tobacco companies from having unrestricted advertisements in the media.

There has been continuing debate among Corporate Social Responsibility experts and practitioners on whether these practices qualify as good and impactful practices (Palazzo & Richter, 2005; Nussbaum, 2009). Yet tensions aside, it seems that the measurement of social impact and social innovation initiatives in the private sector tend to be scattered, only partially following the just measurement principles. The palm-oil and mining sectors have indicated efforts to fulfil the rights of objective measurement. At the same time, the FPIC principles ensure that the right to be objectively measured is fulfilled. By participating in monitoring and periodic evaluation, the beneficiaries and stakeholders are guaranteed to have the right to participate in determining what measures are relevant to the beneficiaries, as well as the right to benefit from measurement practices that involves the beneficiaries. However, a large proportion of the private sector in Indonesia struggles to appropriately measure Corporate Social Responsibility. Since many companies still use Corporate Social Responsibility activities as a pure extension of their business interests, such as using it as marketing and sales strategies in highly regulated sectors, the rights of the beneficiaries are often relegated to secondary or tertiary business objectives.

In contrast, the social impact measurement landscape is different in the non-profit (or the third) sector. Non-profit organisations were previously highly controlled during the authoritarian Suharto's administration. Non-Government Organisation permits were often used a means to control the ideologies and the activities of civil society during the administration. In the post-Suharto period, there was no requirement that Non-Government Organisations receive a license and registration from the government. Thus, the post-Suharto administration period was a golden moment, due to the shift to the democracy, for third sector organisations to flourish. During this period, many foreign-funded Non-Government Organisations operated in Indonesia and introduced tools and social impact measurement principles that were successfully utilised elsewhere around the world. As an example, Oxfam (Great Britain) had substantial activities in Indonesia from the late 1990s to the late 2000s. During this period, Oxfam supported sustainable development initiatives, disaster relief, and campaigning, as well as advocacy to influence government policies. As an organisation, Oxfam developed a methodology of evaluation that promoted beneficiary engagement by ensuring beneficiaries are consulted and involved in developing the plan together, allowing a space for negotiation and collective decision (Oxfam, 2007). Additionaly, many local Non-Government Organisations, using the internet, adapted various participatory tools and used them in their daily activities (Nugroho, 2010). Thus, third sector social innovation impact measurement activities appear to involve the beneficiaries in the process, especially those that were driven by foreign donors—as part of the funding requirement. The use of participatory assessments and evaluation methods in Non-Government Organisation projects seems to reflect the intention to ensure the rights of objective measurement and the rights to be objectively measured.

8.6 Social Impact in the Social Entrepreneurship and Impact Investment Sector

Despite the longstanding history of social entrepreneurship activities in Indonesia (Idris & Hati, 2013), there has been limited social impact measurement in the social enterprise sector. There are several reasons for limitations in social impact measurement. First, social enterprises—the organisations that apply business methods to achieve social objectives (Austin et al., 2006; Margiono et al., 2019)—only recently obtained popularity in Indonesia and many of them are self-proclaimed social enterprises. This means that there is less accountability on the social objectives that they aim to achieve because there are no external mechanisms to validate their claims. Second, most social enterprises in Indonesia have no legal recognition as outlined by the British Council (2018) report on The State of Social Enterprise Report in Indonesia. This implies that many social enterprises are managed in an informal manner and are yet to conduct measurement activities. Third, social enterprises are often struggling to balance between their financial performance and their social objectives, often experiencing mission drift, and therefore they often place impact measurement, as a form of accountability, as less of a priority (Ebrahim et al., 2014). This particular phenomenon has been widely discussed in the hybrid tension literature (e.g. Battilana & Lee, 2014; Doherty et al., 2014). A recent longitudinal research highlighted the fact that social enterprises have to constantly adjust themselves along the social-business poles (Smith & Besharov, 2019) and this makes consistent measurement difficult.

Despite the impact measurement challenges that many social enterprises face in Indonesia, several measurement initiatives have taken place in the social entrepreneurship sector. An example is a social enterprise in the environmental sector, PT SOBI (*Sosial Bisnis Indonesia*). PT SOBI operates in the forestry sector, offering sustainable teakwood that uses Forest Stewardship Council and local *SVLK* (Sistem Verifikasi Legalitas Kayu) standards. These standards provide a measurement scheme that ensure that the products protect the rights of stakeholders as well as the environment. Further, the increasing popularity of impact investment also brings forward the need for social impact measurement. Several measurement tools are being introduced to the social entrepreneurship sector. SROI, among others, is one of the most popular measurement tools among impact investment practitioners (Arvidson et al., 2013). IRIS+, an impact measurement initiated by the Global Impact Investment Network (GIIN), has also started to gain ground in many companies.

The social entrepreneurship and impact investment sectors seem to be consistent in gradually introducing social impact measurement that promotes the rights of objective measurement (see Chap. 6). However, there appears to be less emphasis on the ways in which beneficiaries are involved in the measurement process, leaving the right to be objectively measured unfulfilled. This seems to be true across Indonesia, with the exception of those social enterprises in the environmental industries that, due to the similar reasons with those companies in the plantation sector, require a 'social license to operate' and/or certification.

8.7 The Importance of Context in Social Impact Measurement

Just measurement practices are important in ensuring that beneficiaries and stakeholders are at the centre of the processes and their rights—the rights to objective measurement and the rights to be objectively measured—are guaranteed. Social impact measurement practices in Indonesia started to receive attention during Suharto's regime. Further, the private sector and the third sector begun to embrace social impact measurement following the fall of the authoritarian regime in 1998; in the last decade or so, social enterprises and impact investment started to practice social impact measurement. There are variations in the way each period embraced measurement practice, as discussed in the previous sections, and their approach to fulfilling the rights of a just society. The Suharto administration was very focused on fulfilling the rights of objective measurement, but there were limitations in the practices to fulfil the rights of people to be objectively measured. While social impact measurement in the private sector was scattered and diverse, social impact measurement in the social enterprise sector was rather new and social impact measurement activities in this sector were still limited.

There have been important developments over time; for example, the government has begun to promote participatory approaches in development planning. Indeed, the introduction of the Law No. 25 on national development planning mandated the government to conduct a series of consultation processes with a diverse group of stakeholders, especially those who would become the subject of development (such as people experiencing disadvantage and inequality) in development planning. This extends the just measurement principle for fulfilling the rights of objective measurement that has traditionally been embraced since the Suharto administration, ensuring that the beneficiaries take part in the process and fulfil their rights to be objectively measured. However, despite this progress, there are gaps in the practice of social impact measurement. One gap relates to the ways in which the right to be objectively measured were practiced. Akbar et al. (2020) observed that while the design of the government planning processes was participatory, many of the activities that involved beneficiaries and stakeholders were often misaligned, due to a lack of knowledge integration, learning processes, and power struggles among stakeholders.

In *Musrenbang*, a forum where citizens and government met to discuss policy planning, knowledge integration and exchange among participants did not happen smoothly because the format and setting of the meetings did not encourage participation (Akbar et al., 2020). The *Musrenbang* often used a classroom setting where the 'elites' sat in comfortable chairs, at the front, and communication was often one-way (Akbar et al., 2020). Despite good intentions, one of the reasons for this to happen was because there seemed to be a disconnect between the universal principles of just measurement and day-to-day practice within communities. In many cases, measurement activities were often reduced to 'tick-box' practices—to ensure the formalities of the measurement activities were fulfilled. This 'tick-box' approach in conducting social impact measurement contradicts the principle of just measurement. In the Musrenbang example, while the consultation activities were 'fulfilled'—and therefore the formalities had been met—the participatory process did not consider the local power dynamics among rural elites and communities. An example of the adaptation to the local dynamics would be to adjust the format of the meeting to facilitate a more egalitarian interaction between the elites and the community members.

Understanding local context becomes important in moderating just measurement principles. There is a need for universal just measurement principles to be contextualised and rooted in day-to-day cultural practices. In this case, context may serve as a 'where' and 'when' prism that diffuses universal principles into different shades of contextualisation practices that are rooted in local cultures.

An example of how local context plays an important role can be seen in the Project CERITA (Community Empowerment for Raising Inclusivity and Trust through Technology Application) initiated by The Habibie Center (a think-tank established by the third Indonesian President B.J Habibie) in 2017. Project CERITA was established to promote universal principles of tolerance through the use of technology to break cultural barriers and bridge cultural gaps. This is due to concerns over rising intolerance and sectarianism in Indonesia in the last few decades. Project CERITA runs in five major cities in Indonesia (Bandung, Jakarta, Yogyakarta, Malang, and Solo) that display high levels of intolerance, such as, using storytelling as a humanistic approach that is deemed to be culturally-fit, and easily integrated into daily conversation in a non-threatening manner.

This particular approach, and the use of technology, allow for positive contact with people from marginalised groups that leads to finding common ground, promoting tolerance and inclusivity. As for impact measurement, using the same curriculum and approach obtained in the workshop and through contextual (for example, local culture) adaptation, the graduates of Project CERITA are expected to hold a replication workshop. Equal opportunity is applied in selection recruits, with recruits representing wider groups. Indicators of achievements are the numbers of snowballed replication workshops promoting tolerance and inclusivity. In Project CERITA, the participants are the beneficiaries who are heavily involved in the processes of storytelling, contextualisation, and replication alongside the objectives of promoting universal principles of tolerance and co-existence.

This discussion on contextualism mirrors recent calls to introduce contextual elements in political science. One relevant perspective is that of Joseph Carens who encourages political theorists to look at existing community practices in their attempt to make sense of citizenship. This is primarily because existing practices may contain a 'form of wisdom' (Carens, 2000) that reflects how agents 'do' context (Welter & Baker, 2020). Project CERITA embodies the 'form of wisdom' in how they recruit youth leaders as participants meticulously and in contextualisation of stories to each locality. Stories also serve as a vehicle for the participants in many social entrepreneurship activities to express their particular contexts, helping the audience to get transported to a different realm (Margiono et al., 2019) and to create contextualisation of the universal principles. Each of the recruits needs to be culturally sensitive and able to engage with people of different worldviews and perspectives, through storytelling and dialogue that is culturally embraced.

There is, of course, a danger that local contextualism may sustain and promote existing injustice; for example, there is a risk that working with the 'wisdom' of local elites in Indonesia may sustain existing patriarchal relationships and gender injustice. To avoid this, context needs to be seen as an important addition to the universal principles of justness and fairness and it should never replace them (Carens, 2004).

Embracing SDGs as a universal anchor in just measurement practice may become a way to avoid the traps of localism in Indonesia. This is primarily because SDGs offer universal principles for just and fair principles for all societies, yet it also offers opportunities for appropriate contextualisation. One of the areas where SDGs depart from the previous Millennium Development Goals (MDGs) is the fact that the formulation of SDGs was essentially a political consensus involving leaders of all countries. Unlike MDGs, that were designed specifically for developing countries, SDGs are designed as universal principles; and, in the formulation of SDG targets and the monitoring of the progress there seems to be a strong effort to fulfil the rights of objective measurement.

The discourse of contextualisation also resonates in many discussions on the measurement of the SDGs; one of the challenges appears to be in the measurement of the progress of the SDGs targets. For example, finding a balance between what to measure that fulfils the global and local demands has proven to be difficult and therefore needs to accommodate local complexities. SDGs target 3.3. attempts to eradicate diseases and experts have chosen HIV and tuberculosis as two indicators that represent global and local problems respectively (MacFeely 2018).

8.8 Contextualism and Localism

This chapter illustrates that social impact measurement in Indonesia is diverse, and while some initiatives have followed Rawlsian just measurement principles, the practices are often misaligned. The misalignment challenge seems to be widespread; even the implementation and measurement of SDGs is not immune to this particular disparity. To rectify this matter, this chapter proposed incorporating a contextualism approach in just measurement practice. Contextualism is necessary to ensure that measurement and the practice of measuring is rooted in local practice and local institutions. This is important to avoid the disconnect between the universal principles in just measurement, such as the right to objective measurement, and the right to be objectively measured.

As a recommendation to the government, the private sector, and the civil society sector, including the social enterprise sector, measurement initiatives need to acknowledge and embed local wisdom and local practice while linking to the universal just measurement principles. At this point, SDGs might become a starting point for the government, private sector, and the civil society sector to consider how a common good framework may help to ensure just measurement principles can be fulfilled. However, even the implementation of SGDs is not without challenges. There are tensions that linger in the way indicators are chosen. Thus, project owners in each sector need to ensure the practices and the institutions of stakeholders can serve to contextualise the universal principles that have become the standards in measurement. In many cases, this requires stamina as it involves a lengthy process of negotiation, knowledge integration, and learning processes in the multi-stakeholder measurement processes. The devil is very much in the detail.

Another important lesson from the brief survey of social impact measurement initiatives in Indonesia is that there seems to be limited partnership in the development and implementation of social impact measurement. Social impact measurement tends to be sectoral, scattered, and ad-hoc. Cross-sector partnership, as an implementation of the SDGs (Sustainable Development Goals), in establishing social impact measurement initiatives will become necessary. This is primarily because cross-sector partnership may serve as a platform for the government, business, and civil society sectors to jointly address social and environmental challenges effectively (Selsky & Parker, 2005) and to develop a common platform in measuring the success of social impact activities. At the end, it is the people who will benefit from these effective interventions; having a sectoral, interest-based approach in social impact activities was seen as less desirable to achieve this objective (Ellis & Biggs, 2001). At the same time, much research has highlighted that cross-sector partnerships are quite successful in balancing different interests and perspectives at different levels, e.g. at individual and cognitive level (Stadtler & Van Wassenhove, 2016), as well as at the institutional level (Seitanidi et al., 2010); and thus, provide an avenue for better social impact measurement practices. The cross-sector partnership approach may help to solve the emerging tensions between the top-down approach that characterises many universal principles and the requirement of inclusivity as well as contextualism in just measurement practices.

References

Akbar, A., Flacke, J., Martinez, J., & van Maarseveen, M. F. (2020). Participatory Planning Practice in Rural Indonesia: A Sustainable Development Goals-Based Evaluation. *Community Development, 51*(3), 243–260.

Arvidson, M., Lyon, F., McKay, S., & Moro, D. (2013). Valuing the Social? The Nature and Controversies of Measuring Social Return on Investment (SROI). *Voluntary Sector Review, 4*(1), 3–18.

Austin, J., Stevenson, H., & Wei–Skillern, J. (2006). Social and Commercial Entrepreneurship: Same, Different, or Both? *Entrepreneurship Theory and Practice, 30*(1), 1–22.

Battilana, J., & Lee, M. (2014). Advancing Research on Hybrid Organizing–Insights from the Study of Social Enterprises. *Academy of Management Annals, 8*(1), 397–441.

Beisland, L. A., Djan, K. O., Mersland, R., & Randøy, T. (2020). Measuring Social Performance in Social Enterprises: A Global Study of Microfinance Institutions. *Journal of Business Ethics*, 171, 1–21.

Booth, A. (1993). Counting the Poor in Indonesia. *Bulletin of Indonesian Economic Studies, 29*(1), 53–83.

Booth, A. (2000). Poverty and Inequality in the Soeharto Era: An Assessment. *Bulletin of Indonesian Economic Studies, 36*(1), 73–104.

British Council. (2018). "The State of Social Enterprise in Indonesia". Retrieved on September, 15, 2021. Available at https://www.britishcouncil.org/sites/default/files/the_state_of_social_enterprise_in_indonesia_british_council_web_final_0.pdf

Carens, J. H. (2000). *Culture, Citizenship, and Community: A Contextual Exploration of Justice as Even-handedness*. Oxford University Press on Demand.

Carens, J. H. (2004). A Contextual Approach to Political Theory. *Ethical Theory and Moral Practice, 7*(2), 117–132.

Demuijnck, G., & Fasterling, B. (2016). The Social License to Operate. *Journal of Business Ethics, 136*(4), 675–685.

Doherty, B., Haugh, H., & Lyon, F. (2014). Social ENTERPRISEs as Hybrid Organisations: A Review and Research Agenda. *International Journal of Management Reviews, 16*(4), 417–436.

Ebrahim, A., Battilana, J., & Mair, J. (2014). The Governance of Social Enterprises: Mission Drift and Accountability Challenges in Hybrid Organisations. *Research in Organizational Behavior, 34*, 81–100.

Ellis, F., & Biggs, S. (2001). Evolving Themes in Rural Development 1950s–2000s. *Development and Policy Review, 19*(4), 437–448.

Idris, A., & Hijrah Hati, R. (2013). Social Entrepreneurship in Indonesia: Lessons from the Past. *Journal of Social Entrepreneurship, 4*(3), 277–301.

Kroeger, A., & Weber, C. (2014). Developing a Conceptual Framework for Comparing Social Value Creation. *Academy of Management Review, 39*(4), 513–540.

Kula, W. (2014). *Measures and Men*. Princeton University Press.

Lewis, J. M. (2015). The Politics and Consequences of Performance Measurement. *Policy and Society, 34*(1), 1–12.

Maas, K., & Liket, K. (2011). Social Impact Measurement: Classification of Methods. In *Environmental Management Accounting and Supply Chain Management* (pp. 171–202). Springer.

Macfeely, S. (2018). "The 2030 Agenda An Unprecedented Statistical Challenge." Retrieved on September 15, 2021. Available at https://library.fes.de/pdf-files/iez/14796.pdf

Maier-Knapp, Naila. (2020). "The European Commission's palm oil conundrum". East Asia Forum. Retrieved on September 15, 2021. Available at https://www.eastasiaforum.org/2020/02/28/the-european-commissions-palm-oil-conundrum/

Margiono, A., Kariza, A., & Heriyati, P. (2019). Venture Legitimacy and Storytelling in Social Enterprises. *Small Enterprise Research, 26*(1), 55–77.

Mursitama, T. N., Hasan, M. F., and Fakhrudin, I. Y. (2011). *Corporate social responsibility di Indonesia: teori dan implementasi: studi kasus community development Riaupulp.* .

Nugroho, Y. (2010). Non-government Organisations, the Internet, and Sustainable Rural Development: The Case of Indonesia. *Information, Communication and Society, 13*(1), 88–120.

Nussbaum, A. S. K. (2009). Ethical Corporate Social Responsibility and the Pharmaceutical Industry: A Happy Couple? *Journal of Medical Marketing, 9*(1), 67–76.

Oxfam, G. B. (2007). "Impact Measurement and Accountability in Emergencies: The Good Enough Guide". Retrieved on September 15, 2020. Available at https://oxfamilibrary.openrepository.com/bitstream/handle/10546/115510/bk-impact-measurement-accountability-090207-en.pdf;jsessionid=C9B265D387A90A6BA9185766C028C82B?sequence=1

Palazzo, G., & Richter, U. (2005). Corporate Social Responsibility Business as Usual? The Case of the Tobacco Industry. *Journal of Business Ethics, 61*(4), 387–401.

Paoli, G. D., Yaap, B., Wells, P. L., & Sileuw, A. (2010). CSR, Oil Palm and the RSPO: Translating Boardroom Philosophy into Conservation Action on the Ground. *Tropical Conservation Science, 3*(4), 438–446.

Pradhan, M., Suryahadi, A., Sumarto, S., and Pritchett, L. (2000). *Measurements of Poverty in Indonesia, 1996, 1999, and Beyond.* The World Bank.

Rawhouser, H., Cummings, M., & Newbert, S. L. (2019). Social Impact Measurement: Current Approaches and Future Directions for Social Entrepreneurship Research. *Entrepreneurship Theory and Practice, 43*(1), 82–115.

Rawls, J. (1971). *A Theory of Justice*. Harvard University Press.

Rawls, J. (2001). *Justice as Fairness*. Harvard University Press.

RSPO Human Rights Working Group. (2015). "Free, Prior and Informed Consent Guide for RSPO Members". Retrieved on September 15, 2021. Available at https://rspo.org/news-and-events/announcements/free-prior-and-informed-consent-guide-for-rspo-members-2015-endorsed

Sajogyo, P., and Wiradi, G. (1985). Rural Poverty and Efforts for Its Alleviation in Indonesia, .

Santos, F. M. (2012). A Positive Theory of Social Entrepreneurship. *Journal of Business Ethics, 111*(3), 335–351.

Seitanidi, M. M., Koufopoulos, D. N., & Palmer, P. (2010). Partnership Formation for Change: Indicators for Transformative Potential in Cross Sector Social Partnerships. *Journal of Business Ethics, 94*(1), 139–161.

Selsky, J. W., & Parker, B. (2005). Cross-sector Partnerships to Address Social Issues: Challenges to Theory and Practice. *Journal of Management, 31*(6), 849–873.

Siahaya, I. A., & Smits, T. (2021). Sport Corporate Social Responsibility as a Hidden Marketing Strategy? A study of Djarum, an Indonesian Tobacco Company. *Sport in Society*, 24(9), 1–24.

Smith, W. K., & Besharov, M. L. (2019). Bowing Before Dual Gods: How Structured Flexibility Sustains Organisational Hybridity. *Administrative Science Quarterly, 64*(1), 1–44.

Stadtler, L., & Van Wassenhove, L. N. (2016). Coopetition as a Paradox: Integrative Approaches in a Multi-company, Cross-sector Partnership. *Organization Studies, 37*(5), 655–685.

Stein, Z. (2016). *Social Justice and Educational Measurement: John Rawls, the History of Testing, and the Future of Education*. Routledge.

Waagstein, P. R. (2011). The Mandatory Corporate Social Responsibility in Indonesia: Problems and Implications. *Journal of Business Ethics, 98*(3), 455–466.

Weiss, C. (1973). The Politics of Impact Measurement. *Policy Studies Journal, 1*(3), 179.

Welter, F. (2011). Contextualizing Entrepreneurship—Conceptual Challenges and Ways Forward. *Entrepreneurship Theory and Practice, 35*(1), 165–184.

Welter, F., & Baker, T. (2020). Moving Contexts onto New Roads: Clues from Other Disciplines. *Entrepreneurship Theory and Practice*. 1042258720930996.

Whetten, D. A. (1989). What Constitutes a Theoretical Contribution? *Academy of Management Review, 14*(4), 490–495.

9

Social impact Measurement in Public Service Delivery in the Age of Austerity: The Case of Community Libraries in Vietnam

Oanh T. Cao

9.1 Impact Partnerships

Over the last four decades, public service delivery reform has attracted the attention of many researchers and policymakers. Studies on public service delivery focus mainly on the forms of transformation (Torres & Pina, 2002); the types of partnership and collaboration, including public-private partnerships (PPP) and co-production (Needham, 2008); Public Service Mutuals (Hazenberg & Hall, 2016; Le Grand & Roberts, 2018); and community partnership, together with joined-up and entrepreneurial government (Osborne & Gaebler, 1992; Donahue & Zeckhauser, 2011; Alford & O'Flynn, 2012). Previous research also extensively discusses concepts and functions, in addition to the impact of the third sector on the social economy (Nicholls, 2006; Young, 2006), and its involvement in public service delivery (Di Domenico et al., 2010). Given the policy context, where there is an increasing shift to social value

O. T. Cao (✉)
VNU University of Economics and Business, Vietnam National University, Hanoi, Vietnam

R. Hazenberg, C. Paterson-Young (eds.), *Social Impact Measurement for a Sustainable Future*, https://doi.org/10.1007/978-3-030-83152-3_9

creation (SVC) in public service delivery, there is also a need for increasing academic discussion on SVC and social impact in public service delivery. There is a lack of research focusing on the social impact assessment specific to public service delivery, which identifies the main areas where public services could deliver better social impact. Furthermore, social impact assessment in public service delivery is rarely discussed within economies in transition like Vietnam, where resources are scarce. This under-researched area is important, as it can provide recommendations for all stakeholders in understanding the context and the implementation of public service policy within developing contexts. Therefore, this chapter examines a suitable social impact measurement approach to public service delivery, taking the case of community library services in Vietnam, with consideration towards the limited resources of both government and the community. The chapter discusses the partnership between the community, third sector organisations and the government in public service delivery in relation to the contextual factors that affect social impact creation in developing countries. More importantly, the chapter aims to adjust social impact measurement approaches in the context of austerity, where both service providers and government have limited capability to engage in this.

9.2 Public Service Delivery and Social Impact Assessment

With the aim of improving public service quality in the age of austerity, external providers, including the private sector, the third sector, local government, and the community are encouraged to participate in delivering public services (Alford & O'Flynn, 2012). In public service reform, decentralisation was argued to decrease the financial burden and increase the efficiency of public services, as local governments can better mobilise local resources and understand local needs and preferences (Azfar et al., 2004). Decentralisation is discussed in terms of fiscal, administrative and political aspects (Robinson, 2007); however, it can be argued that researchers have rarely discussed decentralisation as a process of enhancing the legitimacy of the state, service providers and community. When local governments are given more autonomy and power, it is also important for them to enhance legitimacy with their local community in order to sustain the improved quality of public services with respect to the community's preferences and demands. Therefore, the decentralisation of public service delivery is more efficient if it is able to increase social interaction and social bonds among the community.

Co-production is defined as the involvement of the community in producing public services (Alford, 1998; Needham, 2008). Interaction between the community and service providers has been argued to develop horizontal relationships and social capital for both services users and services providers (Needham, 2008). Through frontline interactions, staff acquire expertise, while services users become more responsible and involved. Needham (2008) explored co-production as a therapeutic tool that helps to build trust and communication and as a diagnostic tool that reveals users' needs, identifies causes, and finds solutions. The engagement of the community in public service provision and production is an aspect of transformative entrepreneurial government, moving from centralised power to decentralised and participatory management (Osborne & Gaebler, 1992).

As public services are different from commercial ones, the key issue when externalising public services is the selection of service providers who do not ignore the features of public services as a non-profitable, fair, and equal set of values (Torres & Pina, 2002). By focusing on social interaction and social bonds through wider stakeholder involvement, third sector organisations help to build and increase social capital. Essentially, shared norms, values and links can enable people to trust and work together better. The cooperation between sectors in the social economy, while increasing interactions among those sectors, also contributes to the formation of social capital. The collective goods generated by such partnerships do not enhance, but rather transform, existing interactions among partnerships towards innovation rather than smoother functioning (Jordan, 2008).

Social value can be created by many stakeholders; for example, private enterprises with community interests, policymakers, social organisations and even individuals. However, it is important to note that not all social value created can produce added value and have a social impact. Whilst social value created by individuals or charitable organisations might bring positive benefits to the community, such entities may not really participate in added social value creation, but simply the transformation of resources from one to another (Young, 2006). In contrast, social value is created through the involvement of the recipients in both their processes and outcomes. For example, a third sector organisation hires disabled people, and provides training to equip them with living skills, self-confidence and social networks, leading to a more inclusive environment for them. Therefore, social value created by third sector organisations can translate into social impact on a large scale and deliver transformative social change (Young, 2006; Jain, 2018).

Despite the growth of impact measurement in the social economy, there has been little research undertaken about social impact measurement in public service delivery, especially within developing countries. Furthermore, studies show that there are several challenges for organisations in conducting social impact measurement, such as: resource limitation, data collection over time, capability of organisations (Barraket & Yousefpour, 2013). Indeed, the nature of social value and social impact is socially constructed, thus not easily measured (Arvidson et al., 2010; Ebrahim & Rangan, 2010); a universal measurement method of social impact may not be feasible (Lane & Casile, 2011).

There have been a number of social impact measurement tools, such as: Social Return on Investment (SROI), Social Accounting and Audit (SAA) system, Social Cost-Benefit Analysis (SCBA), Social Enterprise Balanced Scorecard (SEBS, or SBSC), and Outcomes Star (OS). Each measurement method has benefits and drawbacks. For example, SROI focuses on tangible outcomes and thus, fail to capture intangible ones that are hard to monetise (Hall & Arvidson, 2013) (see Chap. 3 for further information on SAA, BSC and SROI). By contrast, tools like OS focus on three key ideas: the empowerment of service users; collaboration between users and workers; and the integration of the tool into the everyday working practices of a service (MacKeith, 2011). However, this interactive feature may cause a risk of bias as it relies on subjective discussion about how service users and staff feel (Hall & Arvidson, 2013). Thus, Costa and Pesci (2016) claimed that a universal measurement method is unlikely to be achievable. Instead, the two authors proposed the multiple-constituency approach which requires the involvement of stakeholders at all five steps of social impact measurements, which are: Identifying stakeholders, categorising stakeholders properly, understanding the nature of their interest, assessing relevant metrics, and considering feedback from stakeholders. This theory emerged from the argument that no impact measurement perfectly meets different stakeholder groups interest in relevant social impact as social enterprises, and so as third sector organisations, operate in complex and multi-stakeholder environments.

Whilst the author agrees with this approach in terms of involving different stakeholders in the social impact measurement process of third sector organisations, there are several inherent weaknesses to the approach. First, the proposed theory does not mention the cost of the social impact measurement process. Engaging stakeholders at all stages may cause a high cost because of time and resource consumption. At the end of the process when different social impact measurements are chosen for different groups of stakeholders, it is a challenge for third sector organisations to conduct all measurement methods. This is particularly true for small third sector organisations whose capability is limited. Second, while mentioning the involvement of stakeholders in measuring social impact, there is a lack of cultural and contextual factors that may have considerable influence on how those stakeholders interact.

In developing countries like Vietnam, with nascent social impact ecosystems, the interaction and involvement of all stakeholder such as the government, the investors, third sector organisations, and consumers are not equally effective. Thus, with regard to public services delivered by a third sector organisation, this chapter will discuss the partnership between the community, third sector organisations, and the government in public service delivery in relation to the contextual factors that affect social impact creation in developing countries like Vietnam. In discussing this partnership approach, this chapter draws on semi-structured interviews with participants at community libraries (Case 1 and Case 2) that are community-managed under supervision of the government. This collaboration in public service delivery is relevant to the UN's SDGs 17 which promote multi-stakeholder partnership and voluntary commitment for sustainable development. Through the engagement of community in public service delivery, partnership, knowledge sharing, financial and technical support are established. The impact of this partnership is recognised by SDG17 regarding Capacity Building which both local authority and community support each other to deliver better services. Besides, the mutual understanding achieved through the engagement contributes to the implementation of inter-governmentally agreed development goals and commitments which is maintaining the library services and inspiring all community to learn and acquire more knowledge. Most importantly, the impact created through this service-delivery model is entitled with promoting lifelong learning opportunity for all (SDG4). The library increases the opportunity to access to education for all community groups, especially the poor. SDG4 is also reached through trainings for not only student, but also teachers, and parents in the local, which ensure the supply of qualified teachers in less developed areas and sustainable changes in knowledge sharing in the local areas. Furthermore, the chapter aims to adjust social impact measurement approaches in the context of austerity where both service providers and service users have limited capability of conducting said tasks.

9.3 How Partnership Can Facilitate Social Impact Creation?

In the community libraries impact creation was rooted in a process of "engagement" resulting from a strong partnership between the local authority and the community. The main forms of "engagement" are 'communication' and 'collaboration' with the community, the third sector organisation, and the local authority. Although the library is small, getting readers to come to the library was critical. With a limited budget, the libraries often made use of its network to invite speakers who had a connection with them to give free talks on a specific subject. Annual meetings with representatives of different unions and the community were also held to ensure accountability.

> The library is not only a place to read but also a place to communicate and share good information with each other. (P3—service user case 1)

More importantly, the users in both community libraries showed their trust in the libraries' boards of directors and felt the libraries were a part of their culture and tradition. Therefore, it could be implied that the 'communication' between the service provider and the users depended much more on interaction factors such as 'trust', 'cohesion', 'social bonds' and 'social awareness', which encouraged the community to engage in service provision. This was particularly true as the engagement of volunteers, household and communities was mostly based on their trust in the leaders of the library and their awareness of its necessity. The vision and actions of the library managers in maintaining the libraries were beneficial for all the members of the village, inspiring and encouraging other members to become involved in the library operations, and therefore, in social impact creation (Crosby et al., 2017; Jain et al., 2020). This two-way communication method, with more collaboration and interaction, can develop a sense of mutual responsibility and understanding between professionals and customers (Miller & Wallis, 2011). In both cases, the leaders' "interpersonal connections" were essential. Thanks to the leader's activeness and extensive network with the local authority and the policy-makers at higher levels, and through attending conferences and meetings, the library was well-known and received more support from the policy-makers and other third sector organisations. Shared norms, values and links can help people build trust and teamwork in an organisation, a community or society, thereby impacting upon the development process (Putnam, 1993; Fukuyama, 1995; Gradstein & Justman, 2002). The impact resulted in the changes in behaviours in both cases where the community is inspired to learn and read more often.

> The impact of this library is not only for student, but also parents and teachers, and the whole community. This is an open space for local community to enhance their knowledge, thus change their awareness about many aspects of life (P13—service user case 2)

> the library was founded by the Study promotion fund which is managed by both local authority and the community. Mr. [name], the founder of this fund, has a wide network with donators, experts in the field of community library, and local authority, so that he can help to introduce the library to many local schools, as well as residents in the areas (P10—service user case 2)

Therefore, the engagement process revealed in both cases was not just an act of partnering with the authority or service provider, but a process of transforming the perception and behaviours of service users. Therefore, it is crucial to assess the social impact created through social changes, which implies a shift in society's structure, practices and beliefs (Thekaekara, 2005). These changes in social perception may lead to shifts in behaviour (Ferguson and Bargh 2004; Young, 2006), which in turn promote actions such as volunteering, self-learning, and innovative teaching methods. The awareness changes from students, parents, to teachers in local areas regarding reading habits and the importance of education establish a learning culture of the local areas, which contribute to sustainable development as stated in SDG4. However, whether the impact can lead to sustainable changes in the long term remains to be seen and thus, requires a long-term and frequent impact measurement.

9.4 Does Partnership Benefit or Challenge Social Impact Measurement?

The partnership among service providers and community and local authority in both cases were built upon their mutual understanding and close collaboration. The libraries were aware of the necessity of community events that helped to promote the library and understand the community's needs. Annual meetings with representatives of different unions and the community were also held to ensure accountability. In general, the library understood that they had to make the library become the "heart of the village", where people would come not only to read books, but also to obtain information, talk, and involve themselves in other activities. This engagement of community from designing and delivering (volunteers at the library) to consulting (feedback) represents a form of co-production (Needham, 2008).

> Of course, the library often makes 6-month and annual reports. Representatives of different unions in the village are also invited to the meetings. Consequently, the number of participants has surged rapidly from hundreds of people to the whole village. (P1—Service provider Case 1)

Social impact assessment was not just a formula-derived numerical calculation but an educative social process through collaboration and partnership, which eventually changes the education environment of the local areas (Carley, 1983). Indeed, social impact assessment also encompasses the empowerment of local people and disadvantaged groups, capacity building, and alleviation of unequal opportunity for education (Vanclay, 2003). This is also mentioned in SDG4. Specific to target 4.7 that ensures community get skills and knowledge to promote sustainable development and sustainable lifestyle, the impact assessment in the studied cases should concerns the changes in people's awareness of education and their ability to improve themselves. The impact assessment should also be aligned with target 4.a (upgrading education facilities for an inclusive learning environments) and target 4.c (increasing the supply of qualified teachers). Those impacts guided by SDGs can only be completed with the involvement of community as both service users and service providers. Having social impacts assessed by the community and users is desirable to cause least disruption and able to adapt to community's demand (Fu-Keung IP, 1990).

In contrast, the interview with provincial library officer revealed that there is no social impact measurement conducted by the authority because of limited capability. However, the authority often bases on the reputation of the library to evaluate their efficiency and give them award for appreciation. They support community-led libraries in the sense that this will improve social well-being for a wider community and that is an indicator considered by any form of assessment (Vanclay, 2003). However, there is a lack of concern for actual burdens experienced by the community (Vanclay, 2003). Whilst the government in developing countries like Vietnam lean on a partnership with the community to deliver some public services, they are ignorant in evaluating the social impact and exploring the unequal distribution of impacts to different social groups in order to reform the development plan.

> Social impact measurement? We wish to but we don't have enough capability for that [...] For libraries that are successful, the state will reward them and give them a certificate for their distribution. Of course, the state could not give them a budget; they mainly seek support from publishing houses and charity funds (P9—policymaker case 1)

The partnership also depends on the capabilities of all stakeholders, as part of a wider multi-stakeholder collaboration. People with better education and awareness of their human rights are often engaged more with the community (Di Domenico et al., 2009; Bovaird et al., 2016). This finding may help to explain why some community partnerships do not work because of the lack of attention to people's ability to collaborate with each other. Communities and local authorities in both cases displayed 'solidarity' and 'tradition' that helped them to join together and maintain the library, although they still had limitations in their skills. The founders in both cases are people with well-developed knowledge, which helps them actively approach policymakers for support and convince the community to run the library with them. More importantly, they have high credibility in the community which makes them influencers.

Whilst partnership can bring more social impact to the community, the impact is differently perceived among stakeholders. In general, the libraries receive good feedback on their services. Participants emphasised that the most important impact of the library is to inspire children, their parents, the teacher, and all the community to read and access to knowledge. They aim to deliver influence not only to the readers but also the whole community by transferring knowledge to parents and teachers so that they could improve outcomes for the next generation.

> The impact of this library is not only for student, but also parents and teachers, and the whole community. This is an open space for local community to enhance their knowledge, thus change their awareness about many aspects of life (P13—service user case 2)

Although participants in both libraries reported the social changes as social impact, their perception of social impact measurement indicators do not fully reflect what they perceive as social impact. Library managers only mentioned "tangible indicators" such as numbers of readers, numbers of books borrowed, the number of hours open, the variety of book types, etc. the library managers contended that, they just need to listen to readers' feedback and record some simple indicators with the purpose to improve themselves and serve the reader better. Because of the financial burden of social impact measurement and the small scale of the library, there was a desire for a simple evaluation that was more qualitative than quantitative. However, while agreeing with library managers on "tangible indicators", experts in the field mentioned some more "intangible indicators", such as the influence of the library on local policy, the popularity of the libraries in the media, and the level of recognition amongst the community. This reflects different angles of how social impact should be measure by different stakeholders.

> we need to evaluate the impacts of library on local policy, the popularity of the librarians to the community, as well as the inspiration that the library brings to the community. We need a tool or a guidance of how to measure the impacts (P14—Expert case 2)

The differences among stakeholders' awareness and capability question the efficiency of partnership in evaluating social impact. As professionals are usually more concern with technical measurement and data collection (Rickson et al., 1990), experts' approach to social impact measurement is more comprehensive, but not necessarily compatible with community's ability to understand the method. This may cause conflict if social impact measurement is conducted on a participatory basis.

9.5 Multi-level Social impact measurement Approach

Although there is a strong collaboration between service provider, community and local authority in delivering public services, there is little engagement and collaboration in social impact evaluation among these stakeholders. Social impact measurement is a social construct concept influenced by stakeholders' viewpoints (Herman & Renz, 1997; Chan et al., 2015). Costa and Pesci (2016) contend that in measuring social impacts, organisations should consider stakeholders' needs through the measurement process. Indeed, in both Cases, library managers showed the demand for impact measurement simply to report their performance and to advance perceptions of their service quality. In contrast, experts tend to focus more on both measurable and immeasurable impacts of the library to other stakeholders; whilst policymakers have only a vague understanding of social impact measurement. They seem to focus more on rewarding libraries based on their reputations, which was reported by interviewees as "symbolic" and not realistic. Solutions such as award recognition, short-term training, and book transfers are short term, and there is a lack of a long-term strategy to develop and gain community trust.

While agreeing with multi-stakeholder approaches (Costa & Pesci, 2016), it require strong resources and knowledge to conduct successfully. The main obstacles faced by the libraries were the lack of a guidance on measurement, the capabilities of people to conduct the task of social impact measurement and the associated financial constraints of such measurement. In the context of public service delivery in Vietnam, both service providers and their local authorities are not yet familiar with social impact measurement. Their perception of social impact measurement seems too close to performance evaluation and is based on the reputations of the services. Even though both cases are community-managed, they are still under the mass organisation of the state, which is politically controlled by the local authority. Indeed, some authors contend that Vietnamese social groups are less autonomous than those in Eastern Europe (Womack 1993).

> There is a lack of standardised indicators guided by the government to measure the impact (P11—the library manager-household in Case 2)

> One of the obstacles for impact measurement is the cost (P7—service provider Case 2)

Both library managers mentioned the complex administration systems, with lots of meetings and reports with/for the local authority. Therefore, social impact measurement, if it happens on a multi-stakeholder collaboration basis, could potentially cause more workload for the library managers.

> If the Ministry of Culture has any instruction, they direct us to deploy the plan, and then we report to the Ministry of Culture at the end of the year. The mechanism of operation is very complicated, and sometimes there are things that don't need to go through the Department of Culture—we could report directly to the Ministry (P10-policymakers case 1)

Furthermore, better cooperation with communities when designing and delivering public services is required so as to understand their needs better (Needham, 2008). Therefore, understanding stakeholders' demand regarding social impact measurement is of importance. The collaboration between the authority and community is a form of capacity building that focus on strengthening and maintaining the capabilities of states and societies to design and implement strategies that brings more social impacts and overcome emerging challenges, as stated in SDG17. SDG17 supports the partnership for sustainable development, in which multi-stakeholder and participatory approaches is emphasised. In the context of public service delivery in Vietnam, library services are only provided at provincial level and some districts (but not effectively as reported by public officers due to limited accessibility and poor infrastructure). Therefore, the need for participatory approach as SDG17 emphasises is apparently. Local authorities in both cases understand the strengths of communities and thus promote the model of self-help for community services, which is only appropriate for communities in which social bonds are strong and close-knit (Dunning 1985). Thus, local authority's demand for social impact measurement is also low, as they do not directly deliver the services. In the context of developing countries like Vietnam where resources are limited, social impact measurement is still a new concept in public service delivery. The need for cooperation in social impact measurement, therefore, is of importance.

Impact assessment is a learning process rather than a methodologically management tool (Rickson et al., 1990). Therefore, a participatory social impact measurement will utilise resources and harness barriers to the measurement such as institutional, political, economic constraints. This cooperative approach is recognised by SDG17 as a vehicle for mobilising and sharing knowledge, expertise, technologies and financial resources to support the achievement of the SDGs in all countries, particularly developing countries. Indeed, the partnership in delivering library services will help the local authority to utilise community's resources and support from experts and non-profit organisation in terms of both financial resources and technical support. Therefore, the design of impact measurement approach must be developed based on a multi-level measurement that shows the collaboration and relationship between stakeholders.

The primary-level measurement is conducted by social organisation who deliver the services. The local authority could conduct more middle-range level measurement that refers the evaluation data towards informing policy implementation. The advanced-level measurement should be conducted by experts, and researchers from research institutions whom have interests in the field. The advanced-level measurement is expected to be transferred to service providers and the local authority in the future, when the capability of all stakeholders and the social impact ecosystem in Vietnam is more developed. Conversely, the simple but realistic measurement on the ground can be a good source for the government and researchers to continue to develop social impact measurement approaches in Vietnam. A general framework for measurement such as SDGs could be a good reference which focus not only on numerical indicators but also on the development of different social groups. SDGs could be applied mainly at advanced and middle-range levels with certain indicators and targets. The guideline then should be given to the preliminary level in order to both give them orientation for development and policy implementation. This framework could be a guideline for how three

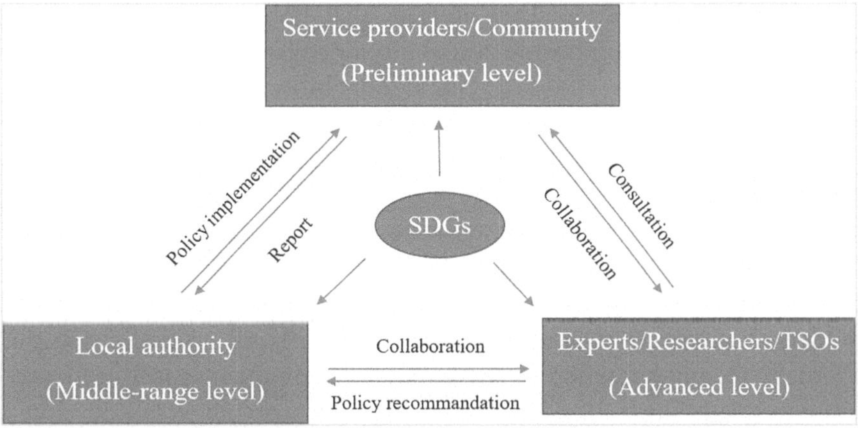

Fig. 9.1 Multi-level social impact measurement approach

stakeholders should focus on their social impact measurement and how they should collaborate to achieves the goals. This collaboration is inextricable to demonstrate social impact in the most comprehensive way given the limited resource and capability. Figure 9.1 demonstrates this approach.

9.6 Transformational Impact in Public service Delivery

This chapter argues that social impact is created through the process of engagement in public service delivery, which is not simply an act of working together, but a transformation of behaviours. Stakeholders experience a process ranging from perception or awareness, to feeling empathy from the service providers, from which trust was built among stakeholders, resulting in a transformation in their behaviours towards engaging more with the service delivery. These changes in social perception, which eventually led to the shift in behaviours, implies social value and social impact creation (Thekaekara, 2005; Young, 2006). The findings also support the important message that the process of engagement needs a vector of 'capability' to encourage the stakeholders to work together based on mutual trust and values. This suggests that policymakers should pay attention to improving people's capability to engage, not just the process of engagement itself. However, the sustainability of the impacts needs further examination, as a culture that favours achievement rather than realistic solutions in Vietnam, is also a barrier for social impact measurement.

The chapter also supports a multi-stakeholder approach to social impact measurement (Costa & Pesci, 2016). However, the development of different social impact measurement tools customised to each stakeholder requires times and resources, which is not suitable in the Vietnamese context, where social impact measurement is still in its preliminary stages. Instead, collaboration between stakeholders to develop a multi-level framework for social impact measurement is more feasible. The primary-level measurement is conducted by social organisation who deliver the services; the middle-range level measurement is conducted by local authority and policy makers; and the advanced-level measurement should be conducted by experts, including researchers from research institutions that have an interest in the field. This data can then be used to develop policy recommendations and consultancy can be delivered to service providers and policymakers to support these. A general framework for all three levels such as SDGs is suggested to provide a better guideline for the collaboration in social impact measurement. This framework and collaboration are important to demonstrate social impact in the most comprehensive way in Vietnam, given the limited resource and capability.

References

Alford, J. (1998). A Public Management Road less Travelled: Clients as Co-Producers of Public Services. *Australian Journal of Public Administration, 57*(4), 128–137.

Alford, J., & O'Flynn, J. (2012). *Rethinking Public Service Delivery: Managing with External Providers*. Palgrave Macmillan.

Arvidson, M., Lyon, F., McKay, S., and Moro, D. (2010). The Ambitions and Challenges of SROI, .

Azfar, O., Kähkönen, S., Lanyi, A., Meagher, P., & Rutherford, D. (2004). Decentralization, Governance and Public Service: The Impact of Institutional Arrangements. In M. S. Kimenyi & P. Meagher (Eds.), *Devolution and Development: Governance Prospects in Decentralizing States* (pp. 19–62). Ashgate.

Barraket, J., & Yousefpour, N. (2013). Evaluation and Social Impact Measurement Amongst Small to Medium Social Enterprises: Process, Purpose and Value. *Australian Journal of Public Administration, 72*(4), 447–458.

Bovaird, T., Stoker, G., Jones, T., Loeffler, E., & Roncancio, M. P. (2016). Activating Collective Co-Production of Public Services: Influencing Citizens to Participate in Complex Governance Mechanisms in the UK. *International Review of Administrative Sciences, 82*(1), 47–68.

Carley, M. J. (1983). In K. Finsterbusch, L. Llewellyn, & C. P. Wolf (Eds.), *A Review of Selected Methods in Social Impact Assessment Methods* (pp. 35–48). Beverly Hills, Calif.

Chan, A., Mook, L., & Kislenko, S. (2015). Stakeholders' Stories of Impact: The Case of Furniture Bank. In J. Quarter, S. Ryan, & A. Chan (Eds.), *Social Purpose Enterprises. Case Studies for Social Change*. University of Toronto Press, Toronto.

Costa, E., & Pesci, C. (2016). Social Impact Measurement: Why Do Stakeholders' Matter? *Sustainability Accounting, Management and Policy Journal, 7*(1), 99–124.

Crosby, B. C., Hart, P., & Torfing, J. (2017). Public Value Creation through Collaborative Innovation. *Public Management Review, 19*(5), 655–669.

Di Domenico, M., Haugh, H., & Tracey, P. (2010). Social Bricolage: Theorizing Social Value Creation in Social Enterprises. *Entrepreneurship: Theory and Practice, 34*(4), 681–703.

Di Domenico, M., Tracey, P., & Haugh, H. (2009). Social Economy Involvement in Public Service Delivery: Community Engagement and Accountability. *Regional Studies, 43*(7), 981–992.

Donahue, J., & Zeckhauser, R. (2011). *Collaborative Governance: Private Roles for Public Goals in Turbulent Times*. Princeton University Press.

Dunning, J. (1985). *Foreword to Village Ventures*. London: Bedford Square Press.

Ebrahim, A., & Rangan, V. K. (2010). *The Limits of Nonprofit Impact: A Contingency Framework for Measuring Social Performance* (Working paper 10–099). Harvard Business School.

Ferguson, M. J., & Bargh, J. A. (2004). How social perception can automatically influence behavior. *Trends in cognitive sciences, 8*(1), 33–39.

Fu-Keung IP, D. (1990). Difficulties in Implementing Social Impact Assessment in China: Methodological Considerations. *Environmental Impact Assessment Review, 10*(1–2), 113–122.

Fukuyama, F. (1995). *Trust: The Social Virtues and the Creation of Prosperity.* Free Press.

Gradstein, M., & Justman, M. (2002). Education, Social Cohesion, and Economic Growth. *American Economic Review, 92*(4), 1192–1204.

Hall, K., & Arvidson, M. (2013). How Do We Know If Social Enterprise Works? Tools for Assessing Social Enterprise Performance. In S. Denny & F. Seddon (Eds.), *Social Enterprise: Accountability and Evaluation Around the World*. Routledge.

Hazenberg, R., & Hall, K. (2016). Public Service Mutuals: Towards a Theoretical Understanding of the Spin-out Process. *Policy and Politics, 44*(3), 441–463.

Herman, R. D., & Renz, D. O. (1997). Multiple Constituencies and the Social Construction of Nonprofit Organisation Effectiveness. *Nonprofit and Voluntary Sector Quarterly, 26*(2), 185–206.

Jain, P. (2018). *Conceptualising Social Value: Perspectives of the Public, Private and Third Sectors in the UK.* Doctoral Thesis. The University of Northampton.

Jain, P. K., Hazenberg, R., Seddon, F., & Denny, S. (2020). Social Value as a Mechanism for Linking Public Administrators with Society: Identifying the Meaning, Forms and Process of Social Value Creation. *International Journal of Public Administration, 43*(10), 876–889.

Jordan, B. (2008). *Welfare and Well-Being: SV in Public Policy*. The Policy Press.

Lane, M. D., & Casile, M. (2011). Angels on the Head of a Pin: The SAC Framework for Performance Measurement in Social Entrepreneurship Ventures. *Social Enterprise Journal, 7*(3), 238–258.

Le Grand, J., & Roberts, J. (2018). The Public Service Mutual: Theories of Motivational Advantage. *Public Administration Review, 78*(1), 82–91.

MacKeith, J. (2011). The Development of the Outcomes Star: A Participatory Approach to Assessment and Outcome Measurement. *Housing, Care and Support, 14*, 98–106.

Miller, F., & Wallis, J. (2011). Social Interaction and the Role of Empathy in Information and Knowledge Management: A Literature Review. *Journal of Education for Library and Information Science, 52*(2), 122–132.

Needham, C. (2008). Realising the Potential of Co-Production: Negotiating Improvements in Public Services. *Social Policy and Society, 7*(02), 221–231.

Nicholls, A. (2006). *Social Entrepreneurship, New Models of Sustainable Social Change*. Oxford.

Osborne, D., & Gaebler, T. (1992). *Reinventing Government: How the Entrepreneurial Spirit Is Transforming the Public Sector*. Addison-Wesley Publishing Company. Inc..

Putnam, R. D. (1993). *Making Democracy Work: Civic Traditions in Modern Italy*. Princeton University Press.

Rickson, R. E., Burdge, R. J., Hundloe, T., & McDonald, G. T. (1990). Institutional Constraints to Adoption of Social Impact Assessment as a Decision-Making and Planning Tool. *Environmental Impact Assessment Review, 10*(1–2), 233–243.

Robinson, M. (2007). Does Decentralisation Improve Equity and Efficiency in Public Service Delivery Provision? *Institute of Development Studies., 38*(1), 7–17.

Thekaekara, S. (2005, June). *A Social Change Manifesto for the Poor, Skoll Centre for Social Entrepreneurship lecture series on social change*. Said Business School, Oxford University.

Torres, L., & Pina, V. (2002). Delivering Public Services—Mechanisms and Consequences: Changes in Public Service Delivery in the EU Countries. *Public Money and Management, 22*(4), 41–48.

Vanclay, F. (2003). International principles for social impact assessment. *Impact assessment and project appraisal, 21*(1), 5-11.

Womack, B. (1993). Political Reform and Political Change in Communist Countries: Implications for Vietnam. In: William, T. and Mark, S. (eds.) *Reinventing Vietnamese Socialism*. Boulder, CO: Westview.

Young, R. (2006). For What It Is Worth: Social Value and the Future of Social Entrepreneurship. In A. Nicholls (Ed.), *Social Entrepreneurship: New Models of Sustainable Social Change* (pp. 56–74). Oxford University Press.

10

Classification of Social Impact Assessment Models in South Korea

Jieun Ryu, Won Jun Lee, Junsu Park, and Heui Jae Choi

10.1 Impact Measurement in South Korea

The question of how to measure organisations' contributions to sustainable development is of considerable interest. Consequently, there are ongoing efforts to develop social impact assessment models to understand exactly how organisations contribute to society. These models often have different purposes, developers, analysis variables, and backgrounds. Therefore, many scholars classify social impact assessment models using different criteria, such as methods (Nicholls, 2005; Karami et al., 2017), impact levels (Becker, 2001), funding feasibility (Clark et al., 2004), and managerial purposes (Maas & Liket, 2011). Some studies further classify social impact models for non-profit organisations (Zappalà & Lyons,

J. Ryu (✉)
Cincinnati, OH, USA

W. J. Lee • J. Park • H. J. Choi
Sungkyunkwan University, Seoul, South Korea
e-mail: jsp2208@skku.edu

R. Hazenberg, C. Paterson-Young (eds.), *Social Impact Measurement for a Sustainable Future*, https://doi.org/10.1007/978-3-030-83152-3_10

2009) and social entrepreneurs (Grieco et al., 2015). Nevertheless, most studies that analyse social impact assessment models and their classification have been conducted from international and Western perspectives.

In this chapter, we introduce and categorise the existing Korean social impact assessment models using seven variables of analysis developed by Grieco et al. (2015). The seven variables include (1) data typology, (2) impact typology, (3) purpose, (4) model complexity, (5) sector, (6) timeframe, and (7) developer dimensions of analysis. We summarise our findings by grouping the Korean social impact assessment models and discuss how our findings are different from the findings of Western social impact assessment classification. In addition, we analyse which United Nation's Sustainable Development Goals (SDGs) are frequently targeted by each Korean social impact assessment model in order to evaluate its potential contribution to the SDGs.

The South Korean context provides unique understanding and use of social impact assessment models insofar as many social impact assessment models are developed and initiated across non-profit organisations, private organisations, and government departments. We found that the Korean government uses social impact assessment models to screen organisations that effectively create social impact in order to further promote their success. For selected organisations, the government provides financial or managerial support, or both. Besides government departments, non-profit and private organisations, such as GuideStar Korea and the SK Group, also use social impact assessment models to support organisations for self-assessment and to reward socially impactful organisations. Unlike most Western social impact assessment models (Grieco et al., 2015), the use of both qualitative and quantitative data with a retrospective timeframe is more common in Korean models. Also, in the Korean context, the government is one of the leading social impact assessment model developers.

From a practical standpoint, this chapter contributes to supporting policymakers and social entrepreneurs in identifying the most suitable models for their organisational purposes. Moreover, it contributes to existing knowledge of Western-focused social impact assessment models by providing a Korean perspective on social impact assessment models. This is the first study to classify Korean social impact assessment models, providing new insights into the development and uses of various social impact assessment models in a different national context. Ultimately, this chapter also discusses how government departments establish and implement social impact assessment models, which can contribute to 'SDG17: Strengthen the means of implementation and revitalise the global partnership for sustainable development.'

10.2 Social Impact Assessment

Social impact assessment helps people, groups, organisations, and communities evaluate the impact they create through a project, plan, program, or policy on people and communities (Vanclay, 1999). Vanclay (2003) defines social impact assessment as a methodology that can analyse, monitor, and manage social outcomes of interventions and social change processes that these interventions caused. In this context, interventions refer to policies, programs, plans, and projects (Vanclay, 1999). Another well-known definition of social impact assessment is developed in the work of Becker (2001). Becker (2001) defines social impact assessment as the process of analysing an expected outcome, as a consequence of a planned or present behaviour (Becker, 2001). Both definitions emphasise the 'consequences of an intervention and action' and 'social change' in terms of the impact on individuals, organisations, and society—whether positive or negative.

Initially, the US government first legalised social impact assessment in 1969 via the National Environmental Policy Act (NEPA). Under the influence of the US government and NEPA, social impact assessment has been used to evaluate the environmental effects of massive construction projects, especially in the 1960s and 1980s (Burdge & Vanclay, 1996). Many other disciplines, such as anthropology (Cottrell, 1951; Sharp, 1952) and development studies (Colson, 1971), have also employed social impact assessment to analyse the social impact of different human behaviours. These days, environmental impact assessment is a part of social impact assessment (Becker, 2001). Also, social impact assessment incorporates technology assessment, as well as economic and fiscal impact assessment (Becker, 2001).

In the process of analysing, monitoring, and managing social impact, various actors become involved, including individuals, communities, governments, and profit and non-profit organisations. These actors apply social impact assessment to evaluate the outcomes of current and future activities across all sectors in order to minimise any adverse impact on people and society (Becker, 2001; Clark et al., 2004). Therefore, social impact assessment is considered a methodology and a philosophy of development and democracy (Vanclay, 1999) with the potential to contribute to sustainability.

As social impact assessment has garnered more attention over the last decade, its scope and models have also expanded (Esteves et al., 2012). Maas and Liket (2011) identified 30 quantitative social impact measurement methods in their study. According to Grieco et al. (2015), as of 2015, there were more than 194 social impact assessment models available online. These models often use different terms such as 'social impact measurement', 'social value creation', 'social impact reporting', and 'social return'—all of which are interchangeable with the term 'social impact assessment' (Emerson, 2003; Clark et al., 2004).

One conventional way of classifying social impact assessment models is to identify them based on method (qualitative or quantitative) (Nicholls, 2005; Karami et al., 2017). Another way of classifying social impact assessment models is to use their impact levels (micro, meso, and macro) (Becker, 2001). In impact level-based classification, each type of social impact assessment analyses different levels of actors and settings. Micro-level social impact assessment analyses the impact of organisations or projects on the behaviour of individuals, while meso-level social impact assessment analyses the impact on organisations, communities, and social networks. Macro-level social impact assessment focuses on social macro systems including national and international political and legal systems (Becker, 2001). These three typologies enable social impact analyses in different settings and levels, which can also be used as a cornerstone of social impact assessment classification (Becker, 2001).

Meanwhile, the work of Clark et al. (2004) analyses eight different social impact assessment models using six variables including (1) functional category (process, impacts, monetisation), (2) credibility risk factors, (3) impact value chain, (4) applicability to lifecycle stages, (5) assessment purposes/functions in the investment process (screening, partnership formation, management operations, scaling, external reporting, exit, retrospective evaluation), and (6) feasibility data as supplied by a practitioner (cost/time, time breakdown—time contributed by management, staff, consultant/third party, investor). With these variables, social impact assessment models can be classified in a comprehensive and detailed manner. Accordingly, this classification is most useful for investors and funders.

Using six dimensions, Maas and Liket (2011) analysed 30 social impact assessment methods from a managerial perspective. Maas and Liket (2011) developed the six dimensions by combining frameworks from the research of Schaltegger and Burritt (2000) and Clark et al. (2004). The six dimensions are (1) purpose (screening, monitoring, reporting, evaluation), (2) timeframe (prospective, ongoing, retrospective), (3) orientation (input, output), (4) length of timeframe (short-term, long-term), (5) perspective (micro, meso, macro), and (6) approach (process methods, impact methods, monetarisation). Classification in the work of Maas and Liket (2011) is widely used to help managers choose an appropriate social impact measurement method for their organisation and social activities.

Most classification variables have been developed to analyse social impact assessment models for corporate actors. Nevertheless, social enterprise, social innovation, and non-profit scholars have also contributed to social impact assessment studies by developing a systemic approach to social impact assessment (e.g. Zappalà & Lyons, 2009; Grieco et al., 2015; Hervieux & Voltan, 2019). For example, the work of Zappalà and Lyons (2009) uses two variables (frameworks and methods) to assess social impact measurement for non-profit organisations. That research emphasises that frameworks and methods should be distinguished from one another insofar as frameworks do not prescribe a particular social impact indicator, while a method does. The work of Grieco et al. (2015) also classifies social impact assessment models for social entrepreneurs using seven variables. This classification (Grieco et al., 2015) is discussed in greater detail later.

As discussed above, the number and scope of social impact assessment studies are growing. Several classification variables have been developed and used to classify various social impact assessment models and assist corporate, government, and non-profit actors in choosing a proper impact assessment model for their organisations and activities. However, most studies on social impact assessment models and their classification have been done from international and Western perspectives. In differentiation, our research introduces seven Korean social impact assessment models developed by various organisations and purposes. Subsequently, we classify the models using the seven variables developed by Grieco et al. (2015) to discuss how they are similar and different from Western social impact assessment models.

10.3 Social Impact Assessment in the Korean Context

In South Korea, the presidential administration of Moon Jae-in emphasised 'social value' in their 100 policy tasks (The Government of Republic of Korea, 2017). Therefore, 'social value' and 'social value assessment' have become more important to public institutions, social economy organisations, and corporations. Moreover, as part of these tasks, several government departments developed social value or social impact assessment models for public entities and social economy organisations.

In the Korean context, social economy organisations include social enterprises, cooperatives, community enterprises, and self-sufficiency enterprises, as well as some social ventures (Ministry of Small and Medium Enterprises and Startups and Korea Technology Finance Corporation, 2019). While social enterprises, cooperatives, community enterprises, and self-sufficiency enterprises have legal organisational forms, social ventures do not have a legal definition or a legal organisational form. Organisations that meet the criteria defined by the 'Social Enterprise Promotion Act (2006)' can be certified as a social enterprise by the Ministry of Employment and Labor. Cooperatives, community enterprises, and self-sufficiency enterprises and their legal entities are recognised by the 'Framework Act on Cooperatives (2012)', the 'Enforcement Rule of Community Enterprise Promotion (2011)', and the 'National Basic Living Security Act (2012)'.

One of the first government-developed social assessment models is the Social Value Index. The Social Value Index was developed by the Ministry of Employment and Labor and the Korea Social Enterprise Promotion Agency in 2017. The Social Value Index is an online survey to gauge social, economic, and innovative aspects of performance, which any social economy enterprise aims to achieve based on its mission. This model is designed to help social economy enterprises self-monitor their levels of social value created by their activities. The Social Value Index also establishes selection criteria that can help private and public sector organisations identify social economy enterprises to which they would be willing to provide financial support for a given period.

The Social Venture Value Measurement Model was developed by the Ministry of Small and Medium Enterprises and Startups and the Korea Technology Finance Corporation in 2019. The Ministry of Small and Medium Enterprises and Startups and Korea Technology Finance Corporation developed this model specifically for social ventures that have been relatively undervalued in comparison to traditional for-profit ventures in deciding which ventures would be financially supported by the government. This model is a web-based platform, where early-stage companies can evaluate their potential to co-create social value and innovation as a social venture.

Lastly, the Social Economy Enterprise Evaluation System is a web-based open platform developed by the Financial Services Commission and the Korea Credit Guarantee Fund in 2020. This model evaluates the social and financial impact that social economy enterprises aim to actualise, with a purpose of screening whether each enterprise is eligible for financial support from the government and other financial institutions. Similar to the previous models, the Social Economy Enterprise Evaluation System also aims to help social economy enterprises overcome their financing difficulties and successfully fulfil their mission via public and private sector investments.

In South Korea, the private sector has also been developing social impact assessment models, mostly for purposes of assessing a company's corporate social responsibility (see Chap. 8 for details on Corporate Social Responsibility). Meanwhile, the SK Group, one of South Korea's five major conglomerate companies, developed an online social impact measurement model for social enterprises called the Measurement of Social Performance in 2015. Together with its associated research centre, the Center for Social Value Enhancement Studies, the SK Group aims to quantify the social performances of social enterprises, subsequently converting performance into monetary incentives that would be rewarded back to the social enterprises. They consider financial rewards for social performance as a critical means to causing more financial and human resources to flow into social enterprises with the potential for social value creation, thereby increasing the ultimate success of social enterprises.

Guidelines in the Impact Accelerating Report developed by a firm called Social Power of Networked Group (SOPOONG) provide a brief but critical template for investee social ventures to use to quantify their social as well as financial impacts. SOPOONG is the first venture capital firm serving as an impact investor and incubator in Korea. Celebrating their tenth anniversary, SOPOONG wanted to self-assess how much they fulfil their role in accelerating the development of new social ventures. In addition to achieving this end, IAR's template functions as mutually beneficial to both parties—in this case, seed-stage social ventures and external investors interested in investing in these ventures.

The non-profit organisation sector has also been developing social impact measurement models for non-profit organisations. Social impact measurement model developers for non-profit organisations often suggest that social economy organisations may also use their models to evaluate their impact. For example, in 2015, the Seoul non-profit organisation centre proposed a framework called the non-profit organisation's Social Impact Framework to help non-profit organisations create assessment tools to best fit their social missions. This approach encourages in-group members to engage in discussions and reach a consensus on the structure and the contents of these tools. On the other hand, in 2018, GuideStar and Community Chest of Korea developed the GuideStar Korea Social Impact (GSK-SI), a web-based platform that measures three different aspects of social impact of non-profit organisations—namely, social change, organisational value change, and human resources change.

10.4 Social Impact Assessment Model Classification Methods

The seven variables developed by Grieco et al. (2015) allow us to classify Korean social impact assessment models with a comprehensive analytical framework. Grieco et al. (2015) developed seven essential variables by combining existing variables from the works of Nicholls (2005), Rinaldo (2010), Clark et al. (2004), Maas and Liket (2011), Zappalà and Lyons (2009), and Rinaldo (2010), together with the Tools and Resources for Assessing Social Impact (TRASI)[1] and the New Economics Foundation (NEF).[2] The seven variables include (1) data typology, (2) impact typology, (3) purpose, (4) model complexity, (5) sector, (6) timeframe, and (7) developer dimensions of analysis.

First, the variable of data typology determines whether a social impact assessment model requires quantitative, qualitative, or mixed (quali-quantitative) data (Nicholls, 2005). Second, impact typology analyses the types of impact that a social impact assessment model focuses on. While a social impact assessment model focuses on the holistic impact, other models focus on assessing differing impact levels on environment, social, economic, and people-based sectors (Rinaldo, 2010; NEF). Third, the work of Grieco et al. (2015) identifies five different organisational purposes of implementing social impact assessment processes. The purpose variable evaluates aspects of (1) screening, (2) assessment, (3) management, (4) certification, and (5) reporting. Fourth, model complexity reveals whether the number of indicators or categories of a social impact assessment model is high. Fifth, the sector variable aims to analyse whether the focus of a social impact assessment model is sector-specific. Sixth, the timeframe variable shows if a model assesses impact from a prospective, retrospective, or ongoing time perspective (Clark et al., 2004; Maas & Liket, 2011). Lastly, the developer variable reveals the main actors in developing the models.

To analyse Korean social impact assessment models, we first made a list of social impact assessment models for social economy organisations

[1] http://trasi.foundationcenter.org/search.php

[2] https://neweconomics.org/

being used in South Korea. Second, we reviewed the social impact assessment models and their criteria. In this process, we only selected social impact assessment models with publicly detailed indicators or categories. Third, we assessed the selected assessment models using the seven variables from the work of Grieco et al. (2015). Fourth, we also analysed common SDGs targeted by each model. The selected social impact assessment models are:

1. Social Value Index (SVI)—Ministry of Employment and Labor (MoEL) and the Korea Social Enterprise Promotion Agency (KOSEA)
2. Social Venture Value Measurement Model (SVVMM)—Ministry of Small and Medium Enterprises and Startups (MSS) and Korea Technology Finance Corporation (KIBO)
3. Social Economy Enterprise Evaluation System (SEEES)—Financial Services Commission (FSC) and Korea Credit Guarantee Fund (KODIT)
4. Measurement of Social Performance (MSP)—SK Group
5. GuideStar Korea Social Impact (GSK-SI)—GuideStar and the Community Chest of Korea
6. Non-Profit Organisation's Social Impact Framework (NSIF)—Seoul Non-Profit Organisation Center
7. Impact Accelerating Report (IAR)—SOPOONG

10.5 Classification of Korean Social Impact Assessment Models

The similarities and differences of the abovementioned social impact assessment models are compared using the seven variables proposed in the work of Grieco et al. (2015). Table 10.1 presents a detailed analysis of the characteristics of the selected models using the seven variables and Table 10.2 shows the frequency of each variable.

First, most models (71.4%) are using a combination of qualitative and quantitative (i.e. quali-quantitative) datasets in the assessment of social impact. For example, the IAR uses quantitative data to materialise a social

Table 10.1 Main features of Korean social impact assessment models

	Main features						
Model	Data typology	Impact typology	Purpose	Model complexity	Sector	Timeframe	Developer
SVI	Quali-quantitative	Social, economic	Screening	Basic	General	Retrospective	Government
SVVMM	Quali-quantitative	Social, economic	Screening	Basic	General	Retrospective	Government
SEEES	Quali-quantitative	Holistic (social, people, economic)	Screening	Basic	General	Retrospective	Government
MSP	Quali-quantitative	Holistic (social, economic, environmental)	Assessment	Simple	General	Retrospective	Research Center
GSK-SI	Quantitative	Holistic (social, people, economic)	Reporting	Simple	Specific	Retrospective	Non-profit organisation
NSIF	Qualitative	Holistic	Management	Basic	Specific	Prospective	Government
IAR	Quali-quantitative	Holistic (social, economic, people)	Reporting	Basic	General	Retrospective	Venture capital company

Table 10.2 Frequency analysis

		Frequency (%)
Data typology	Quali-quantitative	71.4
	Qualitative	14.3
	Quantitative	14.3
Purpose	Screening	42.9
	Reporting	28.6
	Assessment	14.3
	Management	14.3
Complexity	Basic	71.4
	Simple	28.6
Sector	General	71.4
	Specific	28.6
Developer	Government	57.1
	Non-profit network	14.3
	Research centre	14.3
	Venture capitalist	14.3
Timeframe	Retrospective	85.7
	Prospective	14.3
Impact typology	Holistic	71.4
	Social-economic	28.6

venture's financial impact using corporate sales and values due to overall annual growth rates. In addition, the IAR analyses the venture's social impact at different stages—input, activities, outputs, and outcomes—using a logic model from Morgan (2010). For this analysis, the IAR uses a qualitative and multidimensional description of the venture's impact focusing on their key performance indicators. The key performance indicators vary depending on organisations' purposes (e.g. reduced food waste, the number of hours and duration of speech-to-text service for the hearing-impaired, and the rates of revisit to mobile educational applications for young children with learning disabilities). In contrast, GSK-SI only uses quantitative data and NSIF only uses qualitative data.

Second, most Korean social impact assessment models use holistic measurements (71.4%) rather than specific impact typology. For example, SEEES, MSP, GSK-SI, NSIF, and IAR use more than three different types of impact (social, people-based, economic, and environmental) for a multidimensional evaluation of the impact of a venture or project. On the other hand, SVVM measures a social venture's potential using two primary dimensions—(1) sociality and (2) innovation and growth.

Third, the complexity level of most of the Korean social impact assessment models is basic (71.4%), with fewer than 15 indicators. For example, the SVI uses nine indicators, comprising six indicators for social impact (i.e. social mission, the social value attached to business activities, social economy system, reinvestment in the social mission, participative decision making, and employee orientation), two indicators for economic impact (employment creation and labour productivity), and one indicator for innovation impact (organisational innovativeness). Similarly, the SVVMM's level of complexity is basic with a total of 12 indicators—six for evaluating the impact of sociality and six for evaluating innovation and growth. Meanwhile, both the MSP and GSK-SI models are simple models (28.6%), with fewer than 40 indicators. As one example, the GSK-SI consists of seven indicators for each impact type (social change, organisational value change, and human resources change).

Fourth, government-initiated models (42.9%) mainly aim at screening for the purpose of verifying the achievement of specific goals. In comparison, the models developed by non-profit organisations or by the networks of venture capital firms (28.5%) are intended for reporting purposes. For example, the SEEES focuses mainly on screening social economy enterprises in order to offer loans or other financial services to improve their business environment, ultimately contributing to social value creation. In contrast, the purpose of the IAR is not to screen social ventures for funding. Instead, the IAR reports on the impact created by investee social ventures following the receipt of financial investment from SOPOONG. Unlike these models, the MSP prioritises the rewarding of all social enterprises participating in the Social Progress Credit project (sponsored by the SK Group) with cash incentives based on venture outcomes. Specifically, all participating social enterprises are required to report their performance in four key areas of social services, employment, social ecosystems, and environmental impact. Moreover, their performance outcomes are converted into monetary values by the newly developed equations of the MSP for more precise estimation of social performance.

Fifth, most models are explicitly targeted at organisations that belong to the social economy sector in the context of a retrospective (85.7%) timeframe. A retrospective timeframe helps the government identify social economy enterprises with high levels of goal achievement for the sake of supporting these enterprises in building business linkages to external organisations. Only one social impact assessment model, the Seoul Non-Profit Organisation Center's model for non-profit organisation social impact, uses a prospective timeframe and qualitative data analysis (14.3%).

Sixth, five models are generic (71.4%) and two models are sector-specific (28.6%). Most of these generic models aim to assess the impact of social economy-focused organisations rather than any and all organisations in general. Indeed, the sector-specific models are for assessing the impact of non-profit organisations (GSK-SI and NSIF). More specifically, the GSK-SI is developed to establish a comprehensive information network in which the model mainly aims to provide donors interested in investing in non-profit organisations with quantitative data on their social impacts and to assist non-profit organisations in making their impact management more effective. Although non-profit organisations primarily employ this model, the GSK-SI can also be easily applied to social enterprises. Another example of a sector-specific social impact assessment model is the Seoul non-profit organisation Center's NSIF. This framework is characterised as a process in which all members in non-profit organisations are encouraged to gather and deliberate on their identity, organisational effectiveness, social impact, and sustainability. Subsequently, non-profit organisations are prompted to decide what specific actions they can take for creating social value. The framework only has eight indicators; therefore, it is easily applicable to non-profit organisations. Due to heterogeneity in non-profit organisations, however, it remains somewhat difficult to compare social impacts measured by the framework among non-profit organisations.

Lastly, we also analysed how Korean social impact assessment models help social economy organisations to contribute to the SDGs. The models were sorted into the 17 goals based on each model's indicators and its contribution and relation to the SDGs (see Table 10.3).

Table 10.3 The relevance of Korean social impact Assessment models to UN SDGs

Model	SDGs
SVI	4, 8, 9, 16, 17
SVVMM	9, 10, 12, 16, 17
SEEES	4, 8, 16, 17
MSP	8, 9, 10, 11, 14, 15
GSK-SI	8, 11, 16
NSIF	Can be applied to all
IAR	Can be applied to all

SDG 4 = Quality Education; SDG 8 = Decent Work and Economic Growth; SDG 9 = Industry, Innovation, and Infrastructure; SDG 10 = Reduced Inequalities; SDG 11 = Sustainable Cities and Communities; SDG 12 = Responsible Consumption and Production; SDG 14 = Life Below Water; SDG 15 = Life on Land; SDG 16 = Peace, Justice and Strong Institutions; SDG 17 = Partnerships for the Goals

We found that all Korean social impact assessment models contribute to more than three SDGs. Also, the most common targeted SDGs deal with 'Decent Work and Economic Growth (SDG8)', 'Peace, Justice, and Strong Institutions (SDG16)', 'Industry, Innovation, and Infrastructure (SDG9)', and 'Partnerships for the Goals (SDG17)'. Less commonly targeted goals are related to 'Quality Education (SDG 4)', 'Reduced Inequalities (SDG10)', and 'Sustainable Cities and Communities (SDG11)', 'Life Below Water (SDG14)', 'Life on Land (SDG15)', and 'Responsible Consumption and Production (SDG12)'.

10.6 Common Characteristics of Korean Social Impact Measurement Models

Korean social impact assessment models are mostly developed to assess the impacts of social economy organisations, including social enterprises and social ventures. The non-profit organisation sector has developed social impact assessment models, often targeting social economy organisations to adopt their models as well. This section summarises our main findings and how these findings show unique circumstances in social impact assessment models in the Korean context. First, the analysis result shows a higher level of quali-quantitative data (71.4%) usage in Korea in comparison to Western countries. In previous research, Grieco et al. (2015) find that qualitative data is mainly used for Western social impact assessment models (47.4%) and quali-quantitative data is used for 35.5%.

Second, in Korea, the government actively leads the development of the social economy. Importantly, the government has become one of the main developers of social impact assessment models for social economy organisations (57.1%). This finding is contrary to the findings of previous studies, which suggest that not-for-profit networks (31.6%) and not-for-profit organisations (30.2%) are the main developers of social impact assessment models (Grieco et al., 2015). According to Grieco et al. (2015), none of the social impact assessment models in the Western/international context have been developed by a government. Therefore, the Korean government's intervention and efforts in developing social impact assessment models for social economy organisations are a unique endeavour.

Third, the primary purpose of these government developed social impact assessment models is to screen organisations creating social impact in order to prove their growth potential (42.9%). This result reflects the findings in the work of Grieco et al. (2015), also stating that the primary purpose of most Western social impact assessment models is screening (44.6%). It should be noted again that the screening bodies in Korea are different from the screening bodies of other countries, however, and that the government is the primary screening body in Korea.

In Korea, there is no single social impact assessment model for certification. In contrast, the work of Grieco et al. (2015) finds that the purpose of 7.9% of social impact assessment models is for certification. A possible explanation for the lack of a social impact assessment model for certification in Korea might be related to the social enterprise certification system, which was legalised by a law known as the 'Social Enterprise Promotion Act' by the MoEL in 2006. This law certifies any social enterprise that meets given criteria. As of December 2020, there were 3294 certified social enterprises (Korea Social Enterprise Promotion Agency, 2020). The number of certified social enterprises shows that the Act has successfully promoted social enterprise in Korea. It does not indicate a need to develop a social impact assessment model for certifying a social economy organisation.

Fourth, while Grieco et al. (2015) identify several complex (25%) and highly complex (6.6%) social impact assessment models, none of these models exist in Korea. This result may be explained by the fact that there are not many social impact assessment models in Korea, and the nascent models are still in the development stage.

Fifth, regarding impact typology, Korean social impact assessment models use holistic measurements (42.9%) more than specific impact typology (which assess dimensions of people, environment, social, and economic impacts). Indeed, it is not typical for a social economy organ isation to pursue one specific objective due to their characteristic aim to achieve double (or triple) objectives—also known as a 'double (triple) bottom line' (Emerson & Twersky, 1996; Johnson, 2001; Alter, 2004). For social economy organisations, social, economic, and environmental objectives are non-separable—in fact, it is this characteristic that makes a social economy organisation different from traditional non-profit and private organisations. Therefore, it is natural that social impact assessment models for social economy organisations evaluate holistic impact, or more than two aspects of impact, instead of one specific impact.

Based on our findings, we identify common characteristics in Korean social impact assessment models by categorising them into three groups as Table 10.4 shows.

These three groups show that the characteristics of Korean social impact assessment models are different from Western models, which are clustered into four categories: (1) simple social quantitative, (2) holistic complex, (3) qualitative screening, and (4) management clusters (Grieco et al., 2015). First, in Korea, the basic retrospective quali-quantitative group of models (57.1%) is the largest group. All the models that use quali-quantitative data have simple assessment indicators (fewer than 40) with a retrospective timeframe. Second, with the exception of models for

Table 10.4 Common characteristics of in Korean social impact assessment models

Group	Models
Group 1: Basic retrospective Quali-quantitative	SVI, SVVMM, SEEES, IAR
Group 2: General holistic	SEEES, MSP, IAR
Group 3: Government screening	SVI, SVVMM, SEEES

non-profit organisations, most Korean models assess impacts on social, economic, and people in the general sector (42.9%). Third, most government models are used to screen organisations for financial and managerial support from the government. Overall, unlike the findings in the work of Grieco et al. (2015), the use of quali-quantitative data with a retrospective timeframe is the most common in Korean models. The most noticeable finding is that the Korean government's role is essential in promoting and implementing social impact assessment models. In this regard, the Korean government actively initiates and implements sustainable development policies, thereby contributing to 'SDG 17: Strengthen the means of implementation and revitalize the global partnership for sustainable development.'

Further, in terms of the SDGs, Korean social impact assessment models commonly target 'Decent Work and Economic Growth (SDG8)', 'Industry, Innovation, and Infrastructure (SDG9)', 'Peace, Justice, and Strong Institutions (SDG16)', and 'Partnerships for the Goals (SDG17)'. This finding indicates that social impact assessment model developers can integrate other SDGs into their models to encourage users to contribute to a wider variety of the SDGs. In doing so, social impact assessment models can also provide a more comprehensive, inclusive, and future-focused method and framework (Morrison-Saunders et al., 2020).

Most social impact assessment models are developed for measuring the impacts of social economy organisations and non-profit organisations in Korea. In contrast, many Western social impact assessment models target any organisation, including social economy organisations, non-profit, government, and private-sector organisations (Burdge & Vanclay, 1996). Even though the Korean government has included 'social value' as an indicator for assessing government and public organisations since 2017, the metric has not been widely used across the country due to a lack of detailed action plans and financial support (Joint Ministries, 2020). Moreover, Korean people perceive that overall, society's efforts in realising social value are not enough, and have urged the government and National Assembly to take more responsibility in ensuring social value creation in the public sector (Korea Social Enterprise Promotion Agency and LAB2050, 2019).

In the private sector, the SK Group, one of the largest conglomerates in Korea, has developed and used social value assessment indicators (social performance through business, social performance through social contribution, and performance through indirect economic contribution) since 2017 (SK Innovation, 2020). This trend shows that social impact assessment models are becoming widely accepted across sectors in Korea. Nevertheless, most models narrowly target the assessment of social impact in social economy or non-profit organisations only. Insofar as the creation of social impact and contribution to society have traditionally been the responsibilities of only social economy organisations and non-profit organisations, we expect more private and public organisations in the future to develop and use social impact measurement assessment models for creating and evaluating their social impacts on society.

Our findings are useful for organisations and social entrepreneurs when deciding on a model to measure the social impact of their organisations. According to our findings, social economy organisations that seek financial and managerial support should evaluate their impact using SVI, SVVMM, SEEES, and MSP models. If an organisation wants to report its success and achievement in creating impact to the public or potential funders, we recommend using GSK-SI and IAR. The NSIF could be used to develop a bespoke social impact assessment tool for an organisation and to produce an impact report. Because each model has different characteristics, when selecting a model, an organisation should consider available datasets, organisation purposes, assessment purposes, target impacts, and timelines. Moreover, organisations that are considering developing their own social impact assessment model can also use our findings to identify and improve upon gaps in existing models.

Accordingly, further research should explore how social impact assessment models for social economy organisations can be adopted to evaluate the social impacts of organisations and corporations in general. One question raised by this study is whether social impact assessment models for social economy organisations and non-social economy organisations should be differentially developed. Moreover, Korean and Western social impact assessment models and their analysis variables can be compared and contrasted more deeply to determine contextual influences on developing and using the models. In our research, the small sample size did not allow for more in-depth cluster analysis of the existing models. Nevertheless, this study contributes to our understanding of Korean social impact assessment models and their characteristics shaped by the national context.

References

Alter, K. (2004). *Social Enterprise Typology*. Virtue Venures LLC..

Becker, H. A. (2001). Social Impact Assessment. *European Journal of Operational Research, 128*, 311–321.

Burdge, R. J., & Vanclay, F. (1996). Social Impact Assessment: A Contribution to the State of the Art Series. *Impact Assessment, 14*, 59–86.

Clark, C., Rosenzweig, W., Long, D. and Olson, S. (2004). Double Bottom Line Project Report: Assessing Social Impact in Double Bottom Line Ventures.

Colson, E. (1971). *The Social Consequences of Resettlement: The Impact of the Kariba Resettlement Upon the Gwembe Tonga*. Manchester University Press.

Cottrell, W. F. (1951). Death by Dieselization: A Case Study in the Reaction to Technological Change. *American Sociological Review, 16*, 358–365.

Emerson, J. (2003). The Blended Value Proposition: Integrating Social and Financial Returns. *California Management Review, 45*, 35–51.

Emerson, J. and Twersky, F. (1996). New Social Entrepreneurs: The Success, Challenge and Lessons of Non-profit Enterprise Creation.

Esteves, A. M., Franks, D., & Vanclay, F. (2012). Social Impact Assessment: The State of the Art. *Impact Assessment and Project Appraisal, 30*, 34–42.

Grieco, C., Michelini, L., & Iasevoli, G. (2015). Measuring Value Creation in Social Enterprises: A Cluster Analysis of Social Impact Assessment Models. *Nonprofit and Voluntary Sector Quarterly, 44*, 1173–1193.

Hervieux, C., & Voltan, A. (2019). Toward a Systems Approach to Social Impact Assessment. *Social Enterprise Journal, 15*(2), 264–286.

Johnson, S. (2001). Literature Review on Social Entrepreneurship. *Canadian Centre for Social Entrepreneurship, 16*(23), 96–106.

Joint Ministries. (2020). Promotion Strategies for Social Value Realization in the Public Sector. In*:* Ministries, J. (ed.). Seoul.

Karami, S., Karami, E., Buys, L., & Drogemuller, R. (2017). System Dynamic Simulation: A New Method in Social Impact Assessment (SIA). *Environmental Impact Assessment Review, 62*, 25–34.

Korea Social Enterprise Promotion Agency. (2020). *List of Certified Social Enterprise* [Online]. Available online at: https://www.socialenterprise.or.kr/social/ente/company.do?m_cd=D003. Accessed 10 Jan 2020.

Korea Social Enterprise Promotion Agency and LAB2050. (2019). *Survey Results on Perception on Social Value.*

Maas, K., & Liket, K. (2011). Social Impact Measurement: Classification of Methods. In *Environmental Management Accounting and Supply Chain Management.* Springer.

Ministry of SMEs and Startups and Korea Technology Finance Corporation. (2019). *Guidelines for Social Venture Criteria and Value Evaluation Model.*

Morgan, J. P. (2010). *Impact Investments. An Emergent Asset Class.* Global Research.

Morrison-Saunders, A., Sánchez, L. E., Retief, F., Sinclair, J., Doelle, M., Jones, M., Wessels, J.-A., & Pope, J. (2020). Gearing up Impact Assessment as a Vehicle for Achieving the UN Sustainable Development Goals. *Impact Assessment and Project Appraisal, 38*, 113–117.

Nicholls, A. (2005). *Measuring Impact in Social Entrepreneurship: New Accountabilities to Stakeholders and Investors? ERSC Seminar.* Local Government Research Unit.

Rinaldo, H. (2010). *Getting Started in Social Impact Measurement: A Guide to Choosing How to Measure Social Impact.* The Guild.

Schaltegger, S., & Burritt, R. (2000). *Contemporary Environmental Accounting: Issues, Concepts and Practice.* Greenleaf Publishing.

Sharp, L. (1952). Steel Axes for Stone-age Australians. *Human Organization, 11*, 17–22.

SK Innovation. (2020). *SK Double Bottom Line* [Online]. Available online at: http://eng.skinnovation.com/together/happiness.asp Accessed 17 Jan 2021.

The Government of Republic of Korea. (2017). *100 Policy Tasks: Five-year Plan of the Moon Jae-in Administration.*

Vanclay, F. (1999). Social Impact Assessment. *Handbook of Environmental Impact Assessment, 1*, 301–326.

Vanclay, F. (2003). International Principles for Social Impact Assessment. *Impact Assessment and Project Appraisal, 21*, 5–12.

Zappalà, G., & Lyons, M. (2009). Recent Approaches to Measuring Social Impact in the Third Sector: An overview. *CSI Background Paper* [Online], 6.

11

Monetising Social Impact: A Critique of the 'Financialisation' of Social Value

Michael J. Roy and Simon Teasdale

11.1 What Is Value?

Not everything that counts can be counted
Who holds the markets to account?
Not everything that counts can be counted
Not everything that can be counted counts[1]

Seems like everybody's got a price
I wonder how they sleep at night
When the sale comes first, and the truth comes second
Just stop for a minute and smile[2]

[1] Billy Bragg – *Not Everything That Counts Can be Counted* (2017). The original statement is generally credited to Albert Einstein.

[2] Jessie J – *Pricetag* (2011) (lyrics by Cornish, Gottwald, Kelly and Simmons Jr)

M. J. Roy (✉) • S. Teasdale
Glasgow Caledonian University, Glasgow, UK
e-mail: Michael.Roy@gcu.ac.uk; Simon.Teasdale@gcu.ac.uk

R. Hazenberg, C. Paterson-Young (eds.), *Social Impact Measurement for a Sustainable Future*, https://doi.org/10.1007/978-3-030-83152-3_11

Like most of the concepts we seem to grapple with in this field on a daily basis, the concept of 'social value' is a notoriously slippery, imprecise one. People have very different ideas of what has 'value' to them, to other people, and to society at large. Society, meanwhile, is comprised of a myriad of different communities with competing interests and 'values' (that is, what matters to them – see Sayer, 2011). In neoclassical economics, 'value' is how much a desired object or condition is worth relative to other objects or conditions (Keen, 2011) and is often expressed as a function of what people are willing to pay to achieve such objects or conditions (see, for example, Donaldson et al., 1997). The Covid-19 pandemic has vividly brought home some of the paradoxes and disconnects between what we value in society and what we (and/or our representatives) are willing to pay for. In the UK, for example, we were exhorted to demonstrate our support for 'essential' health and social care workers through clapping on our doorsteps every Thursday throughout lockdown in 2020. However, by early 2021 those same 'essential' healthcare staff had been offered a below inflation 1% pay rise by the UK Government which the vast majority of the public believed to be too low (Savage & Tapper, 2021).

The concept of 'social value' as expressed in policy terms has come to the fore over the last couple of decades or so, particularly as third sector organisations have become more involved in the provision of public services as the 'marketisation' agenda (Hall et al., 2012) – the introduction of markets into public services – has radically changed the face of public management (Dunleavy & Hood, 1994; Osborne, 2006). Support for third sector organisations to compete for contracts on a 'level playing field' led to the introduction of the Public Services (Social Value) Act, 2012 which was intended to ensure that public bodies commissioning services take sufficient account of social value (Teasdale et al., 2012). This Act requires public authorities to have regard to economic, social and environmental well-being in connection with public services contracts. Recognising that social value is not an absolute, but a relative, term Social Value UK – the professional body for social value and impact management – explain social value to mean 'the quantification of the relative importance that people place on the changes they experience in their lives.' To be fair to Social Value UK, they then immediately go on to say that 'Some, but not all of this value is captured in market prices' and also stress the power of a compelling narrative: 'An account of social value is a story about the changes experienced by people. It includes qualitative, quantitative and comparative information, and also includes environmental changes in relation to how they affect people's lives.' This dimension is regularly forgotten, though, as we shall soon see.

But *how* we capture value and make decisions on what has value to society is – or at least is supposed to be – a central tenet of the political and policymaking calculus. Politicians are elected to make sometimes difficult decisions on behalf of those who elected them, including whether investing in policy x has greater value to society than investing in policy y or policy z. However, anyone who has ever worked close to politicians, or had significant insight into the policymaking process, will quickly disabuse you of the notion that the world of decision making within the public sector is so straightforward. The rhetoric or discourse of 'evidence' is constantly mobilised by policymakers to support, negotiate and oppose ideas. Rather than being evidence-informed, policy is highly influenced by specific contextual and political factors, such as the vagaries of time and place, prevailing ideologies and cultures, powerful interests, and constraints on time and resources (Cairney et al., 2019; Stoker & Evans, 2016). Whole books have been written on how policies get placed onto the agenda for consideration; a process that can involve considerable time, trouble and significant costs, particularly if professional lobbyists are involved. However, time, energy, and cash to burn are all assets that the third sector does not generally have an over-abundance of to devote to such considerations. So 'what counts' (or what 'gets to count') as evidence to support the work of third sector organisations in delivering social value therefore deserves to be looked at closely.

In this chapter we not only critically examine the concept of 'social value', but also how it has come to be tied up with the commodification of everyday life. Drawing on Karl Polanyi's (1944) concept of 'fictitious commodification', we draw upon two examples to illustrate our points: the funding mechanism known as Social Impact Bonds and the measurement tool known as Social Return on Investment. We show that commodification and monetisation of social value regularly leads to unintended consequences, which can then have troubling implications in furthering what Polanyi identified as the 'market society': a society based around a market economy, where political and economic life are dominated by ideas of individual freedom and self-interest (Polanyi, 1944; see also Block & Somers, 2014). Finally, we outline what may be done to refocus attention on what it means to 'value' the social and offer suggestions for new approaches that could potentially shape a new political economy, particularly as we attempt to recover from the Covid-19 pandemic crisis. First of all, however, what do we mean by 'fictitious commodification'? And what is so wrong with commodifying the social anyway?

11.2 Fictitious Commodification

One of the most important contributions of the economic anthropologist, economic historian and political economist Karl Polanyi was the process he called 'fictitious commodification'. Polanyi defined a market economy as an economic system that is controlled, regulated and directed by market prices. Production and distribution are entrusted to this "self-regulating market system" (Polanyi, 1944, p. 71) where 'self-regulation' implies that all production is for sale on the market, and that all incomes derive from such sales. This effectively translates into the existence of markets for the trading of all elements of industry; so not only goods and services, but also other essential elements such as labour, land and money. Polanyi insisted that land (the environment), labour (people), and money were actually 'fictitious commodities'; 'fictitious' in the sense that they were not created specifically for the purpose of buying and selling in the market. However the propensity of liberal capitalism to treat them as if they were *real* commodities was, according to Polanyi, a major source of contradictions and crisis-tendencies in capitalist development (Jessop, 2007), eventually leading to society fighting back against the environmentally and socially destructive effects of such treatment.[3]

As Sandel (2012, p. 1) explains

No other mechanism for organizing the production and distribution of goods had proved as successful at generating affluence and prosperity. And yet even as

[3] In a process known as the 'double movement.'

> *growing numbers of countries around the world embraced market mechanisms in the operation of their economies, something else was happening. Market values were coming to play a greater and greater role in social life. Economics was becoming an imperial domain. Today, the logic of buying and selling no longer applies to material goods alone. It increasingly governs the whole of life.*

When market forces come to shape almost every aspect of community life – what Polanyi terms the 'market society' – this has significant deleterious consequences for both people and nature. One hallmark of the contemporary market society is the encroachment of market forces into parts of the economy that did not previously work this way, most notably in the public sector. The marketisation of the UK welfare state, to fill the gap caused by retrenchment, is a case in point, combined with

> *engaging in forms of social engineering aimed at producing self-responsibilised individuals and communities who are financially literate, 'investment-ready' and economically productive. New financial instruments such as social impact bonds are deployed to these ends, both to 'solve social problems' and enable cost saving. (Dowling,* 2017, *p. 294)*

It is to Social Impact Bonds that we next turn. Before we do so however, we should acknowledge that global goals and priority setting as an overarching policy instrument – as exemplified in the UN SDGs – regularly creates unintended consequences. Not least, commodifying development into easily digestible performance indicators can divert attention from other important objectives. The race to achieve targets can create distorting effects; most of the Goals are interrelated in some way; so focusing on one may have perverse detrimental impacts on another (Fukuda-Parr et al., 2014).

11.3 Social Impact Bonds

Social Impact Bonds (SIBs) are a variant of 'Payment by Results' aimed at enabling private investment to be levered to fund new models of public service so that service providers do not have to 'front' the costs involved in service delivery. Investors are rewarded if agreed-upon outcomes are met from putative future savings, and lose their investment if outcomes are not met (Roy et al., 2018). Advocates of SIBs believe that they: (1) increase the resources available to support social interventions, with 'socially minded investors' providing the finance to enable innovative new programmes to be tested or scaled-up; (2) give service providers the freedom to prioritise outcomes rather than *outputs* or processes, thus supporting the delivery of better services; (3) helps governments to understand 'what works' through the reporting and evaluation of outcomes attributed to SIB-funded services; and (4) allows governments to 'pay for success' rather than funding interventions that do not work, since the government only pays when providers achieve the social outcomes they specify (Floyd, 2017).

However, despite evidence of success being – at best – patchy, or even absent altogether, SIBs have managed to proliferate around the world (Edmiston & Nicholls, 2018; Fraser et al., 2018; Maier & Meyer, 2017; McHugh et al., 2013). By the end of the first quarter of 2021 there were 210 impact bonds in 35 countries (Gustaffson-Wright et al., 2021) reflecting an enthusiasm that transcends geographic, cultural and political contexts (albeit it should be recognised that most of these are in the highly marketised Anglosphere). The first SIB was launched in HM Prison Peterborough (UK) in 2010, where investors financed a programme combatting recidivism (Disley et al., 2011; Fox & Albertson, 2011) and have since been employed in diverse areas of policy, from addressing homelessness to mental health provision, improving education and combatting unemployment.

The technical challenges that are required to be overcome to set up and operate a SIB are substantial: they are highly complex and involve considerable professional input and thus expense. Perhaps coincidentally, large accountancy and legal firms have been most vocal in pushing the model (Roy et al., 2018). More substantively than the technical challenges to be overcome, however, are the very real dangers that arise from qualitatively changing the nature of public and social service delivery, which the SIB model, at its essence, represents (Sinclair et al., 2014).

A firm rationale for introducing SIBs was that focusing upon delivering outcomes, rather than *outputs*, would encourage experimentation and stimulate innovation. This was based on the premise that the public sector is inherently risk averse and thus prefers to stick with established practices, but that the SIB model would unleash service innovation and lead to exciting new models of service provision. However as yet, there is next to no evidence that has emerged of service innovation as a result of the introduction of SIBs (Tan et al., 2015). Furthermore, service providers regularly report far less flexibility than before the SIB was introduced, have faced increased, rather than decreased, levels of oversight and have seen a significantly increased burden of administration (Edmiston & Nicholls, 2018). Although the design of SIBs brings together investors (private or social) with the stakeholders involved in the arrangement (such as local government, the intermediary, service providers, and service users), the complex nature of contracting arrangements, coupled with the considerable transaction costs often act as a disincentive to leveraging new sources of funding (Fraser et al., 2018). The complexity and size of the contracts generally make them unsuitable for most third sector organisations to be involved in, since they are highly unlikely to have the requisite financial skills or systems in place.

Furthermore, since payments to investors are based on outcomes being met, the contractual arrangements have to be precise regarding outcome measurements in order to avoid legal disputes later. 'Proving' that a certain policy indisputably caused a certain outcome is notoriously difficult in social policy, where we are regularly dealing with highly complex social systems, instead of closed/contained systems (Cairney et al., 2019; Falleti & Lynch, 2009). The unintentional (or otherwise) effect of introducing the SIB model and the logic of the market into a realm of service delivery previously infused with a public service logic qualitatively alters the character of the service. The introduction of a profit incentive fundamentally alters the relationship between service provider and citizen: citizens are, in effect, treated as if they are commodities (Roy et al., 2017) which has potentially dehumanising consequences. Inevitably, we have seen 'parking' of difficult clients and 'creaming' of those most easy to support (Johnson, 2013; Sinclair et al., 2014), leading to increased inequalities. Finally, a payment by results approach to public service delivery requires a reliable means of measuring social outcomes (Marden, 2011), hence the focus on SROI, to which we next turn attention.

11.4 Social Return on Investment (SROI)

SROI was initially developed by Jed Emerson and colleagues at REDF (Roberts Enterprise Development Fund), the San Francisco-based venture philanthropy organisation which supports employment for low-income and formerly homeless individuals through making investments in a portfolio of local third sector organisations that own and operate various local social enterprises. REDF developed its SROI framework in the late 1990s based upon traditional cost-benefit analysis (Gibbon & Dey, 2011) and is described as a framework that identifies and appreciates the social, economic and environmental value created by collating the inputs, outputs, outcomes and impacts made and experienced by stakeholders in relation to the activities of an organisation (Banke-Thomas et al., 2015). Through the use of estimated financial proxies, a monetary value is placed on each of the benefits and/or dis-benefits created (Arvidson et al., 2010) and the outcome (the 'social value' created) is expressed through a ratio: an SROI of 5:1 means that for every unit of currency invested the organisation generates a social value five times that value (net of cost). REDF's model was constructed in parallel with the concept of 'blended value' (Emerson, 2003; Nicholls, 2009) – the notion that all organisations, whether for-profit or not, create value that consists of economic, social and environmental value components. It was REDF's linkup with Harvard Business School's work on blended value that brought SROI to a European audience and, in autumn 2003, a European SROI network was formed. This network involved several UK representatives such as Jeremy Nicholls, then of the New Economics Foundation who integrated REDF's SROI methodology with steps from other forms of analysis methodologies into an 'overarching' SROI framework (Nicholls et al., 2012) to substantially build upon REDF's initial model, including the important integration of stakeholder engagement to the process.

Meanwhile, the methodology caught the attention of the (then opposition) Conservative Party in the UK, who were keen to inject a 'Big Society' flavour into their manifesto commitments. In a May 2008 speech, then leader of the opposition David Cameron declared that:

> *the next Conservative Government will attempt to establish a measure of* social value *that will inform our policy-making when in power...when making decisions, ministers will take account not just of economic efficiency, but also social efficiency* (Wood & Leighton, 2010, *p. 16)*.

Not long after the Conservatives came to power in 2010, a report from the Centre for Social Justice, the think tank established by former Conservative leader Ian Duncan Smith, stated that:

> *Recently, a new approach to public spending has been gathering momentum both within the* UK *and abroad: so-called 'evidence-based policy making' has been adopted by a number of Government bodies and non-Governmental organisations. The (closely related)* 'Social Return on Investment' *(*SROI*) approach is being applied across a steadily increasing proportion of the voluntary sector in Britain, demonstrating to funders a more rigorous approach to performance management while attempting to capture the social and environmental impacts of public spending* (Brien, 2011, *p. 15)*.

However, attempts to demonstrate social value through 'speaking the language of finance' understandably raised a number of anxieties within the third sector. Although they had long been keen to evaluate their impact in outcomes terms and to establish or demonstrate just how cost-effective they are, the use of SROI ostensibly caused third sector organisations to focus most of their attention on what is measurable at the expense of an in-depth understanding of their 'theory of change': the focus is primarily on identifying indicators that can support the calculation of the ratio, and this seems to preclude an in-depth understanding of processes underlying the measured impact (Arvidson et al., 2013, p. 14). Indeed, the trend for outcomes-based approaches, contracts and finance resulted in a number of unintended consequences, at least in part caused by the tendency to 'elevate' or fetishise accounting information as possessing the characteristics of objectivity, credibility and reliability. While there is a degree of economic rationality to doing so, there is an 'oppressive' dimension to privileging accounting information and defining social value through the prism of finance. Through utilising a set of financial proxies that are inherently reductive, such privileging of market behaviours, and the 'logics' of the market exemplifies the types of behaviour that Eikenberry and Kluver (2004) warned would place the vital role of civil society in furthering democracy at risk.

While the initial premise of SROI was to combine qualitative and qualitative information, inevitably the seductive nature of the ratio meant that the numbers took priority. In recent years, though, SROI seems to have fallen somewhat out of fashion, with the number of SROI studies undertaken apparently reaching their peak around 2011 and decreasing in the period since (Banke-Thomas et al., 2015).

11.5 The Evolution of *Homo Economicus*?

Government and the 'third sector'[4] are involved in a complex set of dynamic relationships. Much of the welfare state (as was) in the UK and internationally is built upon the foundations laid by civil society originally through voluntary hospitals, mutual insurance schemes, building societies and so on. From a benign perspective, the institutionalisation of such third sector initiatives into the apparatus of the state could be seen as ensuring the benefits are accessible to all. However, critiques of the welfare state have long suggested that it stifles innovation through bureaucracy and is costly to deliver. From a Foucauldian perspective, commentators such as Carmel and Harlock (2008) and Teasdale and Dey (2019) show how twenty-first century governing seeks to harness the entrepreneurial spirit of civil society and manipulate it towards the creation of (what governments see as having) social value. Early moves in this direction involved the creation of a new political category – the third sector – and the development of statistics to measure economic value (see Kendall, 2000). Considerable resources were invested in measures (such as SROI) to capture social value. While never an explicit goal of SROI, from a governmental perspective knowing which organisations to invest money in to achieve particular policy objectives would allow them to control the third sector and direct its social value towards political purposes. Social

[4] The 'third sector' is itself a political category which can be seen as a form of classification and control (see Alcock & Kendall, 2011).

Impact Bonds and payment by results extend this marketisation 'logic'. In essence, the third sector becomes the delivery arm of government. Third sector organisations compete with each other on the basis of costs to become government's preferred service provider.

SROI and SIBs have not exactly worked as intended. This could be seen simply as a technical issue to be rectified: we simply need better ways of measuring, further checks and balances and control mechanisms to avoid gaming of the system (Mau, 2019). However, as Muller (2015) usefully articulates, fictitious commodification of aspects of society that are not amenable to a market logic rarely work out quite as intended. Muller gives the example of a New York hospital seeking to improve survival rates of coronary bypass patients. The hospital began to compare the performance of surgeons, introducing competition between them. The statistics seemed to support this approach. Survival rates (at least for individual surgeons) increased, although this was partly at the expense of those high-risk patients that surgeons refused to treat, and partly due to significant numbers of patients living for exactly 30 days after treatment (the cut off rate imposed in the performance measures). Financially the hospital faced huge costs keeping people on life support for 30 days! We clearly see patterns in unintended consequences that suggest that such 'fictitious commodification' changes behaviours, such that public officials and third sector practitioners begin to act like *homo economicus*. The problem is that *homo economicus* is likely not the sort of person we would want to perform our heart bypass surgery, educate our children, care for our elderly parents, or provide support and accommodation to homeless people.

11.6 Moving Beyond the Market?

In closing, we should stress that fortunately it would appear that most third sector organisations have little interest in behaving as the entrepreneurs of the self that governmentality seeks to create. Many do game the system, but not necessarily as *homo economicus* seeking to maximise their own income, but rather to re-appropriate government funding towards what they perceive as having social value (see Dey & Teasdale, 2016). But this in itself creates a rather wasteful game, where the innovation and vitality of civil society is directed towards a constant battle to manipulate government funding mechanisms. For Polanyi, the solution was fairly simple. Government (and civil society) acts a bulwark against the market. Therefore, they should be kept separate. This leads to an interesting debate as to whether third sector organisations should be involved in the delivery of public services at all (a discussion we shall sidestep by declaring it to be outside the scope of this chapter). However, we should be mindful that most third sector organisations still remain outside the market. But exploring explicit resistance to marketisation emerging from civil society has considerable productive potential.

Warner and Clifton (2014), for example, describe the efforts of citizens to articulate a radical counter-discourse (which can be thought of as a Polanyian 'double movement') to the ongoing marketisation of public services and thus monetisation of social value, both in the USA and in Europe where the 'hollowing out' of public services has been profound and relentless. Social movements such as Occupy in cities such as Madrid, Barcelona, Seattle and New York City have deliberately pushed back against the intrusion of markets into our everyday lives. More recent social movements such as Extinction Rebellion have deliberately laid the cause of the climate crisis at the door of the political economic system (Doherty et al., 2018) and, at least up until the Covid-19 pandemic, they had conducted a high-profile campaign of civil disobedience, particularly in London.

A more prognostic perspective seeks to examine how civil society might act not simply as a counterbalance to capitalism, but sow the seeds of its eventual replacement. Flomenhoft (2016), for example, contends that the commodification of land, money, and labour are not necessary for a functioning market economy at all and are, in fact, detrimental to it. He suggests that land can be placed in trust, money can be administered as a public utility, and people can reclaim sovereignty over their own labour, such as through worker-owned social enterprise and/or co-operative models of ownership. However such solutions, he argues, "have no chance of succeeding in creating widespread prosperity or sustainability, unless the operating system of the economy can be reformed" (Flomenhoft, 2016, p. 98). Similarly, we have put forward our own suggestions (see Roy et al., 2021) for how the third sector can work to promote democracy and the protection of social rights through the provision of public services guided by the (Polanyian) economic principles of reciprocity and redistribution (as opposed to private profit). Third sector organisations could embed collective decision-making, and facilitate and encourage public deliberation, while guaranteeing protection against marketisation through legal constraints in profit distribution, asset locks and formal democratic decision-making structures. It remains to be seen whether the colossal work to advance the UN Sustainable Development Goals will outweigh the unintended consequences of accelerating the commodification of social value that focusing on numerical targets seems to necessarily entail. We know from history that fictitious commodification can have very grave consequences for people and the planet. In all likelihood, society will eventually act to bring the state, market and civil society back into some semblance of balance. Whether this will be in the form of a progressive or a regressive countermovement – or a combination of both – and what the outcomes for this will be, also remains to be seen.

References

Alcock, P., & Kendall, J. (2011). Constituting the Third Sector: Processes of Decontestation and Contention Under the UK Labour Governments in England. *Voluntas: International Journal of Voluntary and Nonprofit Organizations, 22*(3), 450–469. https://doi.org/10.1007/s11266-010-9178-9

Arvidson, M., Lyon, F., McKay, S., & Moro, D. (2010). The Ambitions and Challenges of SROI. *Third Sector Research Centre, WP49.*

Arvidson, M., Lyon, F., McKay, S., & Moro, D. (2013). Valuing the Social? The Nature and Controversies of Measuring Social Return on Investment (SROI). *Voluntary Sector Review, 4*(1), 3–18.

Banke-Thomas, A. O., Madaj, B., Charles, A., & van den Broek, N. (2015). Social Return on Investment (SROI) Methodology to Account for Value for Money of Public Health Interventions: A Systematic Review. *BMC Public Health, 15*(1), 582. https://doi.org/10.1186/s12889-015-1935-7

Block, F. L., & Somers, M. R. (2014). *The Power of Market Fundamentalism: Karl Polanyi's Critique.* Harvard University Press.

Brien, S. (2011). *Outcome-Based Government: How to Improve Spending Decisions Across Government – A Policy Report from the Social Return on Investment Working Group*. Centre for Social Justice.

Cairney, P., Heikkila, T., & Wood, M. (2019). *Making Policy in a Complex World*. Cambridge University Press. https://doi.org/10.1017/9781108679053

Carmel, E., & Harlock, J. (2008). Instituting the 'Third Sector' as a Governable Terrain: Partnership, Procurement and Performance in the UK. *Policy and Politics, 36*(2), 155–171.

Dey, P., & Teasdale, S. (2016). The Tactical Mimicry of Social Enterprise Strategies: Acting 'As If' in the Everyday Life of Third Sector Organizations. *Organization, 23*(4), 485–504. https://doi.org/10.1177/1350508415570689

Disley, E., Rubin, J., Scraggs, E., Burrowes, N., & Culley, D. (2011). Lessons Learned from the Planning and Early Implementation of the Social Impact Bond at HMP Peterborough. *Research Series, 5*(11). http://socialwelfare.bl.uk/subject-areas/services-client-groups/adult-offenders/ministryofjustice/125755social-impact-bond-hmp-peterborough.pdf

Doherty, B., de Moor, J., & Hayes, G. (2018). The 'New' Climate Politics of Extinction Rebellion? *OpenDemocracy*. https://www.opendemocracy.net/en/new-climate-politics-of-extinction-rebellion/

Donaldson, C., Thomas, R., & Torgerson, D. J. (1997). Validity of Open-Ended and Payment Scale Approaches to Eliciting Willingness to Pay. *Applied Economics, 29*(1), 79–84. https://doi.org/10.1080/000368497327425

Dowling, E. (2017). In the Wake of Austerity: Social Impact Bonds and the Financialisation of the Welfare State in Britain. *New Political Economy, 22*(3), 294–310. https://doi.org/10.1080/13563467.2017.1232709

Dunleavy, P., & Hood, C. (1994). From Old Public Administration to New Public Management. *Public Money and Management, 14*(3), 9–16. https://doi.org/10.1080/09540969409387823

Edmiston, D., & Nicholls, A. (2018). Social Impact Bonds: The Role of Private Capital in Outcome-Based Commissioning. *Journal of Social Policy, 47*(1), 57–76. https://doi.org/10.1017/S0047279417000125

Eikenberry, A. M., & Kluver, J. D. (2004). The Marketization of the Nonprofit Sector: Civil Society at Risk? *Public Administration Review, 64*(2), 132–140. https://doi.org/10.1111/j.1540-6210.2004.00355.x

Emerson, J. (2003). The Blended Value Proposition. *California Management Review, 45*(4), 35–51.

Falleti, T. G., & Lynch, J. F. (2009). Context and Causal Mechanisms in Political Analysis. *Comparative Political Studies, 42*(9), 1143–1166. https://doi.org/10.1177/0010414009331724

Flomenhoft, G. (2016). Escaping the Polanyi Matrix: The Impact of Fictitious Commodities: Money, Land, and Labor on Consumer Welfare. *Real-World Economics Review, 74*, 98–123.

Floyd, D. (2017). *Social Impact Bonds: An Overview of the Global Market for Commissioners and Policymakers*. Centre for Public Impact. http://socialspider.com/wp-content/uploads/2017/04/SS_SocialImpactReport_4.0.pdf

Fox, C., & Albertson, K. (2011). Payment by Results and Social Impact Bonds in the Criminal Justice Sector: New Challenges for the Concept of Evidence-Based Policy? *Criminology and Criminal Justice, 11*(5), 395–413. https://doi.org/10.1177/1748895811415580

Fraser, A., Tan, S., Lagarde, M., & Mays, N. (2018). Narratives of Promise, Narratives of Caution: A Review of the Literature on Social Impact Bonds. *Social Policy and Administration, 52*(1), 4–28. https://doi.org/10.1111/spol.12260

Fukuda-Parr, S., Yamin, A. E., & Greenstein, J. (2014). The Power of Numbers: A Critical Review of Millennium Development Goal Targets for Human Development and Human Rights. *Journal of Human Development and Capabilities, 15*(2–3), 105–117. https://doi.org/10.1080/19452829.2013.864622

Gibbon, J., & Dey, C. (2011). Developments in Social Impact Measurement in the Third Sector: Scaling Up or Dumbing Down? *Social and Environmental Accountability Journal, 31*(1), 63–72.

Gustaffson-Wright, E., Boggild-Jones, I., Nwabunnia, O., & Osborne, S. (2021). *Social and Development Impact Bonds by the Numbers*. Brookings Institute. https://www.brookings.edu/research/social-and-development-impact-bonds-by-the-numbers/

Hall, K., Alcock, P., & Millar, R. (2012). Start Up and Sustainability: Marketisation and the Social Enterprise Investment Fund in England. *Journal of Social Policy, 41*(04), 733–749. https://doi.org/10.1017/S0047279412000347

Jessop, B. (2007). Knowledge as a Fictitious Commodity: Insights and Limits of a Polanyian Perspective. In A. Buğra & K. Ağartan (Eds.), *Reading Karl Polanyi for the Twenty-First Century: Market Economy as a Political Project* (pp. 115–133). Palgrave Macmillan US. https://doi.org/10.1057/9780230607187_7

Johnson, R. (2013, February 20). The Work Programme's Only Success Is at 'Creaming and Parking'. *The Guardian*. http://www.theguardian.com/commentisfree/2013/feb/20/work-programme-success-creaming-parking

Keen, S. (2011). *Debunking Economics – Revised and Expanded Edition: The Naked Emperor Dethroned?* (Second Revised and enlarged). Zed Books.

Kendall, J. (2000). The Mainstreaming of the Third Sector into Public Policy in England in the Late 1990s: Whys and Wherefores. *Policy and Politics, 28*(4), 541–562.

Maier, F., & Meyer, M. (2017). Social Impact Bonds and the Perils of Aligned Interests. *Administrative Sciences, 7*(3), 24. https://doi.org/10.3390/admsci7030024

Marden, R. (2011, July 18). Can SROI Help the Voluntary Sector Measure Value? *The Guardian*. http://www.theguardian.com/voluntary-sector-network/2011/jul/18/sroi-help-voluntary-sector-value

Mau, S. (2019). *The Metric Society: On the Quantification of the Social.* Polity.

McHugh, N., Sinclair, S., Roy, M. J., Huckfield, L., & Donaldson, C. (2013). Social Impact Bonds: A Wolf in Sheep's Clothing? *Journal of Poverty and Social Justice, 21*(3), 247–257. https://doi.org/10.1332/204674313X13812372137921

Muller, J. Z. (2015). *The Tyranny of Metrics*. Princeton University Press.

Nicholls, A. (2009). 'We Do Good Things, Don't We?' 'Blended Value Accounting' in Social Entrepreneurship. *Accounting, Organizations and Society, 34*(6–7), 755–769.

Nicholls, J., Lawlor, E., Neitzert, E., & Goodspeed, T. (2012). *The Guide to Social Return on Investment* (2nd ed.). Cabinet Office. https://www.socialvalueuk.org/app/uploads/2016/03/The%20Guide%20to%20Social%20Return%20on%20Investment%202015.pdf

Osborne, S. P. (2006). The New Public Governance? *Public Management Review, 8*(3), 377–387. https://doi.org/10.1080/14719030600853022

Polanyi, K. (1944). *The Great Transformation: The Political and Economic Origins of Our Time* (Second Beacon Paperback Edition Published in 2001). Beacon Press.

Public Services (Social Value) Act. (2012). https://www.legislation.gov.uk/ukpga/2012/3/enacted

Roy, M. J., Dey, P., & Teasdale, S. (2021). Re-Embedding Embeddedness: What Is the Role of Social Enterprise in Promoting Democracy and Protecting Social Rights? *Social Enterprise Journal*. https://doi.org/10.1108/SEJ-02-2021-0011

Roy, M. J., McHugh, N., & Sinclair, S. (2017). Social Impact Bonds – Evidence-Based Policy or Ideology? In B. Greve (Ed.), *Handbook of Social Policy Evaluation* (pp. 263–275). Edward Elgar Publishing Ltd..

Roy, M. J., McHugh, N., & Sinclair, S. (2018). A Critical Reflection on Social Impact Bonds. *Stanford Social Innovation Review*. https://ssir.org/articles/entry/a_critical_reflection_on_social_impact_bonds

Sandel, M. J. (2012, February 27). What Isn't for Sale? *The Atlantic*. https://www.theatlantic.com/magazine/archive/2012/04/what-isnt-for-sale/308902/

Savage, M., & Tapper, J. (2021, March 6). Ministers Face Public Backlash Over 1% Pay Offer to Nurses. *The Guardian*. http://www.theguardian.com/society/2021/mar/06/ministers-face-public-backlash-over-1-pay-offer-to-nurses

Sayer, A. (2011). *Why Things Matter to People: Social Science, Values and Ethical Life*. Cambridge University Press.

Sinclair, S., McHugh, N., Huckfield, L., Roy, M. J., & Donaldson, C. (2014). Social Impact Bonds: Shifting the Boundaries of Citizenship. *Social Policy Review 26: Analysis and Debate in Social Policy*, 119–136.

Stoker, G., & Evans, M. (2016). *Evidence-Based Policy Making in the Social Sciences: Methods That Matter*. Policy Press.

Tan, S., Fraser, A., Giacomantonio, C., Kruithof, K., Sim, M., Lagarde, M., Disley, E., Rubin, J., & Mays, N. (2015). *An Evaluation of Social Impact Bonds in Health and Social Care*. Policy Innovation Research Unit (PIRU). http://piru.lshtm.ac.uk/assets/files/SIBs%20Trailblazer%20interim%20report%20March%202015.pdf

Teasdale, S., Alcock, P., & Smith, G. (2012). Legislating for the Big Society? The Case of the Public Services (Social Value) Bill. *Public Money and Management, 32*(3), 201–208. https://doi.org/10.1080/09540962.2012.676277

Teasdale, S., & Dey, P. (2019). Neoliberal Governing Through Social Enterprise: Exploring the Neglected Roles of Deviance and Ignorance in Public Value Creation. *Public Administration*. https://doi.org/10.1111/padm.12588

Warner, M. E., & Clifton, J. (2014). Marketization, Public Services and the City: The Potential for Polanyian Counter Movements. *Cambridge Journal of Regions, Economy and Society, 7*, 45–61. https://doi.org/10.1093/cjres/rst028

Wood, C., & Leighton, D. (2010). *Measuring Social Value*. DEMOS.

12

Measuring Outcomes in Social Care

Kelly Hall and Philip Kinghorn

12.1 Social Care Outcomes: An Introduction

Social care covers a range of activities, delivered by a diverse range of organisations and professionals. It has been defined as "all forms of personal care and other practical assistance for children, young people and adults who need extra support" (NICE, 2019). In this chapter, we focus on adult social care, with a particular focus on England. In England, almost 80% of adult social care services are delivered by the private sector (Kearney & White, 2018) with services overall being coordinated by local government and funded either by local government and/or directly

K. Hall (✉)
School of Social Policy, University of Birmingham, Birmingham, UK
e-mail: k.j.hall@bham.ac.uk

P. Kinghorn
Institute of Applied Health Research, University of Birmingham, Birmingham, UK
e-mail: P.Kinghorn@bham.ac.uk

R. Hazenberg, C. Paterson-Young (eds.), *Social Impact Measurement for a Sustainable Future*, https://doi.org/10.1007/978-3-030-83152-3_12

by service users (Kings Fund, 2020). Social care in England, like in many other countries, faces the critical challenge of delivering increasing amounts of care to an ageing population, in a context of tight budget pressures following the 2008 financial crisis and now the Covid-19 pandemic. Local government have responded by restricting eligibility criteria for publicly funded social care, and through lowering the margins of suppliers – leading to concerns around quality and sustainability. At the same time, adult social care is underpinned by a personalisation agenda that seeks to promote choice, tailor services to the individual and empower those who use care services (Needham, 2011).

The ongoing sustainability of the social care system has now reached crisis point, with respect to its financial sustainability and ability to respond to growing inequalities within society (Social Care Institute for Excellence, 2020). Although our focus in this chapter is on adult social care in a high-income country, principles motivating the UN (2015) SDGs, relating specifically to People (eradicating poverty, and promoting dignity and equality) and Prosperity (enabling people to live fulfilling lives), cannot be 'left behind': they should never stop being central principles underpinning the oversight and provision of services to support the most vulnerable groups in society.

SDG3, to 'ensure healthy lives and promote well-being for all at all ages' is arguably the most directly relevant to social care (UN, 2020). However, there are also several other SDG indicators/targets that are relevant, such as the empowerment and inclusion of all people regardless of disability, age or other status (SDG10 and SDG16) – crucial to enabling personalised care. How social care services are funded and allocated will also impact upon labour market participation, particularly when informal care responsibilities disproportionately fall upon women. Such concerns are raised under SDG5 on 'gender equality', which particularly highlights the impact of Covid-19 on women who have taken on additional unpaid care during the pandemic when services like day centres are closed (UN, 2020) (See Chap. 5 for a detailed discussion on 'Impact and gender'). Given the reality of resource scarcity across all contexts, the achievement of individual SDGs or the general principles motivating them, will rely on the prioritisation of services that can fairly and efficiently promote personalised and quality care. We feel that it is important to note the lack of explicit reference to social or long-term care within the SDGs, despite the relevance of care to some of the principles underpinning them and the likely importance of social care to achieving many of the SDGs. Social care is often overshadowed by health, and this is a theme that we will draw on throughout the chapter. As an example, SDG3 focuses on improving mortality ratios and the prevention/reduction of 'disease', whilst wider indicators of wellbeing that are central to social care, including dignity and independence, are largely excluded.

In this chapter, we introduce how economic evaluation could be utilised in social care contexts to promote quality, personalisation and sustainability in social care systems. We begin by introducing economic evaluation, before setting out three outcomes measurement tools utilised in economic evaluations within social care. We do not argue that these tools should be reserved exclusively for use in economic evaluation and/or social care and recognise their potential for use in more general service evaluation, routine data collection and as a framework to initiate discussion between individual service users and care providers. Whilst our analysis focuses primarily on the English context, these evaluation tools are widely used across different countries.

12.2 Economic Evaluation in Social Care

Full economic evaluation is comparative in two respects: first, a comparison of alternative courses of action, and second, a comparison in terms of both costs and consequences (Drummond et al., 2005). Whilst technical skill is needed to identify and value elements on the cost side of the equation, our remit here relates to the identification and measurement of outcomes within economic evaluations. Economic evaluation is commonly used in health, and economists often seek to summarise complex information on health outcomes using a consistent quantitative framework, such as the quality-adjusted life year (QALY). Through the QALY, 'health' is represented on a scale anchored between dead (zero) and full health (one). Because this type of analysis follows a consistent methodology, it can promote an efficient allocation of resources across an entire sector, even though the nature of specific activity (interventions) will be diverse in terms of what is involved and who benefits.

Economic evaluation in social care is however much less developed than in health, and the direct transfer of health economic methodologies from health to social care is not possible (Francis & Byford, 2011). Despite the label of quality-adjusted life years, the QALY is essentially a health-adjustment to life expectancy, and hence this type of approach fails to align with broad social care objectives. Identifying, conceptualising and assessing relevant and important outcomes associated with social care is challenging as social care is not designed to 'cure' health conditions, but instead to enable people to lead fulfilling lives and protect them from harm, despite physical or cognitive impairments. When measuring social care outcomes there is a need to measure less tangible outcomes, such as independence, dignity, social relationships and connectedness. Such outcomes are often overlooked when it comes to national and global priorities, as we noted above in the case of SDGs, which place an almost exclusive emphasis on health. Economic evaluations also often fail to recognise the value of informal (unpaid) care; something that is central to social care (Goodrich et al., 2012). A key strength of the SDGs is the recognition of the importance of unpaid care and the centrality of unpaid care to the continuation of gender inequalities around the world (SDG5).

Several outcome measures have been developed for use in economic evaluation, which conceptualise outcomes in ways that are more relevant to the context of social care. These measures are characterised by scoring systems, allowing complex information to be distilled into a single number using conceptual principles understood by economists. A conceptual framework underpinning two suites of measures that we introduce below (ICECAP and ASCOT) is the Capability Approach of Amartya Sen (Sen, 1979), which suggests that well-being can be understood in terms of *functionings* (the things that people do and be) and *capability* (the ability a person has to achieve valuable functionings). Capability (reflecting freedom and ability) is more valuable than functioning (achieved outcomes) in differentiating between the well-being of different individuals or states of the world. For example, two individuals could be observed to have minimal social interaction (functioning) but will have different levels of capability if one chooses to have minimal social interaction despite opportunities being available to them, whilst the other lacks such opportunities.

In the following section, we outline and discuss three tools that have been used in social care economic evaluations. Adult Social Care Outcomes Toolkit (ASCOT) and ICECAP are questionnaires which define outcomes in terms of a fixed conceptualisation of quality of life (a fixed list of dimensions). In contrast, SROI, is a more flexible approach whereby outcomes are identified as being relevant to a specific context and then quantified in monetary terms.

12.2.1 Adult Social Care Outcome Toolkit (ASCOT)

The ASCOT was designed to provide a social care equivalent of the QALY, but with social care-related quality of life (SCRQoL) as the objective to be maximised (Netten et al., 2012). ASCOT is designed to be applied across user groups and in different care settings to assess 'soft' outcomes, including for example dignity, social participation and control. The initial phase of work to develop the attributes for ASCOT involved systematically reviewing the literature for measures deemed appropriate for social care (Netten et al., 2002). From the review, a need was identified to reflect Sen's notion of capability (Sen, 1979) and introduce an attribute relating to dignity (Netten et al., 2012). Subsequent study phases explored the meaning of social care outcomes with service users and their carers.

Eight attributes of SCRQoL were identified: personal cleanliness and comfort; food and drink; control over daily life; social participation and involvement; occupation; accommodation cleanliness and comfort; personal safety; and dignity (Netten et al., 2012). A value set exists for ASCOT, which ranges from zero (being dead) to one. Whilst the lower anchoring (zero) is the same as that used for the QALY and values could be used in decision making in an almost identical way, an ideal construct of social care-related quality of life replaces a description of perfect health as the upper anchor (1). This 'ideal' state (1) is presented as a preferred state, in which the individual's needs are met to their desired level (Netten et al., 2012).

ASCOT is now the most widely known and used tool to measure social care outcomes and is a central measurement tool in the Department of Health and Social Care's English Adult Social Care Survey, sent to people who use publicly funded care services. A key advantage of ASCOT is that it is now so widely used within social care evaluation that it can facilitate the comparison of outcomes of different services and can be used to compare the findings from a specific study against wider benchmarks. ASCOT can also be used to assess the impact of specific care services as it explicitly asks people about whether or not their care provider helps them to achieve particular outcomes, and whether they would achieve less of that outcome if the service was not there (Needham et al., 2016). This is a key strength, as defining a counterfactual or comparator is difficult in social care (i.e. what would have happened to the person had they not been receiving that specific service). In social impact measurement, comparison against a benchmark is viewed as best practice (Clifford, 2014). Different versions of the tool have been created for people in different care settings e.g. there are self-completion questionnaires, interviews and observation tools. ASCOT therefore tackles the significant hurdle of using self-reported outcome measures in the social care context where people eligible for social care (e.g. who may have cognitive, intellectual, sensory and physical impairments) find it difficult to self-complete questionnaires.

The suitability of ASCOT for social care research has however been questioned, with critics suggesting that the questions are complex, worded awkwardly and that they are not always clearly understood by people using care services (Needham et al., 2016). A further critique is that ASCOT, like many other outcome tools, does not gather information about how outcomes are achieved. Such outcomes tools simply provide a 'summative' evaluation of social care interventions and provide no understanding of how social care actually produces its effects (Bovaird, 2014). This makes it difficult to use such outcomes tools to support the redesign of social care initiatives to improve outcomes. The same challenge can also be applied to ICECAP, which is discussed in the next section, but highlight it here as a recent study (Needham et al., 2016) attempted to overcome this challenge, by combining ASCOT with qualitative interviews to understand both the outcomes and the 'process' of care i.e. how social care produces outcomes. However, the abovementioned awkwardness and rigidity of the questions (compared with qualitative interviewing) along with the length of the ASCOT survey, meant that ASCOT was hard to use in an interview setting. The same study (Allen et al., 2019) also highlighted some of the practical and epistemological tensions between the two dominant paradigms within social care evaluation i.e. participatory research and quantified outcomes. This underpins the argument by Glasby and Beresford (2006, p. 268) that 'objective' evidence created through the use of specialist evaluation tools often overpowers the lived experience of service users.

12.2.2 Broader Measures of Capability Well-Being: ICECAP

Like ASCOT, ICECAP was developed to assess outcomes for inclusion in economic analysis. However, rather than replicating the health element of the QALY model with social care related quality of life, the ICECAP measures were developed to assess quality of life in a broad sense, and hence be suitable for use across both health and social care (Grewal et al., 2006). There is now a suite of different ICECAP measures, for use across different stages of the life-course: ICECAP-A (Al-Janabi et al., 2012) for use with the general adult population; ICECAP-O for older people (Grewal et al., 2006); and ICECAP Supportive Care Measure (SCM) (Sutton & Coast, 2014) for use at the end of life.

Development of the ICECAP measures involved user involvement. ICECAP-O (the first of the measures) began with in-depth interviews with 40 older people, which identified five conceptually exclusive attributes: Attachment; Role; Enjoyment; Security; and Control (Grewal et al., 2006). Although no distinction was made within the interviews between functionings and capability, it was observed that the ability to function was a major theme, and this observation led to a decision to focus the measure on the capability to achieve important outcomes (Grewal et al., 2006). The focus on assessing capability could be said to promote choice and empowerment and potentially provide richer information to distinguish between individuals who, at the level of functioning, are observed to have the same outcomes. As an example, no view is stated that people will or should seek or value social interaction, or indeed that they should desire any specific type of relationship; but instead importance is attached to people having the ability to experience the love, friendship and support that is valuable to them.

Value sets are available for ICECAP-A (Flynn et al., 2014) and ICECAP-O (Coast et al., 2008), with values anchored between zero (no capability) and one (full capability). However, in contrast to ASCOT, there is no assumption that efficiency (the maximisation of outcomes from a fixed budget) should be the sole objective of economic evaluation. Alternative objectives have actively been explored which explicitly incorporate the notion of equity (Mitchell et al., 2015; Kinghorn, 2019).

A recent systematic review (Proud et al., 2019) indicated that the ICECAP-O has good construct validity and responsiveness. A review of ICECAP-A more tentatively concluded that promising evidence of the measure's content and construct validity is beginning to emerge (Afentou & Kinghorn, 2020). However, the reviews revealed that ICECAP measures are almost exclusively included in research as secondary outcome measures (with health measures typically included as the primary outcome measure) and have almost exclusively been used within a health context. Their feasibility and validity in social care contexts is thus unproven. The broad nature of ICECAP measures potentially may make them less sensitive to change, compared to condition specific measures, and this may explain why health specific measures have dominated. It is natural that those involved with developing an intervention will want to demonstrate its efficacy, and this may be easier with a narrow range of health outcomes, compared to broad well-being measures.

12.3 Social Return on Investment (SROI)

Social return on investment has emerged as a preferred technique for measuring social impact and outcomes, including within a health and social care context. Originating in the US in 2000 and later tested and refined in the UK, SROI offers a way of evaluating personal, social and community outcomes by placing financial proxy values on each outcome.

The result is a ratio of monetised social value that outlines the value of social benefits created by an organisation in relation to the relative cost of achieving those benefits (Emerson & Twersky, 1996). For example, a ratio of 3:1 indicates that an investment of £1 delivers £3 of social value. Most commonly used by third sector organisations, SROI uses elements of cost-benefit analysis (CBA) but explicitly attempts to involve stakeholders at every stage (Arvidson et al., 2010) through assessment of how much stakeholders value the service (Millar & Hall, 2013). SROI can therefore empower its participants and promote positive relationships between different groups (Bosco et al., 2019). SROI has also emerged as a favoured measurement tool in some health and social care contexts. For example, when the (previously named) UK Department of Health set up the Social Enterprise Investment Fund (SEIF) to deliver £120 million of grants and loans to social enterprises operating in the health and social care sectors in England, additional funding was provided to some investees to encourage them to undertake SROI (Millar & Hall, 2013). SROI was used as a tool to meet one of the key SEIF goals; to encourage social enterprises to measure and communicate their social return.

Despite being a favoured measurement tool, SROI has been widely criticised. The main critique relates to the difficulty of attributing a financial figure to 'soft' outcomes (Millar & Hall, 2013), such as dignity or happiness. Person-centredness is central to social care provision yet attributing a financial value to personalised outcomes like choice and control will involve subjective value judgments and assumptions (Lingane & Olsen, 2004; Millar & Hall, 2013). Therefore, as outlined in the previous chapter (Roy and Teasdale), the 'value' of something can be interpreted very differently, and so attempting to put a price tag on personalised outcomes is not always possible. Even if it was possible to attribute a financial proxy to these outcomes, it would require an organisation to have sufficient data and a strong evidence base. Furthermore, SROI requires a counterfactual i.e. an idea of 'what would have happened anyway' that is rarely available (New Philanthropy Capital, 2010). SROI findings can therefore have limited generalisability as the analysis and methodology is highly sensitive to the context in which it takes place and rarely include a control group (Bosco et al., 2019). The SROI result is therefore often incorrect and inconsistent data makes it impossible to compare SROI ratios across different organisations (Ryan & Lyne, 2008).

Millar and Hall (2013) also highlight a series of practical problems with SROI, including that it can be costly and requires significant time and expertise to develop. Whilst larger organisations may have the capacity, smaller and voluntary organisations are unlikely to have such resource and instead can see measurement as a burden that takes resource away from front-line service delivery. Indeed, SROI has been reported as overly idealistic and ambitious, particularly in social service contexts. Further, using SROI may even lead to the disempowerment or stigmatisation of service users whose voices may be overpowered by stakeholders who fund or deliver the service (Cheung, 2017). Therefore, in summary, whilst SROI can be beneficial in a social care context to help an organisation understand key elements of their work including the identification of stakeholders and beneficiaries, to elucidate relevant outcomes and highlight areas for improvement (Bosco et al., 2019), the actual SROI ratio often has little meaning outside of the context within which it was produced.

12.4 Comparison of Our Three (Economic) Approaches

The three measurement tools introduced in this chapter offer social care organisations and funders different ways to quantify the value that they create. On the one hand, they all seek to measure quality of life outcomes that are relevant to social care contexts and have involved (or promote the involvement of) different stakeholders, including people who use care services, in their design. They also differ in a number of key areas and we set out the key similarities and differences in relation to the evaluative space, the role of stakeholders, validity and adaptability in Table 12.1. Each has characteristics that may make it relevant for the evaluation of specific types of social care intervention, and it may be valuable – at least in the short-term whilst more evidence is compiled on their relative strengths and psychometric performance (where relevant) – to use more

Table 12.1 A comparison of economic approaches

Comparative variable	SROI	ASCOT	ICECAP
Relevance of evaluative space i.e. are outcomes pre-determined?	Flexibility to identify costs and outcomes to a particular intervention/ context.	Attributes identified as being specifically relevant to social care.	Attributes are not context-specific and have a broad quality of life focus.
Involvement and role of stakeholders	Involvement of stakeholders is a key principle to develop context-specific measures.	'Sunk' stakeholder involvement (various stakeholders involved with identifying attributes; public involvement in valuation) resulting in standard questionnaire format.	'Sunk' stakeholder involvement (qualitative and quantitative work with the public to identify and value attributes) resulting in standard questionnaire format.
Validity, transparency and consistency	Transparency and independent verification are key principles. Costs and outcomes relate to a single project. Valuation of outcomes relies heavily on identifying proxy values.	Increasing body of evidence on validity and sensitivity within a social care context. Consistent outcome assessment, value set and decision-rule across evaluations.	Increasing body of evidence on validity and responsiveness mainly within a health context. Consistent assessment of outcomes and value set for those at same 'life-stage'.
Adaptability for vulnerable groups	Assessment of costs and outcomes decided within project.	Self-, interview-, proxy-completion, easy read and mixed method versions available.	Standard format with limited flexibility but proxy versions used in end of life care context.

Adapted from Kinghorn et al. (2019)

than one approach within the same project. For example, it may be desirable to use both ASCOT and ICECAP, an approach used in a recent project on market shaping and personalisation in English social care (Needham et al., 2020).

12.5 Making Sense of Impact Measurement in Social Care

As outlined at the outset of the chapter, the social care sector is in crisis due to a combination of the Covid-19 pandemic, an ageing population, workforce vulnerabilities, and ongoing cuts to public services. This chapter has focused on the English context where it has been widely noted that further investment in social care is needed to tackle widening inequalities and to ensure the future wellbeing of the most vulnerable people (e.g. Social Care Institute for Excellence, 2020; Kings Fund, 2020). Such challenges are not however unique to the English context. The principles underpinning the SDGs can help us consider how we develop sustainable solutions to tackle what has become known as the 'social care crisis'. The SDGs values in relation to People (eradicating poverty and promoting dignity and equality) and Prosperity (enabling people to live fulfilling lives) are central in exploring how we can reduce inequalities and support vulnerable individuals and groups. The need to empower all people and communities regardless of age, disability or other social status is crucial (SDG10 and SDG16) if we are to develop a sustainable and inclusive care system. We need to tackle gender inequalities (SDG5) that are particularly evident in care work, as women take on the majority of unpaid care work and the Covid-19 pandemic has further exacerbated these challenges. Despite the relevance of the SDGs to care systems, the SDG goals do not directly refer to social care. They present a narrow, and somewhat medicalised focus on health and wellbeing (e.g. SDG3) that largely excludes the key principles of social care (e.g. dignity, independence and control). Understanding and measuring social care outcomes that offer a wider understanding of wellbeing and quality of life are an important step in the allocation of scarce resources. Economic evaluation is crucial within this context.

Economic evaluation is, however, at an early stage in the social care sector and as we have demonstrated in this chapter, transferring methodologies and measurement tools from health is problematic. There is no 'one size fits all' approach to measuring outcomes and any approach to identifying, defining and measuring outcomes should be relevant to the needs and objectives of key stakeholders, which will include service users, funders, provider organisations and the care workforce. In reality, these diverse stakeholder groups may have competing objectives and perceptions of acceptable methods for assessing outcomes. For example, local authority funders of social care often impose their own requirements in terms of outcome measurement and may impose targets or key performance indicators (KPIs) as part of the commissioning process (Millar & Hall, 2013). Funders often focus on monetary metrics in social care contexts, neglecting more meaningful approaches to impact measurement valued by provider organisations. Prior research has indicated a preference among some health and social care organisations for outcomes measures that encourage 'bottom up' engagement with users (Millar & Hall, 2013).

Collaborative and participatory approaches are viewed as central principles in social care (Social Care Institute for Excellence, 2020) and fundamental if personalisation and equality are to be achieved. This reflects a wider acceptance of co-production principles within social care that can also be extended to outcomes measurement. Returning to the SDGs, the development of participatory outcome measures can help the achievement of SDG target 16.7 that aims to "Ensure responsive, inclusive, participatory and representative decision-making at all levels" as a means to support the empowerment and inclusion of all people.

Whilst SROI represents the most participatory approach, it is widely criticised for its inability to apply financial values to 'soft' outcomes that are so central in social care settings. ASCOT and ICECAP are better able to measure soft outcomes and indicators relevant to social care. They can promote consistency in the evaluation of different social care services or interventions, and hence facilitate the type of comparative analysis that is favoured by researchers, and economists in particular. However, they can represent a top down approach, imposing a pre-defined set of outcomes/dimensions. As such, measurement tools like ASCOT and ICECAP can create tensions when used in co-produced research. As Allen et al. (2019) have observed, participatory approaches and the need for validated outcomes measure are two central yet competing priorities in social care evaluation and practice. There may be a need for sensitivity and education to overcome fears that the quantification of outcomes using tools such as ASCOT or ICECAP will fail to demonstrate the value of services against their stated objectives.

12.6 Empowerment in Social Care

Key funding bodies are making an increasing commitment to social care, and economic methods are available (and encouraged) for use in this context. We have highlighted some of the challenges associated with measurement tools for economic evaluation in social care, and we argue that it is unlikely that a single approach will ever be acceptable when used in isolation. We instead advocate the use of several approaches (to the extent to which this is feasible and affordable) as a way of triangulating evidence and understanding 'the big picture' (i.e. analysing and interpreting findings intelligently). For this to happen, there must be meaningful representation and involvement of relevant stakeholders (a plurality of views and perspectives), but without losing or compromising the integrity of specific disciplinary approaches. Approaches for impact measurement are however often developed through rigid, top-down frameworks. This is reflected in the SDGs that refer to user empowerment, but policymakers and practitioners need to ensure that user voices are fully represented in their implementation. The SDGs also present a narrow view of what constitutes 'quality of life' and 'care', with a focus on medicalised definitions of health to the detriment of social care-related outcomes like independence and control. Finally, given the complexity of social care interventions and provider organisations, effort should be devoted to understanding not only what the desired outcomes are, but also how outcomes are achieved; qualitative and participatory research methods may be most suitable for addressing this question.

References

Afentou, N., & Kinghorn, P. (2020). A Systematic Review of the Feasibility and Psychometric Properties of the ICEpop CAPability Measure for Adults and its Use So Far in Economic Evaluation. *Value in Health, 23*(4), 515–526.

Al-Janabi, H., Flynn, T., & Coast, J. (2012). Development of a Self-Report Measure of Capability Wellbeing for Adults: The ICECAP-A. *Quality of Life Research, 21*(1), 167–176.

Allen, K., Needham, C., Hall, K., & Tanner, D. (2019). Participatory Research Meets Validated Outcome Measures: Tensions in the Co-Production of Social Care Evaluation. *Social Policy and Administration, 53*(2), 311–325.

Arvidson, M., Lyon, F., McKay, S., & Moro, D. (2010). *The Ambitions and Challenges of SROI, Third Sector Research Centre*. Working Paper 49. Third Sector Research Centre, University of Birmingham.

Bosco, A., Schneider, J., & Broome, E. (2019). The Social Value of the Arts for Care Home Residents in England: A Social Return on Investment (SROI) Analysis of the Imagine Arts Programme. *Maturitas, 6*(124), 15–24.

Bovaird, T. (2014). Attributing Outcomes to Social Policy Interventions – 'Gold Standard' or 'Fool's Gold' in Public Policy and Management? *Social Policy and Administration, 48*, 1–23.

Cheung, J. C. (2017). A Social Work Perspective on Using Social Return on Investment (SROI) in Humanistic Social Care. *Australian Social Work, 70*(4), 491–499.

Clifford, J. (2014). *Proposed Approaches to Social Impact Measurement*. European Commission. Available online at: https://op.europa.eu/en/publication-detail/-/publication/0c0b5d38-4ac8-43d1-a7af-32f7b6fcf1cc#. Accessed on Apr 2021.

Coast, J., Flynn, T., Natarajan, L., Sproston, K., Lewis, J., Louviere, J., & Peters, T. (2008). Valuing the ICECAP Capability Index for Older People. *Social Science and Medicine, 67*, 874–882.

Drummond, M., Sculpher, M., Torrance, G. W., O'Brien, B., & Stoddart, G. (2005). *Methods for the Economic Evaluation of Health Care Programmes*. Oxford University Press.

Emerson, J., & Twersky, F. (1996). *New Social Entrepreneurs: The Success, Challenge and Lessons of Non-profit Enterprise Creation*. The Roberts Foundation.

Flynn, T., Huynh, P. T., Al-Janabi, E., Moody, H., Clemens, A., & Coast, J. (2014). Scoring the ICECAP-A Capability Instrument. Estimation of a UK General Population Tariff. *Health Economics, 24*(3), 258–269.

Francis, J., & Byford, S. (2011, December). *SCIE's Approach To Economic Evaluation in Social Care*. SCIE Report 51. SCIE.

Glasby, J., & Beresford, P. (2006). Who Knows Best? Evidence-Based Practice and the Service User Contribution. *Critical Social Policy, 26*(1), 268–284.

Goodrich, K., Kaambwa, B., & Al-Janabi, H. (2012). The Inclusion of Informal Care in Applied Economic Evaluation: A Review. *Value in Health, 15*(6), 975–981.

Grewal, I., Lewis, J., Flynn, T., Brown, J., Bond, J., & Coast, J. (2006). Developing Attributes for a Generic Quality of Life Measure for Older People: Preferences or Capabilities? *Social Science and Medicine, 62*, 1891–1901.

Kearney, J., & White, A. (2018). *The Economic Value of the Adult Social Care Sector – UK.* https://www.skillsforcare.org.uk/Documents/About/sfcd/Economic-value-of-the-adult-social-care-sector-UK.pdf. Accessed Aug 2019.

Kinghorn, P. (2019). Using Deliberative Methods to Establish a Sufficient State of Capability Well-Being for Use in Decision-Making in the Contexts of Public Health and Social Care. *Social Science and Medicine, 240*, 112546.

Kinghorn, P., Afentou, N., Betts, G., Coast, J., Tudor, R., Edwards, R., Knapp, M., & Malley, J. (2019). *Embracing the Different: Overcoming the Challenges Associated with Conducting Economic Analysis in Social Care, and Identifying Opportunities and Priorities for Future Research.* Health Economists' Study Group.

Kings Fund. (2020). *Social Care 360.* Available online at: https://www.kingsfund.org.uk/publications/social-care-360. Accessed on Mar 2021.

Lingane, A., & Olsen, S. (2004). Guidelines for Social Return on Investment. *California Management Review, 46*(3), 116–135.

Millar, R., & Hall, K. (2013). Social Return on Investment (SROI) and Performance Measurement: The Opportunities and Barriers for Social Enterprises in Health and Social Care. *Public Management Review., 15*(6), 923–941.

Mitchell, P., Roberts, T. E., Barton, P., & Coast, J. (2015). Assessing Sufficient Capability: A New Approach to Economic Evaluation. *Social Science and Medicine, 139*, 71–79.

Needham, C. (2011). *Personalising Public Services: Understanding the Personalisation Narrative*. Policy Press.

Needham, C., Allen, K., Burn, E., Hall, K., Mangan, C., Al-Janabi, H., Tahir, W., Carr, S., Glasby, J., Henwood, M., McKay, S., & Brant, I. (2020). *Shifting Shapes: How Can Local Care Markets Support Personalised Outcomes?* https://www.birmingham.ac.uk/documents/college-social-sciences/social-policy/publications/shifting-shapes.pdf. Accessed Apr 2021.

Needham, C., Allen, K., & Hall, K. (2016). *Micro-Enterprises and Personalisation: What Size Is Good Care?* Policy Press.

Netten, A., Burge, P., Malley, J., Potoglou, D., Towers, A.-M., Brazier, J., Flynn, T., Forder, J., & Wall, B. (2012). Outcomes of Social Care for Adults: Developing a Preference-Weighted Measure. *Health Technology Assessment, 16*(16).

Netten, A., Ryan, M., Smith, P., Skatun, D., Healey, A., & Knapp, M. (2002). *The Development of a Measure of Social Care Outcome for Older People.* Available online at: https://kar.kent.ac.uk/27339/. Personal Social Services Research Unit, University of Kent.

New Philanthropy Capital. (2010, April). *Social Return on Investment Position Paper.* Available online at http://www.philanthropycapital.org/publications/improving_the_sector/charity_analysis/sroi_position_paper.aspx. Accessed on Apr 2020.

NICE: National Institute for Health and Care Excellence. (2019). *Glossary.* Available online at: https://www.nice.org.uk/Glossary?letter=S. Accessed on Apr 2021.

Proud, L., McLoughlin, C., & Kinghorn, P. (2019). *ICECAP-O*, the Current State of Play: A Systematic Review of Studies Reporting the Psychometric Properties and Use of the Instrument over the Decade since its Publication. *Quality of Life Research, 28*(6), 1429–1439.

Ryan, P. W., & Lyne, I. (2008). Social Enterprise and the Measurement of Social Value: Methodological Issues with the Calculation and Application of the Social Return on Investment. *Education, Knowledge and Economy, 2*(3), 223–237.

Sen, A. (1979). *Equality of What? The Tanner Lecture on Human Values.* Stanford University.

Social Care Institute for Excellence. (2020). *Beyond COVID: New Thinking on the Future of Adult Social Care.* SCIE.

Sutton, E., & Coast, J. (2014). Development of a Supportive Care Measure for Economic Evaluations of End-of-Life Care Using Qualitative Methods. *Palliative Medicine, 28*(2), 151–157.

United Nations. (2015). *Transforming Our World: The 2030 Agenda for Sustainable Development.* Available online at: https://sdgs.un.org/sites/default/files/publications/21252030%20Agenda%20for%20Sustainable%20Development%20web.pdf. Accessed on Apr 2021.

United Nations. (2020). *The Sustainable Development Goals Report 2020.* Available online at: https://unstats.un.org/sdgs/report/2020/The-Sustainable-Development-Goals-Report-2020.pdf. Accessed on Apr 2021.

Section IV

Power, Accountability and Ethics

13

Enhancing Impact Materiality: Lessons from Evidenced-Based Policy Making

Alex Nicholls and Edward Yee

13.1 Impact and Policy Evidence

This chapter takes a critical lens to the emerging landscape of impact measurement and management and considers what lessons can be learned from the established field of evidence-based policymaking. In this context we consider three questions:

- What constitutes impact materiality in terms of data validity and how can it best be measured?
- What are impact materiality data risks associated with different levels of data validity?
- What is the impact materiality of end-user voice in impact measurement and management practices?

A. Nicholls (✉) • E. Yee
University of Oxford, Oxford, UK
e-mail: Alex.Nicholls@sbs.ox.ac.uk; Edward.Yee.MBA20@said.oxford.edu

R. Hazenberg, C. Paterson-Young (eds.), *Social Impact Measurement for a Sustainable Future*, https://doi.org/10.1007/978-3-030-83152-3_13

This chapter is structured as follows. First, we consider the current landscape of impact measurement and management and set out impact materiality. After this overview, the chapter sets out three impact materiality issues: data validity; data risk; end-user voice. Following this, we set out an alternative context for impact data measurement in terms of evidence-based policymaking. This leads us to consider how established evidenced-based models offer opportunities to enhance impact measurement and management practices with data validity and risk (the Hierarchy of Evidence Model) and end-user voice (the Ladder of Citizen Participation Model). Finally, we offer conclusions concerning what can be learnt from bringing in models from evidence-based policymaking into impact measurement in terms of developing more effective models to underpin better-informed decision-making.

13.2 Impact Measurement and Materiality

Materiality is a foundational concept in financial accounting. The materiality of data is determined by the judgement of the professional accountant in terms of the relevance to investor decision-making of the available data. Consequently, according to the Generally Accepted Accounting Principles, financial data is generally considered 'material' if its omission or misrepresentation could influence the economic decisions of anyone for whom the information is relevant. This depends on the significance of the data relative to the circumstance and is often viewed as a threshold.[1]

However, impact materiality is more contested, primarily because—lacking any regulatory guidelines—the definition of what constitutes *relevant* impact data is far less clear. In contrast to financial materiality, the dimensions of impact relevance cannot—*sui generis*—be confined only to financial metrics (though see the discussion of impact monetization below). Furthermore, the definition of what constitutes 'good' or 'bad' impact performance may differ depending on different stakeholder perspectives. Whilst the investor (or grant-maker) perspective may still be expected to dominate, this may lead to sub-optimal sustainable finance

[1] See: https://www.accounting.com/resources/gaap/

capital allocations if it fails to recognise the calibrations of impact performance offered by other stakeholders (most obviously the end-users, who actually 'experience' the impact) (Nicholls, 2018).

Despite the material importance of valid non-financial, 'impact', performance data in terms of organisational decision-making, the landscape of impact measurement and management remains under-institutionalised and lacks both the standards of metrics and disclosure, and the regulatory structures of financial reporting. In this context, there is an increasing demand for impact reporting standards to be developed following the model of financial reporting standards. In recent years, some significant progress towards standardisation has been made, most notably in the work of the Global Impact Investment Network, the Impact Management Project (IMP), the United Nations SDG Impact Project, the International Finance Corporation (IFC), and the International Financial Reporting Standards Foundation (IFRS). In addition, moves towards standardisation have also been linked to models of data comparability based on the monetization of impact. Finally, new data collection and analysis technologies are also playing a role in innovations around data reliability and validity, as well as improving end-user participation and voice. Next, we consider two critical issues concerning impact materiality: data validity and risk; the role of end-user voice.

13.3 Impact Materiality: Validity of Data and Risk

The IMP—a global coalition aiming to establish impact reporting standards—defined impact risk as 'the likelihood that impact will be different than expected, and that the difference will be material from the perspective of people or the planet who experience impact' (Impact Management Project, n.d.). In this context, the IMP also set out nine categories of impact risk probability (Evidence Risk, External Risk, Stakeholder Participation Risk, Drop-off Risk, Efficiency Risk, Execution Risk, Alignment Risk, Endurance Risk, and Unexpected Impact Risk) focussed on issues around data validity, organisational impact performance, stakeholder perceptions, and external issues. However, the IMP did not provide any guidance on how to determine the impact materiality of data validity on the relative impact risk of these nine categories.

A further set of challenges in terms of the impact materiality of data validity relate to claims of green-, SDG- or impact-washing (see 2Degrees Investing Initiative, n.d.). Absent clear regulation on impact reporting and disclosure—and absent any common standards or metrics—the opportunity for investors to over-claim their impact will always be a material issue[2] (see Chap. 15 for discussion on ethical issues in social impact measurement'). Despite the substantial growth of green finance over recent years, there remain material concerns around transparency, disclosure and the potential for 'greenwashing'.[3] For example, the World Economic Forum reported that whilst 63% of the companies in its ESG Index had a policy in place to reduce their emissions, only 35% had specific reduction targets.[4] Furthermore, according to the Bank for International Settlements, in a survey of >200 firms in 2015–18, ESG investing was biased towards firms that tended to be cleaner in the first place.[5] Over 70% of issuers had a carbon intensity equivalent to, or lower than, a multi-national consumer products firm, such as Procter and Gamble. In contrast, carbon-intensive, or highly polluting, companies rarely issued green bonds for fear of being accused of greenwashing. Moreover, many green bonds are simply used to refinance already green projects without an additional reduction in carbon dioxide emissions. Such critiques have also been raised against the wider sustainable finance sector,[6] as several mainstream investment banks have developed impact investing funds, advisory services and consultancy expertise, for example,

[2] See: https://www.privatedebtinvestor.com/investor-interest-grows-will-dangers-impact-washing/

[3] See: https://www.economist.com/finance-and-economics/2019/12/07/climate-change-has-made-esg-a-force-in-investing

[4] See: https://www.weforum.org/agenda/2020/01/sustainable-finance-starts-with-data/

[5] See: https://www.bis.org/publ/othp31.pdf

[6] See, for example critiques of ESG ratings systems – https://www.economist.com/finance-and-economics/2019/12/07/climate-change-has-made-esg-a-force-in-investing – as well as warnings over 'greenwashing' funds, https://www.ftadviser.com/investments/2020/07/16/be-critical-of-esg-credentials-to-avoid-greenwashing-funds/

JP Morgan;[7] Credit Suisse;[8] Barclays;[9] and UBS.[10] The entry of the mainstream investment banks into the impact investing market will, inevitably, grow it substantially over time, though there remain some concerns over the potential for green- or, more recently, impact-washing.[11]

13.4 Impact Materiality: End-User Voice

Understanding the dimensions of impact materiality in terms of data validity and risk are essential to support effective impact management and decision-making. Establishing impact materiality involves establishing *which* types of valid data matter most in terms of their materiality for decision-making. With respect to the impact measurement of human welfare and other social goods, the input of key stakeholders—notably end-users—plays an important role in materiality analysis. By paying attention to the lived experiences of service users in terms of the design and implementation of impact methodologies, better quality (richer and more valid) data can be collected. Such processes also create ancillary impact as they serve to empower often disempowered populations by giving them voice.

New technology also offers an important set of opportunities to improve the integration of end-user voice in impact materiality assessments. Central to this is a set of innovations that have emerged under the heading of 'lean data'. In 2014, the Acumen Fund (Acumen, 2015) created the Lean Data initiative to apply the principles of lean design to the collection of impact data. The core philosophy behind Lean Data is to

---

[7] See: https://privatebank.jpmorgan.com/gl/en/services/investing/sustainable-investing/impact-investing

[8] See: https://www.credit-suisse.com/uk/en/private-banking/secure-your-legacy/sustainable-investing.html

[9] See: https://www.barclays.co.uk/smart-investor/investments/funds-etfs-and-investment-trusts/impact-investing/

[10] See: https://www.ubs.com/uk/en/asset-management/institutional-investors/investment-themes/sustainable-impact-investing.html

[11] See, for example: https://www.bloomberg.com/news/articles/2020-04-09/-social-washing-is-becoming-growing-headache-for-esg-investors and https://www.theimpactivate.com/new-impact-management-principles-aim-to-safeguard-against-impact-washing/

build, from the ground up, a data collection mindset and methodology that prioritizes the voice of the end-users.[12] The Lean Data model aims better to understand how investments impact the lives of low-income people.[13] Rather than collecting data on 'impact', the Lean Data approach coined the term 'social performance measurement' better to represent its end-user-centric measurement approach to capturing social change at the individual or group level (Acumen, 2015).

However, despite these important innovations, the impact materiality of end-user voice remains poorly conceptualised across the impact measurement and management field more generally where the precedence of investor or funder voice still perpetuates. Next, we turn to an analysis of impact measurement in evidence-based policymaking to set out the relevance of such an established field of practice to improve and enhance impact measurement as described above.

13.5 Evidence-Based Policy Making

Despite the significant innovations in impact measurement and management noted above, the focus has been, primarily, on adapting existing models from financial accounting to the impact domain. This is largely a consequence of a dominant, strategic, focus on growing the impact investment market by designing a taxonomy of impact data consistent with mainstream capital markets norms and expectations (see Chap. 6). This agenda has also driven a shift towards the establishment of *sustainability*, rather than impact, standards that aim to consolidate existing Environmental, Social and Governance systems rather than build a distinctive domain of impact measurement and management (Impact Management Project, n.d.). Consistent with this agenda has been a lack of attention to other, established, non-financial market systems of impact measurement in other sectors, specifically evidence-based policymaking.

[12] See: https://www.youngfoundation.org/publications/nothing-about-us-without-us-lived-experience-insight-social-investment/

[13] See: https://acumen.org/lean-data/

In this context, we suggest there is value in exploring cognate approaches from evidence-based policymaking. Here, evidence-based policymaking refers to the research methods used to build reliable evidence around interventions that first emerged in the 1930s;[14] and the application of such evidence for public and private resource allocators to make allocation decisions in interventions shown to be effective (Baron, 2018). These approaches aim to improve public policy decision-making by providing valid, comparative, data to optimize both the efficiency and effectiveness of the allocation of public funding (VanLandingham, 2020). This practice has been developed over decades and can prove, with a high degree of confidence, the causal relationships between the allocation of public finance and its impact.

Evidenced-based policy approaches encompass a range of methodologies contingent on the materiality of impact data to different stakeholders (Parker & Robinson, 2013). The utility of this data comes first, leaving a strong bent towards experimental and observational designs that establish causal relationships. Having high confidence in such relationships are material for decision making as decision-makers can trust that their decisions would lead to the intended outcomes. Some materiality variables include external validity; internal validity; user participation; cost-effectiveness. To address the complexity of materiality judgements, a range of methodological innovations have emerged (Better Evaluation, 2014) including observational design, meta-analyses, participatory approaches, and quality-adjusted life-years (QALYs). Moreover, conceptualizations of what constitute material data range from prioritizing community-based participatory research (CBPR)—that gives voice to end-users (Viswanathan et al., 2004)—to well-established social-science models such as RCTs (Cartwright, 2007). Brief descriptions of some key methods (borrowed from the hierarchy of evidence in Fig. 13.1 below) and their examples are as follows:

[14] Evidence-based policymaking first emerged with the landmark Cambridge Somerville Youth Study (Powers & Witmer, 1951). Seen as one of the first Randomised Controlled Trials (RCTs), it selected youths to partake in counselling and group recreational activities to reduce rates of juvenile delinquency.

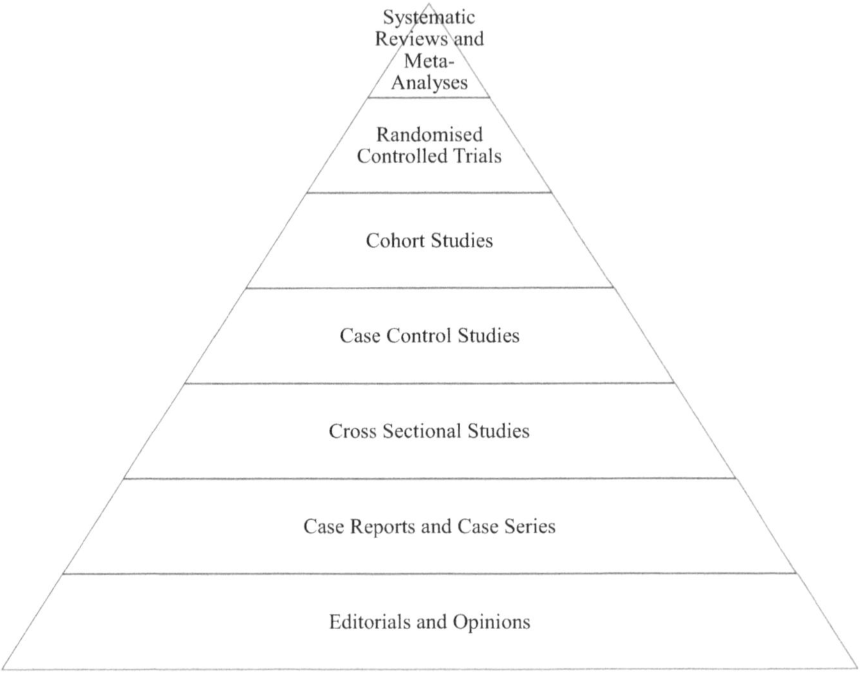

Fig. 13.1 Hierarchy of Evidence Model (Pinchbeck & Archer, 2018)

Systematic Reviews A systematic review is designed to collate results from existing studies of a particular intervention and then select and evaluate the contributions of each study, analysing and synthesizing their data. The amalgamation of conclusions from various studies in differing contexts is more valid than any individual study (Denyer & Tranfield, 2009). Van Rooyan et al. (2012) is an example that examined the impact of micro-finance in Sub-Saharan Africa. This case amalgamed 15 other relevant studies by searching through a variety of databases and data sources.[15] Other examples of systematic reviews can be found at the

[15] These studies were screened for relevance including full-text screening by two researchers. The researchers then coded these studies and synthesised their results in terms of the impact of micro-finance across financial, health, nutrition, education, child labour, women's empowerment, housing, job creation, and social cohesion outcomes.

Cochrane Library.[16] Meta-analysis A meta-analysis is a type of systematic review that uses quantitative statistical techniques to weigh and combine impact data points from other relevant individual studies. Doing so creates greater confidence in the validity of findings. This is typically performed using RCTs (Lipsey & Wilson, 2001; Ab, 2005). An example is by Masi et al. (2010) on interventions that reduce loneliness. Taking a similar approach to systematic reviews, it proceeded one step further by combining 20 randomised studies to obtain greater power levels and hence confidence levels. This data, as usually the case, was plotted on a forest plot. Randomised Controlled Trials A form of experimental study—drawn from social science—that has become central to evidence-based policymaking, RCTs focus on identifying the causal relationships between an intervention and its expected outcome. RCTs have several key features that make them unique and distinct (Sibbald & Roland, 1998): Random allocation of end-users into intervention and control groups

- All end-users are treated identically aside from the experimental treatment
- End-users are analysed within the treatment group they were allocated
- Analysis focuses on estimating the effect size—the difference in outcomes between the groups

An example is the parenting for lifelong health programme that was a partnership between the University of Oxford, the World Health Organisation, UNICEF, and the University of Cape Town. The programme conducted fourteen parent and adolescent workshops to improve parenting practices and reduce abuse at home in South Africa (University of Oxford, n.d.; WHO, n.d.; Cluver et al., 2018, 2020).[17]

[16] See: https://www.cochranelibrary.com/

[17] The programme recruited over a thousand participants in forty villages and towns. An RCT approach matched 20 treatment and 20 control villages with each other—with one group receiving the intervention and one group not receiving it. The RCT demonstrated positive outcomes in terms of reducing abuse, corporate punishment, and generally improving parenting behaviours. This program was so successful that it was replicated by its sponsors across multiple countries including the Philippines and Thailand.

Cohort Study

A cohort study takes a longitudinal approach to observe large groups of end-users (a cohort) over time, comparing subsets of a cohort to examine the differences between people who have and have not been exposed to a particular intervention. A cohort study is typically categorised as a form of observational study and is different from other experimental models in that researchers only passively observe the strength of a relationship between a cause and outcome that can be either prospective or retrospective in design. (Song & Chung, 2010; MacGill, 2018) An example was an intervention to improve sewerage coverage within a Brazilian city from 26% to 80% of households. The study investigated this intervention's ability to reduce diarrhoea morbidity amongst children less than three years old (Genser et al., 2008; Barreto et al., 2018).[18]

Case-Control Study

A case-control study is another form of observational study that compares end-users in a specific outcomes case with a control group. The method identifies end-users in a population who have specific positive or negative outcomes from an intervention. Typically using a retrospective design, the case then compares the causal factors that might have resulted in the difference in outcomes through interviews or secondary data (Song & Chung, 2010). One such study was on serious suicide attempts by young people. The study attempted to investigate the causal factors that cause a young person to commit suicide (Beautrais, 1996).[19]

[18] Two cohorts of children were observed for eight months to determine the effect of improved sewerage coverage, comparing the children across time to determine the effect of the intervention. As researchers had no control over the treatment of the sewerage intervention, an RCT was not possible, and researchers had to use an observational design. This intervention was found to be successful, reducing diarrhoea by over 20%.

[19] This was performed by identifying 129 young people who had made an attempt against a control of 153 control subjects chosen from the same communities. The study then attempted to identify underlying risk factors and differences between the subjects that could explain the attempt. Factors found included:

Cross-sectional Study

A cross-sectional study is an observational method that examines a population at one specific point in time. These studies are not designed to understand causal mechanisms, but, instead, describe characteristics in a population. The method is often used prior to subsequent research of greater validity (Cherry, 2019). An example of a cross-sectional study examined the relationship between psychosocial work, environment and cardiovascular disease prevalence in Sweden (Johnson & Hall, 1988).[20]

Case Report and Case Series

A case report or series study is a descriptive method that reports on a series of observations, at the individual level, of the experiences of a small group of participants who experience the same intervention, usually without a control group. These observations are then aggregated in a write-up. The median number of participants in case reports and series are typically four and seven respectively (Sayre et al., 2017; Murad et al., 2018). An example of a case report focussed on infants at risk of developing autism. Researchers recruited eight infants to be inducted into a parent-mediated, video-aided and interaction-focused intervention. Designed as a proof of concept for larger and more comprehensive studies it helped demonstrate the feasibility of such an intervention for researchers (Green et al., 2013).

- Low socioeconomic backgrounds and lack of formal education
- Childhood and family adversity
- Neuroticism and hopelessness
- Affective and substance use disorders
- Higher rates of reported life events

[20] This study used the Swedish government's Living Conditions Survey as well as phone interviews. The study compared end-users' working environment (survey) to the prevalence of the disease (interview). While the study suggested that people with more stressful working environments had a higher prevalence of disease, the method only tests for correlations not causal relationship.

Editorial and Opinion

Editorial and opinion data usually take the form of an article based on an expert author's experience or opinions without and control for biases. (Burns et al., 2011). These data typically avoid empirical evidence. An example of editorial and opinions data was Kenneth et al. (2003), commenting on the construction of four types of communities: the community as a setting, target, agent, and resource.

13.6 Impact Materiality: Validity of Data

Evidenced-based data focuses, primarily, on validity. Here 'validity' refers to the 'truth' of an inference and the extent to which relevant evidence supports that inference being true (Shadish et al., 2002). For policy-making, such data is material in decision-making. To date, the development of evidence-based approaches has largely focussed on improving the validity of its study designs. There are four types of validity in policymaking (Calder et al. 1982):

- *Statistical conclusion* validity: whether the statistical inference is appropriate in determining whether the independent and dependent variables covary.
- *Internal* validity: whether there is a causal relationship from an observed covariation.
- *Construct* validity: whether variables used to observe covariation can be interpreted in higher-order constructs.
- *External* validity: whether the observed causal relationship is generalisable across different situations.

Ideal-type models attempt to maximise all four types of validity for each methodology, but each type is material in different situations. In this context, policymakers have used various approaches to determine the *type* and *level* of validity of their models and attendant data.

One of the most common is the Hierarchy of Evidence Model. Originally proposed by the Canadian Task Force on Periodic Health

Examination (Canadian Task Force on the Periodic Health Examination, 1979) and later expanded by Sackett (Sackett, 1989; Burns et al., 2011), the hierarchy is used to rank different research methods according to the validity of their findings (Evans, 2003). Methods higher in the hierarchy are argued to have greater validity and, hence, a lower likelihood of bias, giving greater confidence to a study's data (Evans, 2003). Figure 13.1 shows the Hierarchy of Evidence Model and Table 13.1 discusses each level of the hierarchy's validity, risk, and cost.

This Hierarchy is used to classify, and weight, data based on their level of bias and validity between similar interventions. While various limitations have been suggested around such a hierarchy and various other classification systems have been proposed—such as typographies (Muir Gray, 1996; Petticrew & Roberts, 2003), spectra of internal and external validity (Bhattacherjee, 2012), and rankings based on effectiveness, appropriateness, and feasibility (Evans, 2003)—the Hierarchy Model remains the most popular and well-used within policymaking.

We suggest here that a Hierarchy of Evidence Model approach can also be used to rank the materiality risk of impact metrics and methodologies more generally within the impact measurement and management. While the idea of ranking impact-risk is not new (for example the IMP nine categories of impact risk in Fig. 13.1 above), there have yet to be any analyses of the material data validity of each method that may rank them accordingly to risk. The Hierarchy of Evidence Model ranking of methodologies would enhance the IMP categories by determining the material validity of impact data across categories. Data from methods higher up the hierarchy are more valid and could be trusted more and, therefore, provide more materially valid data to inform decision-making and impact management. Materially valid data reduces the 'evidence risk'—noted by the IMP—within the decision-making process. Moreover, reducing/managing evidence-risk also reduces other categories of IMP impact data risks such as drop-off, execution, unexpected impact, and efficiency (Impact Management Project, n.d.). Furthermore, many of the methodologies set out in Table 13.1, if used correctly, would also address other IMP data risks—such as external risk, stakeholder participation risk, drop-off risk, execution risk, endurance risk, and unexpected risk.

Table 13.1 Validity, risk, and cost in the Hierarchy of Evidence

Method	Data validity, risk and cost
Systematic review and meta-analysis	A systematic review or meta-analysis offers the highest level of data validity. This is because it weighs and combines findings from various studies. However, such approaches are constrained by a reliance on the existence of completed studies. They also have high transaction costs.
Randomised controlled trial	An RCT offers a high level of data validity using comparative, experimental, and randomisation models. This data validity allows interventions tested by RCT to be replicated in other contexts. However, the RCT approach may be constrained by practical or ethical issues around the type of intervention or end-user population. RCTs also have high transaction costs and cannot, typically, report results quickly (Hariton & Locascio, 2018).
Cohort study	A cohort study has lower data validity—as well as lower internal validity—than an RCT as it does not randomise comparable groups to eliminate sample biases(Choueiry, n.d.). Moreover, a cohort study requires a large sample size and long follow-up times that result in high transaction costs. These may still be lower than comparable RCT costs, however.
Case-control study	As a form of observational study, case-control methods have lower data validity and less internally validity when compared to experimental designs. Furthermore, as these studies track causal factors after the fact, data tends to be difficult to validate and may suffer from recall bias. The rates of exposure to causal factors are also difficult to determine in such a design. These factors place it lower than cohort studies in terms of data validity. However, case control studies are typically affordable due to their retrospective design and the need to only collect data from a relatively small group of end-users.
Cross-sectional study	As a form of observational study, a cross-sectional study does not attempt to understand causal relationships. As such it has lower data validity than, case-control studies or experimental methods. Limitations include being unable to measure incidence, lack of ability to make causal inferences, and susceptibility to bias (Wang & Cheng, 2020). However, since a cross-sectional study generally uses data at a single point in time it is typically lower cost than other observational methods.

(*continued*)

Table 13.1 (continued)

Method	Data validity, risk and cost
Case report and case series	Case report and series methods are descriptive by design, lack a counterfactual or control group, and, as a result, have lower data validity compared to other observational designs. Furthermore, the small number of participants may introduce significant biases affecting the analysis of any causal relationships. These studies are generally much more affordable than experimental or other observational designs due to the small number of participants involved.
Editorial and opinion	Editorial and expert opinion data is not linked to end users' experience and has very low data validity. However, this type of data is affordable with low transaction costs and no requirement to recruit participants.

For example, a well-performed systematic review would rely on multiple RCTs in different contexts to draw conclusions. This helps mitigate external risk by understanding the range of external and contextual factors that could disrupt an intervention's ability to deliver impact. Similarly, guides from constituent RCTs for a variety of contexts would help minimise the execution risk of the intervention. These RCTs, if well done, would, in turn, also account for stakeholder participation, drop-off, endurance, and unexpected impacts within intervention groups.

However, despite the attraction of RCTs in terms of establishing impact data materiality and validity, a problematic issue is cost. RCTs are, typically, expensive and many impact organisations lack the resources to carry them out. Whilst the use of RCTs across all impact decisions would be ideal, this level of confidence is not always required or material for most decisions. As demonstrated in Table 13.1, other methods are available to practitioners to use that, while lower in validity, are lower in cost. Interestingly, the level of validity is generally inversely correlated with cost. That is, while validity decreases with methods lower in the hierarchy, so does the cost of the methods. Hence, practitioners could select methods based on the level of validity required in relation to their costs. In this context, we argue that the primary utility of the Hierarchy of Evidence Model may lie in its analytic approach to establishing the relationship between data validity, data risk and methodology (and cost). The Hierarchy allows impact organisations to understand what level of impact risk is both material and affordable in terms of informing decision-making. The equivalence in financial analysis is being able to understand risk-return trade-offs as opposed to depending only on return data.

13.7 Impact Materiality: End-User Voice and Accountability

Established approaches from within evidence-based policymaking also offer insights into the impact materiality of end-user voice, specifically in terms of policy evaluation and accountability. Such evaluations typically engage end-users in the policy intervention design and evaluation process (Garaway, 1995; King et al., 1998), something that is less common in impact measurement and management (Ely & Hearn, 2021).[21] There are both pragmatic and accountability reasons for this. From a pragmatic perspective, involving end-users in the intervention and evaluation design process may create more material data to inform decision-making, process improvements, lower drop-off rates, and increase uptake. From an accountability perspective, it is may also be seen as the 'right thing' to do as users have the right to be involved in designing and evaluating policy interventions that affect their own lives (Guijt, 2014). Engaging end-user voice and participation can be seen as a strategic approach, adaptable in context, rather than a specific methodology (Canadian International Development Agency, 2001), working in concert with other impact metrics and methodologies (Guijt, 2014). In this context, participatory approaches have been applied across a range of study designs from RCTs to quasi-experimental designs.

Figure 13.2 sets out a Ladder of Citizen Participation that shows the extent to which end-users' voices can be incorporated into an evaluation via such models as Community Based Participatory Research (CBPR) (Wallerstein et al., 2017). Through such an approach, end-users are actively engaged throughout the policy process, from the design of an intervention (for example, through 'citizen assemblies'(Involve UK,

[21] See Lean Data models such as Keystone and 60 Decibels, as well as the underpinning principles of SROI.

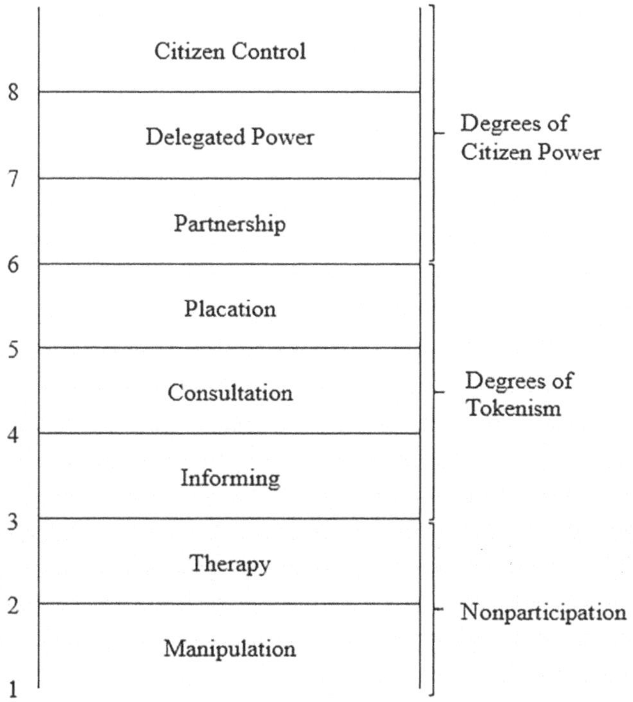

Fig. 13.2 Ladder of Citizen Participation (Arnstein, 1969)

n.d.-a) to the data collection process in (as 'citizen science': see Irwin, 1995), to weighting the importance of outcomes (via 'citizen juries': see Involve UK, n.d.-b). The Ladder has eight 'steps' moving downwards from 'citizen power' to 'tokenism' and 'non-participation'. Each element of the Ladder is considered next.

Citizen Power—Citizen Control Citizen Control cedes complete control of an intervention to citizens. This happened in the UK with the National Community Land Trust Network, a trust that is set up and run by ordinary people to develop and manage their assets. They act as long-term stewards that ensure prices remain affordable for current and future occupants. By giving citizens complete control over their communities and direct access to sources of funds, this approach allows end-users to deploy resources exactly as they see fit, without any intermediaries (National Community Land Trust Network, n.d.). This model sits on the highest rung of the Ladder because citizens design and manage the intervention entirely by themselves.

Citizen Power—Delegated Power Delegated power offers communities control throughout an intervention, from design to execution stage. An example is the Communities Mobilizing for Change on Alcohol Project (Wagenaar et al., 1998). The project aimed to reduce young people's access to alcohol in America's Midwest. It enacted a multi-pronged community organising strategy—designed by community members themselves—that combined policy, law enforcement, and communications strategies to prevent underage drinking. Researchers designed the intervention and evaluation as an RCT together with a CBPR. Evaluation of the intervention indicated that it successfully reduced driving under the influence arrests amongst eighteen- to twenty-year-old participants and increased identification checking of buyers' during alcohol transactions. In particular, the improved participation was attributed to the CBPR design of the intervention.

Citizen Power—Partnership A partnership approach creates a collaboration between the designers and implementers of interventions with local communities. The favelas in Rio de Janeiro's are an example of this approach since they created themselves through various partnerships with different groups across local communities. These communities came together to self-design, self-regulate, and self-build the favelas over a century. Such a model allows different groups of stakeholders to work with intervention designers and policymakers to co-create their environment and community over time. Such an approach gives power and control to citizens during the design stage of the intervention (Farnham, 2014).

Tokenism—Placation In placation approaches, citizens are not given power or control within any aspect of the intervention. An example of a placation approach is a Model City advisory and planning committee. Such a committee allows citizens the freedom to advise or plan interventions or changes to their communities. However, policymakers retain the right to choose the form of implementation and execution. This leaves citizens with a voice within the intervention designs, but one that has limited influence (Arnstein, 1969).

Tokenism—Consultation Consultation occurs when citizens' opinions are sought when designing or implementing an intervention. An example is the Appalachian Trail MEGA-Transect in the U.S. This intervention used a citizen survey to empower everyday people to collect various forms of natural data along the Appalachian Trail. This included deer tracks, plants, and other environmental markers that researchers might not otherwise be able to collect on their own. The data collectors were de facto everyday people who had a passion for the outdoors and were willing to go out of their way to contributing to research that might preserve it. Such an approach mobilised far greater research resources and reach across the trail's 2175 miles than they otherwise would have been the case (Cohn, 2008).

Tokenism—Informing Informing is when citizens are informed of an intervention but have little or no voice or involvement within the intervention itself. An example of this was the Growth Acceleration Program in Rio de Janeiro which developed a cable car system in Complexo do Alemão. Communities in the favelas were informed that this intervention would be happening and that it would help improve their quality of life. This lack of consultation resulted in the eventual failure of the intervention to meet its intended outcomes of increasing mobility and social integration (Freitas, 2013).

Non-participation—Therapy Therapy is not considered a genuine form of participation (Arnstein, 1969). In fact, it is considered harmful in some cases due to the tokenistic involvement of end-users that might be used to cover up more insidious problems. One example of this was a public housing programme that use tenant groups to promote clean-up campaigns to hide serious problems such as slow-building repairs, unjustified evictions, and segregation.

Non-participation—Manipulation This refers to the manipulation of participants by policymakers to achieve their objectives. In this approach, citizens have no voice or involvement. An example of this approach was when UNICEF asked children to make drawings of their perfect playground, without informing them of the purpose of this exercise. Designers of the intervention who then take these drawings to design an actual playground are considered to be using a manipulation approach as the children have no idea how their ideas are being used (Hart, 1992).

While some principles of participation (similar to the positive approaches in the Ladder) have been adopted within the impact measurement and management field—particularly in some SROI models (see Chaps. 3 and 11 for further information on SROI) and Lean Data technologies—stakeholder voice often remains only a marginal consideration in the majority of impact data collection and decision-making. This adds a data risk in terms of missing key information that is material to making good impact decisions. It may also disempower and alienate end-users. Its equivalence in the commercial world would be ignoring the demands and voices of customers when making product or service design decisions. Evidence-based policymaking demonstrates the value of including end users' voices within the decision-making process that can enhance impact measurement and management practices more generally.

13.8 Accountable Impact Models for Evidence-Based Policy-Making

We have suggested here that the established practices within evidence-based policymaking can offer insights to organisations focussed on impact measurement and management more generally—specifically in terms of material validity of impact data, impact risk and end-user participation. Adopting such approaches will support better decision-making and increase impact. Table 13.2 compares impact measurement and management and evidenced-based policymaking practices to suggest opportunities for enhancing the material validity of impact data in the former.

In this chapter, we have explored how established practice from evidence-based policymaking can enhance impact measurement and management. Specifically, we have suggested that impact materiality—and the attendant data risks inherent in different methods and metrics—is poorly understood and lacks best practices in impact measurement and

Table 13.2 Comparison of practices in evidenced-based policy making and impact measurement and management

Dimension	Impact measurement and management practice	Evidence-based policy making practice	Opportunities for better practice in impact measurement and management
Prime focus of data	Reporting to investors and funders. Data maps onto investor/funder requirements and is not materially used in decision-making.	Decision making by policymakers. Data provides materially valid data on whether an intervention works.	Focus on material validity of data and data risk to focus on decision making.
Methods	No common standards of methodology. No analysis of the link between data risk and methods. Methods are often outputs driven and do not establish causal relationships between an intervention and outcome.	An established hierarchy of evidence demonstrates methods/data risk. External studies used to establish causal relationships between intervention and outcome.	Use external studies to establish causal links between interventions and outcomes to improve impact data materiality and validity. Causal analysis also provides evidence of the level of data risk and builds trust with end-users that the intervention will lead to intended outcomes.
Material validity	Material validity of data is not, typically, considered. 'Evidence-risk'—as a category—lacks utility in informing effective decision making.	Hierarchy of evidence Model offers an analysis of data material validity links to methods. These validity scales are often used by policymakers to weight data and make decisions.	Use the hierarchy of evidence Model to establish material validity of data across method and categorise the level of data risk.

(continued)

Table 13.2 (continued)

Dimension	Impact measurement and management practice	Evidence-based policy making practice	Opportunities for better practice in impact measurement and management
End-user voice and accountability	Stakeholder accountability is, typically, focused on investors and funders. End-user voice is typically absent or marginalized (Ely & Hearn, 2021).	Participatory and qualitative approaches are regularly used—often in conjunction with other methods. Policymakers retain power but efforts to reduce data validity risk often eliminate such biases through methods such as double-blinding models.	Incorporate participatory approaches to integrate end-users in impact measurement and management design. Prioritise end-user voice in establishing impact accountability.

management particularly around data validity and end-user voice and accountability. We have also set out how established approaches from evidence-based policymaking could be adopted in impact measurement and management practice to improve decision-making and the allocation of capital.

First, impact measurement and management practice could adopt models from evidence-based policymaking models in terms of better establishing the causal relationships between interventions and their outcomes. This will lead to better decision-making and end-user accountability. Second, impact measurement and management practice could categorise impact materiality data risk in terms of the choice of methods following the Hierarchy of Evidence Model. This Model also allows an analysis of the trade-offs between data materiality, validity and cost-effectiveness. Third, impact measurement and management practice could focus more on incorporating end-user voice within their existing methods. Incorporating end-user voice in impact measurement and management practice will both increase impact materially valid data to inform better decision-making, as well as increasing organisational accountability.

In addition to the recommendations above, it is also useful to note that evidence-based policymaking provides a range of evaluation models to assess the cost-effectiveness of interventions and policies (Bumbarger & Owen, 2009). Developed to help policymakers and implementors of social interventions maximise the use of their resources, these tools focus on cost-benefit analysis (CBA), cost-utility analysis, and cost-effectiveness analysis (CEA) (Belfield & Levin, 2010; Fca, 2018) and quantify the benefits of different interventions using common units of measure. Such models include life-years gained, QALYs, Healthy Years Equivalents (HYES), money (NICHSR, 2016), and Well-being Year (WELLBYs) (Cylus et al., 2020). An example of how such data can be used is the Unit Cost Database developed by New Economy, the Greater Manchester Combined Authority (New Economy, 2015; Greater Manchester Combined Authority, 2019), and verified by the UK government, that brings together over 800 cost estimates for a variety of outcomes. These approaches have also underpinned a turn towards outcomes-based public sector contracting, known as payment-by-results or pay-for-success models. In this case, evidence-based policy has already informed the development of impact bonds (Nicholls & Tomkinson, 2015a, 2015b)—one of the fasted growing impact investing models globally. It is the intention of this chapter to suggest that there is now significant utility in the adoption of other approaches from evidence-based policymaking to improve the effectiveness and efficiency of the field of impact measurement and management more generally going forward.

References

2Degrees Investing Initiative. (n.d.). *Impact Washing Gets a Free Ride*. Available online at https://2degrees-investing.org/resource/impact-washing-gets-a-free-ride/

Ab, H. (2005). Meta-Analysis in Medical Research. In Meta-Analysis in Medical Research (2010, 1). Wiley. https://doi.org/10.1002/9780470994894

Acumen. (2015). *The Lean Data Field Guide – Tips for Collecting Customer Data to Build more Impactful Businesses.* Available online at: https://acumen.org/wp-content/uploads/2015/11/Lean-Data-Field-Guide.pdf.

Arnstein, S. R. (1969). A Ladder of Citizen Participation. *Journal of the American Planning Association, 35*(4), 216–224. https://doi.org/10.1080/01944366908977225

Baron, J. (2018). A Brief History of Evidence-Based Policy. *The Annals of the American Academy of Political and Social Science, 678*(1), 40–50. https://doi.org/10.1177/0002716218763128

Barreto, M. L., Genser, B., Strina, A., Teixeira, M. G., Assis, A. M. O., Rego, R. F., Teles, C. (2018). *Asian Development Bank: Strategy 2030 – Prosperous, Inclusive, Resilient, Sustainable. Asia and the Pacific.* https://doi.org/10.22617/TCS189401-2

Beautrais, A. L. (1996, August). *Serious Suicide Attempts in Young People: A Case Control Study*. Department of Psychological Medicine.

Belfield, C., & Levin, H. M. (2010). Cost-Benefit Analysis and Cost-Effectiveness Analysis. In *International Encyclopaedia of Education* (pp. 199–203). Elsevier Ltd. https://doi.org/10.1016/B978-0-08-044894-7.01245-8

Better Evaluation. (2014). *Choose Methods and Processes* | Better Evaluation. https://www.betterevaluation.org/en/choose-methods-and-processes

Bhattacherjee, A. (2012). *Social Science Research: Principles, Methods, and Practices.* http://scholarcommons.usf.edu/oa_textbookshttp://scholarcommons.usf.edu/oa_textbooks/3

Bumbarger, B. K., & Owen, J. (2009). The Impact and Cost-Effectiveness of Taking Evidence-Based Prevention to Scale: Lessons Learned from One State's Experience. https://www.purdue.edu/hhs/hdfs/fii/wp-content/uploads/2015/07/s_ncfis05c05.pdf

Burns, P. B., Rohrich, R. J., & Chung, K. C. (2011). The Levels of Evidence and their Role in Evidence-Based Medicine. *Plastic and Reconstructive Surgery, 128*(1), 305–310. https://doi.org/10.1097/PRS.0b013e318219c171

Calder, B. J., Phillips, L. W., & Tybout, A. M. (1982). The Concept of External Validity. Journal of Consumer Research, https://d1wqtxts1xzle7.cloudfront.net/6629388/calderphillipstybout_jcr82_external_validity-with-cover-page-v2.pdf?Expires=1631273547&Signature=HPqL8snUHOAEOoi94eEC1RLa-DivwRc1p3eprsdkMCY7j6TL9H2AoGjFzcfhwFUPr1NJB944zor5a7x-CgPlJYRUff2uh9EFIFF8tXfTf2-Uxh~nTySF8baQrPDL4i6ameWFQji48jrA97iNxRj~Drn~nZzI7VXmhaTnlmjatjxlCUymhSuE-e2GWxzWWlZGr-Ys8X0~t6dCSKBnFX6ucdyBYC98BKZQKmCeVK3j444d4tFMOZvTy-

ic2XLXkkqDsWZBfueb8kuKwwSyjtVhjSdHuteZPbq1pwm0FLRMrJ9Amiw~6HJwf38g-XuUanddyYJX0nouQ9upzEC2aFEVDSPA__&Key-Pair-Id=APKAJLOHF5GGSLRBV4ZA

Canadian International Development Agency. (2001). *How to Perform Evaluations Participatory Evaluations*.

Canadian Task Force on the Periodic Health Examination. (1979). *The Periodic Health Examination*.

Cartwright. (2007). *Are RCTs the gold standard?* 11–20. https://doi.org/10.1017/S1745855207005029

Cherry, K. (2019). *The Definition and Use of a Cross-Sectional Study*. https://www.verywellmind.com/what-is-a-cross-sectional-study-2794978

Choueiry, G. (n.d.). *Cohort vs Randomized Controlled Trials: A Simple Explanation – Quantifying Health*. Retrieved April 16, 2021, from https://quantifyinghealth.com/cohort-vs-randomized-controlled-trials/

Cluver, L. D., Meinck, F., Steinert, J. I., Shenderovich, Y., Doubt, J., Romero, R. H., Lombard, C. J., Redfern, A., Ward, C. L., Tsoanyane, S., Nzima, D., Sibanda, N., Wittesaele, C., de Stone, S., Boyes, M. E., Catanho, R., Lachman, J. M. L., Salah, N., Nocuza, M., & Gardner, F. (2018). Parenting for Lifelong Health: A Pragmatic Cluster Randomised Controlled Trial of a Non-commercialised Parenting Programme for Adolescents and Their Families in South Africa. *BMJ Global Health, 3*(1), 539. https://doi.org/10.1136/bmjgh-2017-000539

Cohn, J. P. (2008). Citizen Science: Can Volunteers Do Real Research? *Bioscience, 58*(3), 192–197. https://doi.org/10.1641/B580303

Cylus, J., Smith, P. C., & Smith, P. C. (2020). The Economy of Wellbeing: What Is it and What Are the Implications for Health? *The BMJ, 369*. https://doi.org/10.1136/bmj.m1874

Denyer, D., & Tranfield, D. (2009). *The Sage Handbook of Organisational Research Methods*. Sage Publications Ltd. https://psycnet.apa.org/record/2010-00924-039

Ely, A., & Hearn, D. (2021). To Advance Equity, Impact Investors Must Examine Power, Not Just Provide Capital. *Stanford Social Innovation Review*. https://ssir.org/articles/entry/impact_investors_need_to_share_power_not_just_capital#

Evans, D. (2003). Hierarchy of Evidence: A Framework for Ranking Evidence Evaluating Healthcare Interventions. *Journal of Clinical Nursing, 12*(1), 77–84. https://doi.org/10.1046/j.1365-2702.2003.00662.x

Farnham, K. (2014). *The Ladder of Citizen Participation*. Retrieved April 17, 2021, from https://catcomm.org/ladder-participation/

FCA. (2018). How We Analyse the Costs and Benefits of Our Policies.

Freitas, C. (2013). *Rocinha and Alemão Plan to Sue the State Over Cable Car*. Retrieved April 17, 2021, from https://www.rioonwatch.org/?p=11466

Garaway, G. B. (1995). Participatory Evaluation. *Studies in Educational Evaluation, 21*(1), 85–102. https://doi.org/10.1016/0191-491X(95)00007-H

Genser, B., Strina, A., dos Santos, L. A., Teles, C. A., Prado, M. S., Cairncross, S., & Barreto, M. L. (2008). Impact of a City-Wide Sanitation Intervention in a Large Urban Centre on Social, Environmental and Behavioural Determinants of Childhood Diarrhoea: Analysis of Two Cohort Studies. *International Journal of Epidemiology, 37*(4), 831–840. https://doi.org/10.1093/ije/dyn101

Muir Gray. (1996). *Evidence-based Healthcare and Public Health*. Churchill Livingstone. http://sutlib2.sut.ac.th/sut_contents/H126376.pdf

Greater Manchester Combined Authority. (2019). How Can I Estimate the Programme Costs in My Charity's Funding Proposal? https://www.inspiringimpact.org/resource-library/unit-cost-database/

Green, J., Wan, M. W., Holsgrove, S., and Mcnally, J. E. (2013). *Intervention for Infants at Risk of Developing Autism: A Case Series Attention Training for Infants at Risk of ADHD (INTER-STAARS)* View project PACT-Pre-school Autism Communication Trial and Follow-up Study View project. *Journal of Autism and Developmental Disorders*. 10.1007/s10803-013-1797-8

Guijt, I. (2014). *Participatory Approaches*. www.unicef-irc.org

Hariton, E., & Locascio, J. J. (2018). Randomised Controlled Trials – The Gold Standard for Effectiveness Research: Study Design: Randomised Controlled Trials. *BJOG : An International Journal of Obstetrics and Gynaecology, 125*(13), 1716. https://doi.org/10.1111/1471-0528.15199

Hart, R. (1992). "Children's Participation, from Tokenism to Citizenship". *UNICEF*.

Impact Management Project. (n.d.). *Risk*. Impact Management Project. Retrieved April 17, 2021, from https://impactmanagementproject.com/impact-management/impact-management-norms/risk/#anchor2

Involve UK. (n.d.-a). *Citizens' Assembly*. Retrieved April 7, 2021, from https://www.involve.org.uk/resources/methods/citizens-assembly

Involve UK. (n.d.-b). *Citizens' Jury*. Retrieved April 7, 2021, from https://www.involve.org.uk/resources/methods/citizens-jury

Alan Irwin. (1995). Citizen Science: A Study of People, Expertise and Sustainable Development – Alan Irwin, Irwin a Staff – Google Books. https://books.google.co.uk/books?hl=en&lr=&id=MFiuIsC5hAUC&oi=fnd&pg=PR-

9&dq=citizen+science&ots=1wtj4csea5&sig=y3Ywe68z95kASIwSwOd-2uMjF3Y&redir_esc=y#v=onepage&q=citizen%20science&f=false

Johnson, J. V., & Hall, E. M. (1988). *Job Strain, Work Place Social Support, and Cardiovascular Disease: A Cross-Sectional Study of a Random Sample of the Swedish Working Population* (Vol. 78, pp. 1336–1342). Journal of Public Health.

King, J. A., Cousins, J. B., & Whitmore, E. (1998). *Making Sense of Participatory Evaluation: Framing Participatory Evaluation Construct Validity in Program Evaluation* View Project Evaluation Capacity Building View Project. *New Directions for Evaluation*. https://doi.org/10.1002/ev.226

Lipsey, M. W., & Wilson, D. B. (2001). Practical Meta-Analysis. In *Applied Social Research* (p. 49). Sage Publications. https://psycnet.apa.org/record/2000-16602-000

MacGill, M. (2018). Cohort Study: Finding Causes, Examples, and Limitations. *Medical News Today*. https://www.medicalnewstoday.com/articles/281703

Masi, C. M., Chen, H.-Y., Hawkley, L. C., & Cacioppo, J. T. (2010). A Meta-Analysis of Interventions to Reduce Loneliness. *Personality and Social Psychology Review*. https://doi.org/10.1177/1088868310377394

McLeroy, K. R., Norton, B. L., Kegler, M. C., Burdine, J. N., & Sumaya, C. V. (2003). Community-Based Interventions. *American Journal of Public Health, 93*, 529–533. https://doi.org/10.2105/AJPH.93.4.529

Murad, M. H., Sultan, S., Haffar, S., & Bazerbachi, F. (2018). Methodological Quality and Synthesis of Case Series and Case Reports. *Evidence-Based Medicine, 23*(2), 60–63. https://doi.org/10.1136/bmjebm-2017-110853

National Community Land Trust Network. (n.d.). *What Is CLT?* Retrieved 17 April 2021, from http://www.communitylandtrusts.org.uk/what-is-a-clt

New Economy. (2015). *Unit Cost Database*. https://golab.bsg.ox.ac.uk/knowledge-bank/resources/unit-cost-database/

Nicholls, A. (2018). A General Theory of Social Impact Accounting: Materiality, Uncertainty and Empowerment. *Journal of Social Entrepreneurship, 9*(2), 132–153.

Nicholls, A., & Tomkinson, E. (2015a). The Peterborough Social Impact Bond. In A. Nicholls, R. Paton, & J. Emerson (Eds.), *Social Finance* (pp. 331–378). Oxford University Press.

Nicholls, A., & Tomkinson, E. (2015b). Risk and Return in Social Finance: 'I Am the Market'. In A. Nicholls, R. Paton, & J. Emerson (Eds.), *Social Finance* (pp. 278–306). Oxford University Press.

NICHSR. (2016). *Health Economics Information Resources: A Self-Study Course: Module 4*. U.S. National Library of Medicine.

Parker, R., & Robinson, E. (2013). *Evidence-based Practice and Service-Based Evaluation | Child Family Community Australia*. https://aifs.gov.au/cfca/publications/evidence-based-practice-and-service-based-evaluation

Petticrew, M., & Roberts, H. (2003). Evidence, Hierarchies, and Typologies: Horses for Courses. *Journal of Epidemiology and Community Health, 57*, 527–529. http://www.evidencenetwork.org/

Pinchbeck, G. L., & Archer, D. C. (2018). How to Critically Appraise a Paper. *Equine Veterinary Education, 32*(2), 104–109. https://doi.org/10.1111/eve.12896

Powers, E., & Witmer, H. (1951). *An Experiment in the Prevention of Delinquency; the Cambridge-Somerville Youth Study*. – PsycNET. Columbia University Press. https://psycnet.apa.org/record/1952-00430-000

Sackett, D. L. (1989). *Rules of Evidence and Clinical Recommendations on the Use of Antithrombotic Agents* 95(2), 2S–4S. https://doi.org/10.1378/chest.95.2_supplement.2s

Sayre, J. W., Toklu, H. Z., Ye, F., Mazza, J., & Yale, S. (2017). Case Reports, Case Series – From Clinical Practice to Evidence-Based Medicine in Graduate Medical Education. *Cureus, 9*(8). https://doi.org/10.7759/cureus.1546

Shadish, W., Cook, T. D., & Campbell, D. T. (2002). *Experimental and Quasi-Experimental Designs for Generalized Causal Inference*. Houghton Mifflin.

Sibbald, B., & Roland, M. (1998). Understanding Controlled Trials: Why Are Randomised Controlled Trials Important? *BMJ, 316*(7126), 201. https://doi.org/10.1136/bmj.316.7126.201

Song, J. W., & Chung, K. C. (2010). Observational Studies: Cohort and Case-Control Studies. *Plastic and Reconstructive Surgery, 126*(6), 2234–2242. https://doi.org/10.1097/PRS.0b013e3181f44abc

University of Oxford. (n.d.). *Parenting for Lifelong Health*. Retrieved April 16, 2021, from https://www.ox.ac.uk/research/research-impact/parenting-lifelong-health

van Rooyen, C., Stewart, R., & de Wet, T. (2012). The Impact of Microfinance in Sub-Saharan Africa: A Systematic Review of the Evidence. *World Development, 40*(11), 2249–2262. https://doi.org/10.1016/j.worlddev.2012.03.012

VanLandingham, G. (2020). Evaluation in the Age of Evidence-Based Policymaking: Promises, Pitfalls and Paths Forward. *Evaluation Journal of Australasia, 20*(3), 129–139. https://doi.org/10.1177/1035719X20928164

Viswanathan, M., Ammerman, A., Eng, E., Garlehner, G., Lohr, K., Griffith, D., Rhodes, S., Samuel-Hodge, C., Maty, S., Lux, L., Webb, L., Sutton, S., Swinson, T., Jackman, A., and Whitener, L. (2004). Community-Based

Participatory Research: Assessing the Evidence: Summary . AHRQ. https://www.ncbi.nlm.nih.gov/sites/books/NBK11852/.

Wagenaar, A. C., Murray, D. M., Gehan, J. P., Wolfson, M., Forster, J. L., Toomey, T. L., Perry, C. L., and Jones-Webb, R. (1998). Communities Mobilizing for Change on Alcohol: Outcomes from a Randomized Community Trial*.

Wallerstein, N., Duran, B., Oetzel, J., & Minkler, M. (2017). *Community-Based Participatory Research for Health: Advancing Social and Health Equity*. Google Books. John Wiley and Sons. https://books.google.co.uk/books?hl=en&lr=&id=GLg4DwAAQBAJ&oi=fnd&pg=PA31&dq=CBPR&ots=lGszxsDvzK&sig=360yFVQnIBNzX04szcVzdmOiqGc&redir_esc=y#v=onepage&q=CBPR&f=false

Wang, X., & Cheng, Z. (2020). Cross-Sectional Studies: Strengths, Weaknesses, and Recommendations. *Chest, 158*(1), S65–S71. https://doi.org/10.1016/j.chest.2020.03.012

WHO. (2020). *Parenting for Lifelong Health (PLH) programme manuals.* WHO; World Health Organization. http://www.who.int/violence_injury_prevention/violence/child/PLH-manuals/en/

WHO. (n.d.). *Parenting for Lifelong Health*. Retrieved April 16, 2021, from https://www.who.int/teams/social-determinants-of-health/parenting-for-lifelong-health

14

Mapping SDGs in Sub-Saharan Africa: Highlighting System Effects

Chantal Hervieux and Margaret C. McKee

14.1 Mapping SDGs in Sub-Saharan Africa: Highlighting System Effects

On August 4, 2015, the United Nations unveiled 17 goals as part of its 2030 Agenda for Sustainable Development (SDGs) (UN, 2015a). These new SDGs replaced the Millennium Goals, a framework of eight goals introduced in 2000 that had motivated international development efforts targeting poverty reduction over the previous 15 years (UN, 2015b). Since that time, supra-national institutions, individual governments, for-profit and not-for-profit organisations, educational institutions, and scholarly researchers around the world have initiated programs and activities in support of these ambitious goals. While good work has undoubtedly been done, as we will highlight in this introduction, many involved in these initiatives have noted the special nature of the underlying

C. Hervieux (✉) • M. C. McKee
Saint Mary's University, Halifax, NS, Canada
e-mail: Chantal.Hervieux@smu.ca; Margaret.McKee@smu.ca

R. Hazenberg, C. Paterson-Young (eds.), *Social Impact Measurement for a Sustainable Future*, https://doi.org/10.1007/978-3-030-83152-3_14

problems being addressed by the SDGs and the need for new ways of monitoring and assessing progress in addressing the underlying problems.

Specifically, the problems being addressed by the SDGs have been described as "wicked problems" (Dentoni et al., 2016; Manning & Reinecke, 2016) with the potential to promote innovation, catalyse transformational change (Norström et al., 2014), and redefine outcomes in terms of the health of societies and civil liberties rather than simply economic growth (Moore, 2015). Others have noted the highly inter-related nature of the SDGs (Le Blanc, 2015; Nilsson et al., 2016; Weitz et al., 2018), and the UN itself has characterised the goals as "integrated and indivisible" (UN 2015a, p. 1). This has prompted scholars to propose that innovative approaches are required to understand their inter-relationships, as well as to assess the impact of efforts being undertaken in addressing SDGs (Boas et al., 2016; Le Blanc, 2015; Vladimirova & Le Blanc, 2016), and to the SDGs as a complete system (Nilsson et al., 2017; Weitz et al., 2018). Indeed, shedding light on how SDGs interact with each other has been described as central to the successful implementation of the UN's 2030 agenda (Weitz et al., 2018). In response to this, we developed a longitudinal research project with the aim to answer the following question: Can we account for the effect of systems in a more comprehensive assessment model showing the inter-relationships between SDGs?

In this chapter, we present findings from our research mapping the inter-relationships between the SDGs linked to the food system in sub-Saharan Africa. Our findings highlight several significant and perhaps unexpected relationships between the SDGs and how some of the least powerful actors in the system – specifically women – are at risk of being disadvantaged if such inter-relationships are not recognised and accounted for by policymakers. This chapter is organised into sections as follows. First, we discuss relevant literature related to wicked problems, systems theory, and research that has looked at SDGs as a system of relations. Second, we present the methodology and findings from our research. Lastly, we discuss the relevance of our findings, and limitations of our approach.

14.2 Wicked Problems and the SDGs

The term wicked problem is said to have been first used by Horst Rittel to describe social problems that share the characteristics of being part of a broader system that is not well understood and that typically involves many stakeholders representing different interests (Churchman, 1967). Recognising the challenges associated with locating and defining wicked problems, Rittel later collaborated with a colleague to develop a framework of 10 characteristics that would assist social planners to identify wicked problems and address them effectively. They also highlighted the importance of being able to determine whether a given solution has been effectual, and especially to identify any unintended negative consequences that might negate hoped-for benefits (Rittel & Webber, 1973).

More contemporary scholars have adopted the term wicked problem to characterise some of the environmental disasters, such as massive fires, floods, and droughts, that are being attributed to climate change (Manning & Reinecke, 2016). They proposed that classifying them as such is appropriate given (1) the magnitude of these environmental problems, (2) their complexity, and (3) the fact that multiple parties are involved, with often little to no effective means of ensuring integrated action. They also highlighted that developing effective interventions to address these urgent issues is further complicated by our lack of in-depth understanding of causal relationships, resulting in interventions sometimes producing unintended negative effects. (Manning & Reinecke, 2016). More recently, equally significant and pressing issues such as poverty and food insecurity, as well as climate change and environmental degradation, have been described as addressing wicked problems (Dentoni et al., 2016).

Head and Alford (2015) reviewed research done since the 1970s on wicked problems in domains ranging from health care policy and programs to natural resource management and cybernetics. They maintained that the very nature of public policy development and management – in terms of its structures and processes – makes it challenging for people working in these areas to understand wicked problems and to develop appropriate and effective responses. They noted that more recently published research has shown that efforts to address these challenging problems can have poor outcomes and/or generate unintended results. Such results would seem to support a systems approach for addressing and studying the SDGs.

14.3 Systems Theory

As mentioned, previous scholars have noted the inter-related nature of the SDGs and proposed various approaches to uncover the type and strength of these relationships. We advocate for a system thinking approach for a variety of reasons. Rittel and Webber (1973) spoke in terms of a planning and governance system required for complex problems and noted there were many obstacles to the creation of such a system, including a lack of effective theory for forecasting purposes, insufficient intelligence about the system, and variability in political agendas that made it challenging to identify common causes. Other scholars in the social planning sphere have also highlighted the benefits of a non-technical systems thinking approach such as that of Senge (1992), noting that it helped promote an examination of causes and effects that was holistic and integrated, considering not simply the desired results but also the elements necessary to secure these results, e.g., inputs or key processes.

More specific to our research, other scholars have noted the importance of monitoring systemic links – especially those that might not be immediately apparent from the SDGs and targets themselves (Le Blanc, 2015). Researchers have also suggested that the existence of the various targets underlying each of the larger SDGs is evidence of the recognition of the inter-related nature of the goals and creates a broader system (Le Blanc, 2015). The fact that the SDGs address both social and economic issues also makes them ideal for consideration from a systems perspective, as social planners have argued that, for economic and social problems to be well understood and addressed effectively, they cannot be considered in isolation (Head & Alford, 2015). Weitz et al. (2018) have suggested that, despite the need to understand the overall systemic impact of actions undertaken by various parties addressing the SDGs, there have been few advances in such research and therefore limited progress on efforts to maximise overall effectiveness. They note that the UN itself has recognised this as a significant gap in knowledge.

Scholars have identified several possible unintended, but nonetheless negative, consequences of failing to adopt a holistic approach to addressing the SDGs. These include the development of policies which are not coherent (Boas et al., 2016), the continuation of siloed decision making and the inability to identify which grouping of SDGs to concentrate on and with what policies or interventions (Nilsson et al., 2016). There is also the suggestion that decision makers may be relying on outdated or simply unfounded notions about the SDGs and their inter-relationships, and so addressing SDGs individually may be highly problematic (Nilsson et al., 2016). Others note that while the UN encourages countries to address the entire suite of SDGs, this is challenging due to differences in priorities and available budgets (Weitz et al., 2018). Scholars have argued that the properties of the system are not well understood (Nilsson et al., 2017), promoting the development of a framework for evaluating SDG interactions (Nilsson et al., 2017).

14.4 Mapping the SDGs as a System

Given that the SDGs were only introduced in 2015, research in this domain is at a nascent stage. In a 2016 review of 642 Web of Science articles, identified using the search terms SDGs and Agenda 2030, Weitz et al. (2018) found that most research to date had been on one SDGs and its links to others, or a subset of SDGs and their relationships, referencing a few studies as exemplars (see Collin & Casswell, 2016; Jha et al., 2016; Yumkella & Yillia, 2015). Weitz et al. (2018) concluded that there has been limited empirical study of how all the SDGs interact as a system and, therefore, little associated discussion of the implications for policy. Table 14.1 briefly summarises the studies that we found to have used a systems perspective to map interactions amongst SDGs.

Specific to food, Le Blanc (2015) noted that SDG2 had a high level of linkages to other SDGs, as such this would seem an appropriate area of investigation using a systems approach. Given that over 820 million

Table 14.1 Previous mapping of SDG system interactions

Year	Author(s)	SDG Focus	Findings
2014	Weitz, Nilsson and Davis	Examined draft SDGs and targets for water, energy, and food	Most SDG targets were inherently cross-sectoral; distinct types of interactions existed between targets; and mapping helped identify shared resource interests and impact on SDGs linked in an ecosystem.
2015	Le Blanc	Considered first 16 SDGs and their targets	SDG12 and SDG10 were key to connections amongst some goals and to ensuring a tightly linked network. SDG2 had the fifth highest number of linkages to other goals, as well as targets linked to reducing food losses and sustainable food production systems.
2016	Vladimirov and Le Blanc	Focused on SDG4 and its relationship to other 16 SDGs	SDG4 linked to all other SDGs except SDG14, with variation in extent of linkages and causal direction. There is limited or uneven discussion of constraints or policy implications.
2018	Weitz, Carlsen, Nilsson and Skånberg	Examined relations between two targets of each of the 17 SDGs	Work being done in Sweden on individual SDG targets was positively influenced by work on other SDGs, with few negative relationships. Some SDGs were particularly influential, signalling the need for policy makers to be aware of these relationships, and opportunities for reinforcement.
2020	Lawrence, Ihebuzor and Lawrence	Examined SDG4 and relationships with other 16 SDGs	SDG4 identified as foundational goal with many direct and indirect relationships, acting as enabler for other SDGs. To maximise benefit from SDG-related interventions, developing countries should prioritise those focused on multiple SDGs to generate positive multiplier effects.

people in our world are reported to chronically undernourished it is certainly a widespread issue (UN-FAO, 2019), and the UN itself has highlighted the interconnected nature of the world's food system and the importance of food security to the attainment of future sustainable development (UN-FAO, 2018a, b). The World Bank also highlights the link between hunger and poverty, citing that close to 767 million people are below the world's poverty line of $1.90 a day (World Bank, 2016).

Ringler, Bhaduri and Lawford (2013) propose that an integrated systems approach to the management of the inputs to our food security system, specifically water, energy, and land, will ensure greater efficiency in terms of these resources. However, to accomplish this greater efficiency, they argue that we need to acquire a much better appreciation for the system's dynamics and its feedback loops. This is not surprising given that food has multiple aspects, including production, cooking, access, and health, and is thus a good topic to explore to assess interconnected issues. In this, it can also provide good insights as to where and how power, in various forms, can positively or negatively affect various SDGs. It is therefore an appropriate area to investigate in our work, as we aim to provide insights into a deeper understanding of the complex linkages between issues associated with the SDGs.

That said, challenges related to food vary from one continent to the next, and within specific continents, between regions, and countries (Ringler et al., 2013; Weitz et al., 2018). Therefore, we chose to look at the topic of food in the context of Sub-Saharan Africa. This enables us to contextualise our analysis. This context was selected because of the significant issues this part of the continent faces, as well as the fact that while the continent had made some progress towards attaining the previous Millennium goals, such as increasing access to education and reducing mortality rates for children and their mothers during childbirth,[1] too many goals remain unresolved. For instance, Sub-Saharan Africa has the highest child mortality rate, and 57% of the global 57 million children of

[1] https://www.africa.undp.org/content/rba/en/home/sustainable-development-goals.html Last visited Jan 11, 2021.

school age that remain out of school.[2] With data being available to do our analysis, we therefore felt that basing our analysis on this part of Africa's continent was timely.

14.5 Mapping SDGs in Sub-Saharan Africa

This chapter focusses on one element of a larger research project, conducted in two steps, following the approach of Vladimirova and Le Blanc (2015) in relying on UN reports as our primary data source. In the first step, we focused on the synthesis provided of the "related news" section on the individual UN SDG web pages. On 6 January 2018, we downloaded the first three webpages of news stories for each SDG, with 204 UN news briefs downloaded and coded. In the second step, we used publicly available web-based material from the UN and partner institutions. We sourced 25 reports associated with the topic of food (identified in the reference list with an asterisk). In this step we explored the topic of food, in Sub-Saharan Africa, as it emerged as an important topic from the data sourced in step 1. We coded this data with ATLASti software using both a deductive and inductive approach. Deductive coding was done using UN SDG goals as pre-established codes and inductive coding was done by coding topics and aspects within reports that emerged as we read the reports. Coded citations were then extracted from reports and re-entered in a separate hermeneutic unit to code relations between SDGs and identify positive and negative relationships.

For the first step, global relations between SDGs, we used both deductive and inductive coding for issues related to multiple SDGs as well as relationships between SDGs. In the second, more topic oriented and context specific coding, we coded for all interrelated issues connecting SDGs and associated with the topic of food in the specific context of Sub-Saharan Africa. We used a deductive approach when we coded specifically looking for SDG related elements, followed by an inductive approach to identify aspects and relations that emerged from the data. Data was entered into GEPHI software for network mapping and

[2] https://sustainabledevelopment.un.org/topics/africa Last visited Jan 11, 2021.

analysis, enabling the identification and production of visual graphs that provide a weighted relationship map of the social system of interaction between SDGs. In the figures presented in our chapter, the thickness of an edge is an indication of its weight, and the size of a node is an indication of its importance in the network.

Our initial mapping of relationships between the 17 UN SDGs identified 1270 relations, and 199 edges. This web of relations between the SDGs is only a picture in time and represents issues discussed or addressed at that time. It is not a complete picture of all issues related to SDGs; however, it presents a view of the complexity of the relations between UN SDGs and the issues they aim to address. There are many important relations, and some SDGs stand out as more related than others.

We examined the triad of SDG 8, 9 and 10, as an example. We found industry has a strong role to play in meeting the objectives of other UN SDGs. For instance, SDG9 is strongly related to SDG8 and SDG10, indicating the potential positive or negative effect of industry innovation on the direction of the economy. At the same time, central to the reduction of inequalities (SDG10) and growth (SDG8) is SDG16. This demonstrates that the objective of "No Poverty" cannot be attained if one does not also seek to address the issues of conflict, crime, and all forms of violence.[3]

As a second example, we extracted the egos network (i.e., the relations between one node and all other nodes in a network) for SDG1. We found a strong relationship between SDG1, SDG2, SDG4, and SDG 10, but also some important, if not as strong, relations with SDG3 and SDG13. It is not surprising that poverty and hunger are related, and it has been estimated that 800 million of the one in eight people that still live below the poverty line remain hungry (SDG2) (UN, 2016). There is a reduction in the number of individuals living below the poverty line (UN-DESA, 2017); however, continued inequalities (SDG10) trap people into recurrent poverty (UN-FPA, 2017). While mortality rates are decreasing, our planet's poorest children are chronically malnourished

[3] https://www.peacedirect.org/us/sustainable-development-goals-peace/?gclid=CjwKCAiA9bmABhBbEiwASb35V-SEr_kkr0p59oaPqIqg0E3WYQv174GRhO910SABpaaGEoxDy9D0TRoCh-WkQAvD_BwE Last visited Jan 25, 2021.

and remain twice as likely to die before the age of five (UNICEF, 2017). Furthermore, climate change (SDG13) continues to impact the poor more severely because of inequalities (SDG10) (UN-DESA, 2016). And, while exports of tropical fruits can help reduce poverty, since much of the production is done in developing economies (UN-FAO, 2018a, b), existing income inequalities can contribute to unrest and violence (UN-DESA, 2017), complicating efforts to attain SDG objectives.

On a more encouraging note, looking at the egos network for SDG2, we found that positive associations also exist. Looking at how specific SDGs affect and are affected by SDG2, we saw some evidence that when an overall system outlook is adopted in rural areas, and investments in the agriculture sector are made, that this is linked to economic growth (SDG8) and reduced hunger (UN-FAO, 2017a, b, c). In the section titled *The Influence of Urbanisation*, that has a focus on agriculture, urbanisation, and rural-urban linkages, we further develop the importance of actions that can provide solutions to issues faced by both the rural and urban poor.

Our initial mapping of the relations between issues addressed by SDGs provides support for the importance of using a systems approach in addressing SDGs, by illustrating the complex network of relations and interconnected issues between SDGs. However, since context matters, and issues vary according to geographical regions, we now focus on the specific issues related to the topic of food in Sub-Saharan Africa.

We choose food as an area to investigate further because of the important previously recognised linkages it has with many issues, as well as our own analysis that brought forth its importance in the system of relations mapped in step 1. The SDG relationship map of interrelated issues linked to food in Sub-Saharan Africa was the focus of step 2. In our data sources, we identified 1899 relations and 100 edges connecting the various SDGs in this context. Many issues are associated with each individual SDG and attaining their objectives requires a deep understanding of how they interact to ensure that policies are comprehensive and account for systemic effects (Head & Alford, 2015).

14.6 Interacting Issues Related to Cooking

Considering food in the context of poverty in Sub-Saharan Africa, we chose to focus on cooking because of the complexity it highlights in the web of relations between issues and SDGs (see Fig. 14.1). From our analysis, SDGs related to cooking include SDG1, SDG2, SDG3, SDG5, SDG7, SDG 8, SDG10, SDG13, SDG15, and SDG16. Those with the strongest relationships appear to be SDG1, SDG2, SDG3, SDG8 and SDG10 as well as SDG16, which like all our models, is strongly related to poverty. While the stronger relations provide information, some of the weaker interactions provide important insights.

For instance, poverty (SDG1), health (SDG3), gender (SDG5), and energy (SDG10) all interact with food in its relationship with cooking. Lack of clean, sustainable energy is of vital importance in relation to cooking and its impact. Women in Sub-Saharan Africa are responsible for collecting material, such as wood and charcoal, to meet the energy needs of the family unit. This can create negative health impacts for women and create time inequity between genders (Habtezion, 2012). For African women in rural areas such work has been described as physically strenuous as well as potentially dangerous (UN-EP, 2017). When burning biomass for cooking and heating, people are also exposed to air pollution, with an estimated 41,000 people dying each year due to Chronic Obstructive Pulmonary Disease (COPD) and another 350,000 people dying because of Acute Lower Respiratory Infection (ALRI) (Ndwiga et al., 2014). Sadly, in Sub-Saharan Africa, young women are reported to die more often because of exposure to fumes and smoke from their in-home cooking fires than they are to die from malnutrition or malaria (UN-EP, 2017).

There is also a serious inequity issue here in terms of accessibility to affordable energy, where the poorest pay the most for their energy. It is estimated that some $10 billion a year is spent by Africa's poorest people to purchase basic energy sources. This energy, in the form of charcoal or kerosene, is estimated to be 20 times more expensive than the cost of energy purchased by those connected to the grid (UN-EP, 2017).

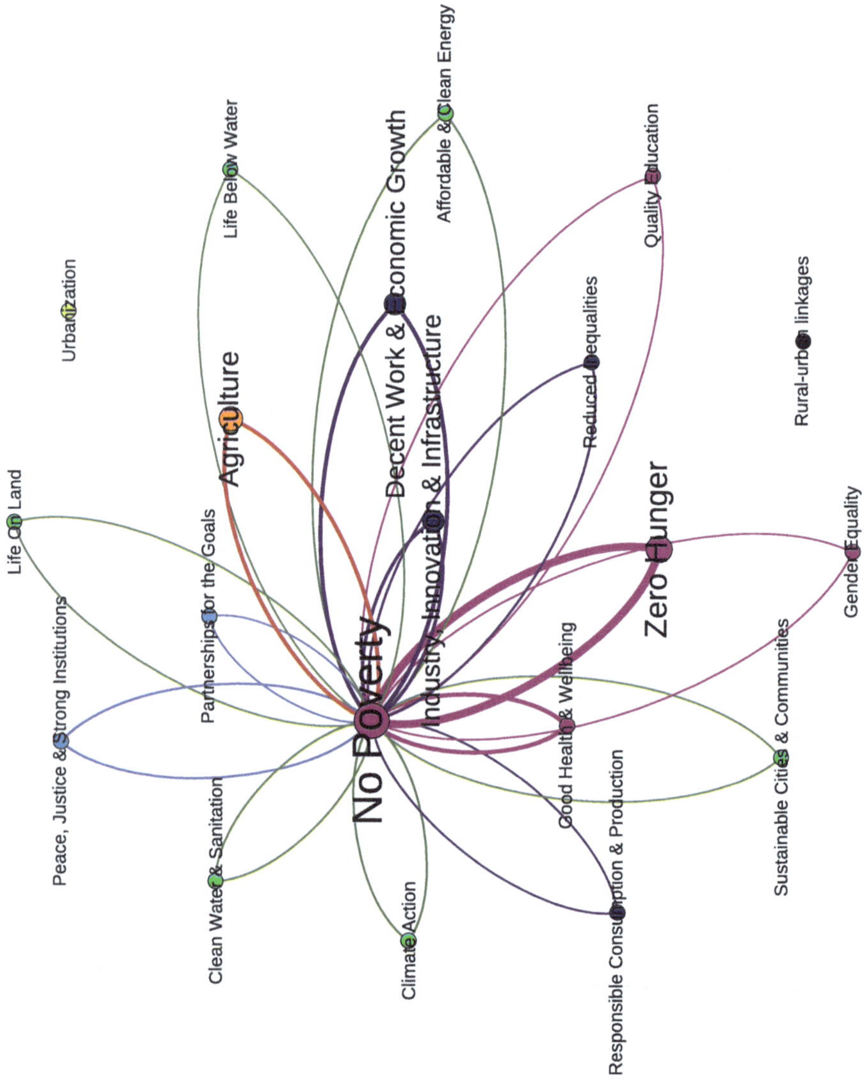

Fig. 14.1 SDG 1 Relations to other SDGs in the context of food in Sub-Saharan Africa

As noted, time spent gathering biomass fuel for household energy requirements can create a time inequity between men and women (SDG5, SDG10). This has been linked to poverty and gender inequality as women then have less time for education, as well as seeking employment outside the home (Wodon & Blackden, 2006). In Sub-Saharan Africa, lower literacy rates for women and school enrolments (primary, secondary, and tertiary) for girls could partially be explained by this time inequity (UN-DESA, 2010). Unfortunately, if no action is taken to improve access to affordable renewable energy, climate change will likely increase this time inequity by increasing natural resource scarcity (Habtezion, 2012). Yet access to affordable modern fuels could reduce health issues and reduce the time inequity issues by freeing women from the requirements of gathering biomass fuel.

As if this was not enough, in many regions, regional unrest has led to population displacements and refugee camps (SDG16) (UN-DESA, 2017). This displaced population has its own energy requirements, and often suffer from a lack of available financial resources; thus, increasing competition for the available biomass fuel (wood) (SDG7) (WEF, 2019). This creates pressure on an already stressed natural system (SDG15), as well as tensions between local populations and the refugees (SDG16). When one adds to this the effects of climate change (SDG13), we again increase stress on natural systems. With women having primary responsibility for meeting the energy needs for the family, the time inequity is only increased by these factors, further limiting the time women have for other things, such as education (SDG4). Clearly, interventions on any of the above-mentioned SDGs that do not consider context and systemic effects are likely to miss some essential elements that will influence the impact of such initiatives. In fact, the impact could be reduced or even negative because of interacting effects and issues. We now turn our attention to food and urbanisation as, in our overall analysis, there were important relationships that indicated differences in the connections between the most relevant SDGs as compared to rural areas.

14.7 The Influence of Urbanisation

During our phase of inductive coding, three important concepts emerged related to food, Sub-Saharan Africa and the SDGs. These were urbanisation, rural-urban linkages, and agriculture. For cooking in the context of Sub-Saharan Africa, we chose to focus on this because of the complexity of relations; however, in the analysis related to agriculture it was the importance of the concepts themselves as evidenced by the number of times they emerged as codes in our analysis. As Fig. 14.2 illustrates, agriculture is central to the relations between food and SDGs, and the system's complexity increases when urbanisation is considered. It shows that the most important relations are between agriculture and SDG2, SDG8, SDG9 and, to a lesser degree, SDG1 and SDG3.

Adding these three concepts provides new insights into issues related to the topic of food in the context of Sub-Saharan Africa, specifically when we isolate SDG2. Agriculture alone is perceived as extremely important for the attainment of UN SDGs in Africa. The African Development Bank Group with business leaders and the African green revolution forum seek to transform agriculture to end hunger (SDG2), poverty (SDG1) and malnutrition (SDG3) (IFPRI, 2017). Through investments in infrastructure, they aim to increase productivity and positively impact employment and income of small producers (SDG8).

When one looks at urbanisation, we find that, while investments in agriculture would increase quantity of food produced, it will not necessarily increase the availability of food to the urban poor. Urbanisation in many regions of Africa is linked to questions of food security. The urban poor rely to a great extent on the informal economy to provide them with readily available sources of food that they can afford (SDG1, SDG2). Government attempts to control this informal urban economy have led to greater regulation, and sometimes eradication, of these important sources of affordable food for the urban poor (IFPRI, 2017).

Our research identifies further issues related to UN SDG system. The linkages we traced between poverty and urbanisation highlight a broken, disconnected system. Like Le Blanc (2015), we note that many systemic links between SDGs are missing and efforts to trace the links between their sub-components have not been systematically explored. Our analysis seems to suggest that things have not changed substantively since Ringler

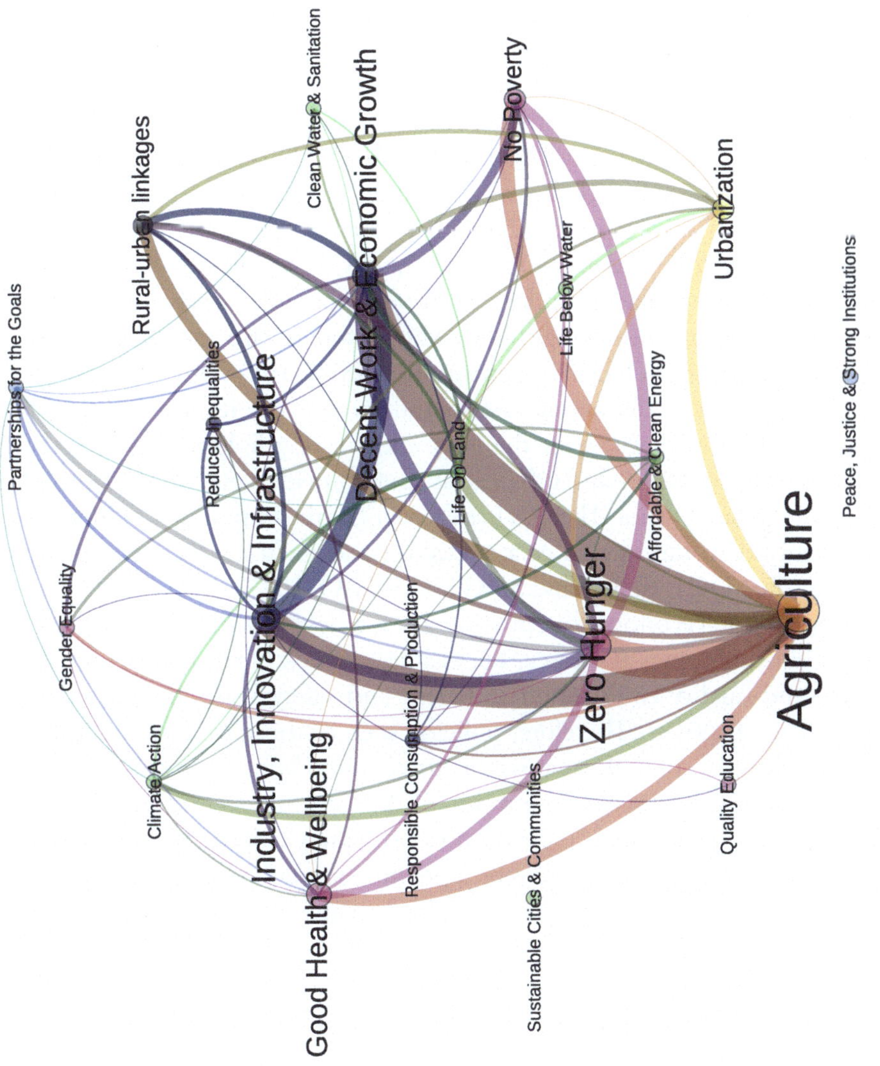

Fig. 14.2 SDG mapping with agriculture, urbanisation, and rural-urban linkages

et al. (2013) commented on the siloed approach of policymakers and government officials, as well as their self-interest in maintaining the status-quo.

The potential impact of the new ways to provide solutions to the wicked problems of poverty and climate change require a deep understanding of systems, and these differ between rural and urban areas. Our analysis brings forth the issue of policies and initiatives that aim to control the informal economy, yet strongly impact the poor and vulnerable. Examples of these include Malawi's Operation Order (2006, 2015), Nigeria's Zero Tolerance Campaign (2009), South Africa's Operation Clean Sweep (2013), Keep Zambia Clean and Healthy Campaign (2007, 2015) and Zimbabwe's Operation Restore Order (2005) (IFPRI, 2017). Yet, in urban areas, our analysis highlights that this informal economy provides access to resources for the urban poor; removing this access therefore further increases poverty (SDG1), hunger (SDG2), and inequalities (SDG10). While policies are required, a look at the overall system and the role the informal economy plays in improving access for the poor and creating linkages between the rural agricultural sector and urban areas could provide a path to solutions to these interrelated issues. The UN itself recognises the importance of improving rural-urban linkages to create effective and inclusive food systems to address the SDG1, SDG2 and SDG3 (UN-FAO, 2017a, b, c).

The informal economy can provide access to low-cost food for the urban poor, but this comes at a price. For example, a lack of regulation on food safety and quality could result in health and safety issues for the urban poor (IFPRI, 2017). Therefore, policies, such as those we have discussed above relative to the informal sector, are required but, at the same time, a better understanding and accounting of the informal sector's role in providing food to the urban poor need to be acknowledged. Making use of the informal linkages could also be a preliminary path to connecting rural and urban areas, and in this way partially formalise the informal economy.

14.8 Food Supply, Hunger and the SDGs in Africa

This chapter set out to assess whether we could account for the effect of systems in a more comprehensive assessment model of the interrelationships between SDGs and their associated issues. We feel that our modelling of issues related to food in Sub-Saharan Africa illustrates that it is possible to map such a system and its interrelationships. The output of such system modelling could be used to identify key, problematic areas in the system so that policy makers and development organisations could identify interventions and design policies that consider systemic effects and prevent siloed responses. Our approach also allows for replication and extension of the assessment of such systems in other regions, using readily available UN and partner documents and data sources. By using a longitudinal approach, and identifying key actions (for example, new policies or interventions), it should be possible to repeat the modelling analyses at different points in time to identify and assess change within the system.

Specific to food, we see our approach as supporting the FAO's desire to develop new, innovative ways to address the wicked problem of hunger (UN, 2018). Food, when looked at through the lens of interrelated impacts and issues, is a complex area, but also one with opportunities for entrepreneurs and innovators. With purposeful actions taken to develop value chains inclusive of the informal food economy, the socio-economic conditions of the poor in rural areas can be addressed, while providing food to those in urban areas (IFPRI, 2017). Improved supply chains have shown promise in reducing gender inequalities, as well as poverty through the provision of employment in rural areas (Maertens & Swinnen, 2012).

As emphasised by Boas et al. (2016), SDGs are interconnected and yet the approach to addressing these issues through policy remains siloed. Resolving the underlying issues of SDGs cannot be accomplished without recognising their interdependencies and developing policies that account for this interconnectedness. Therefore, we see partnerships (SDG17) as key to the success of any effort to develop initiatives based on our approach to SDG system modelling. Without a coordinated and collaborative effort, that includes ongoing dialogue with stakeholders and partnerships with system actors, there is a risk that policies and interventions will not realise their stated objectives. Such dialogue and partnerships can bring deeper understanding of these complex and ever-changing problems that is significantly more nuanced than a "simple picture in time" offered by any system modelling approach, including our own.

References

Boas, I., Biermann, F., & Kanie, N. (2016). Cross-Sectoral Strategies in Global Sustainability Governance: Towards a Nexus Approach. *International Environmental Agreements: Politics, Law and Economics, 16*(3), 449–464.

Churchman, C. W. (1967). Wicked Problems. *Management Science, 14*(4), B141–B142.

Collin, J., & Casswell, S. (2016). Alcohol and the Sustainable Development Goals. *Lancet (London, England), 387*(10038), 2582–2583.

Dentoni, D., Bitzer, V., & Pascucci, S. (2016). Cross-Sector Partnerships and the Co-Creation of Dynamic Capabilities for Stakeholder Orientation. *Journal of Business Ethics, 135*(1), 35–53.

Habtezion, S. (2012). *Gender and energy. Gender and Climate Change: Capacity Development Series*. Africa Training Module 3, United Nations Development Programme, New York.

Head, B. W., & Alford, J. (2015). Wicked Problems: Implications for Public Policy and Management. *Administration and Society, 47*(6), 711–739.

IFPRI. (2017). *Global Food Policy Report*. International Food Policy Research Institute. https://www.ifpri.org/publication/2017-global-food-policy-report-synopsis (148pp.).

Jha, A., Kickbusch, I., Taylor, P., & Abbasi, K. (2016). Accelerating Achievement of the Sustainable Development Goals. *BMJ, 352*, i409.

Lawrence, A. W., Ihebuzor, N., & Lawrence, D. O. (2020). Comparative Analysis of Alignments Between SDG16 and the Other Sustainable Development Goals. *International Business Research, 13*(10), 1–13.

Le Blanc, D. (2015). Towards Integration at Last? The Sustainable Development Goals as a Network of Targets. *Sustainable Development, 23*(3), 176–187.

Maertens, M., & Swinnen, J. F. M. (2012). Gender and Modern Supply Chains in Developing Countries. *Journal of Development Studies, 48*(10), 1412–1430.

Manning, S., & Reinecke, J. (2016). We're Failing to Solve the world's 'Wicked Problems.' Here's a Better Approach. *The Conversation, 3*, 1–5.

Moore, H. L. (2015). Global Prosperity and Sustainable Development Goals. *Journal of International Development, 27*(6), 801–815.

Ndwiga, T., Kei, R. M., & Jepngetich, H. (2014). Assessment of Health Effects Related to the Use of Biomass Fuel and Indoor Air Pollution in Kapkokwon Sub-Location, Bomet County, Kenya. *Open Journal of Air Pollution, 3*, 61–69.

Nilsson, M., Griggs, D., & Visbeck, M. (2016). Policy: Map the Interactions Between Sustainable Development Goals. *Nature News, 534*(7607), 320–322.

Nilsson, M., Griggs, D., Visbeck, M., Ringler, C., & McCollum, D. (2017). Introduction: A Framework for Understanding Sustainable Development Goals Interactions. In D. J. Griggs, M. Nilsson, A. Stevance, & D. McCollum (Eds.), *A Guide to SDG Interactions: From Science to Implementation* (pp. 18–30). International Council for Science (ICSU).

Norström, A., Dannenberg, A., McCarney, G., Milkoreit, M., Diekert, F., Engström, G., Fishman, R., Gars, J., Kyriakopoolou, E., Manoussi, V., & Meng, K. (2014). Three Necessary Conditions for Establishing Effective Sustainable Development Goals in the Anthropocene. *Ecology and Society, 19*(3), 1–8.

Ringler, C., Bhaduri, A., & Lawford, R. (2013). The Nexus across Water, Energy, Land and Food (WELF): Potential for Improved Resource Use Efficiency? *Current Opinion in Environmental Sustainability, 5*(6), 617–624.

Rittel, H. W., & Webber, M. M. (1973). Dilemmas in a General Theory of Planning. *Policy Sciences, 4*(2), 155–169.

Senge, P. M. (1992). The Fifth Discipline, Australia.

UN-DESA. (2010). *The Millennium Development Goals Report.* United Nations Department of Economic and Social Affairs (UN-DESA).

UN-DESA. (2016). *World Economic and Social Survey Climate Change Resilience: An Opportunity for Reducing Inequalities.* United Nations Department of Economic and Social Affairs. https://www.un.org/development/desa/dpad/publication/world-economic-and-social-survey-2018-frontier-technologies-for-sustainable-development/

UN-DESA. (2017). *The Sustainable Development Goals Report.* The United Nations Department of Economics and Social Affairs. https://www.un.org/development/desa/undesavoice/more-from-undesa/2016/08/27589.html (64pp.).

UN-EP. (2017). *Atlas of Africa Energy Resources.* United Nations Environment Program; African Development Bank. https://wedocs.unep.org/bitstream/handle/20.500.11822/20476/Atlas_Africa_Energy_Resources.pdf?sequence=1&isAllowed=y (342pp.).

UN-FAO. (2017a). *The State of Food and Fast Agriculture 2017: Leveraging Food Systems for Inclusive Rural Transformation.* The United Nations Food and Agriculture Organization. http://www.fao.org/policy-support/tools-and-publications/resources-details/en/c/1046886/ (181pp.).

UN-FAO. (2017b, September). *Crop Prospects and Food Situation.* United Nations Food and Agriculture Organization. http://www.fao.org/3/i7830e/i7830e.pdf (40pp.).

UN-FAO. (2017c, December). *Crop Prospects and Food Situation.* United Nations Food and Agriculture organization. http://www.fao.org/3/i8278e/i8278e.pdf (40pp.).

UN-FAO. (2018a). *Food Outlook – Biannual Report on Global Food Markets.* United Nations Food and Agriculture Organization. http://www.fao.org/3/CA2320EN/ca2320en.pdf (108pp.).

UN-FAO. (2018b, December). *Crop Prospects and Food Situation.* United Nations Food and Agriculture Organization. http://www.fao.org/3/CA2726EN/ca2726en.pdf (42pp.).

UN-FAO. (2019). *The State of Food and Agriculture 2019. Moving forward on food loss and waste reduction.* Rome. http://www.fao.org/3/ca6030en/ca6030en.pdf (156pp.).

UN-FPA. (2017). *Worlds Apart: Reproductive Health and Rights in an Age of Inequality.* State of the World Population 2017. United Nations Population Fund. https://reliefweb.int/sites/reliefweb.int/files/resources/UNFPA_PUB_2017_EN_SWOP.pdf (140pp.)

UNICEF. (2017). *The State of the World's Children 2017: Children in a Digital World.* https://www.unicef.org/media/48581/file/SOWC_2017_ENG.pdf (215pp.)

United Nations. (2015a). *17 Sustainable Development Goals Are Set and Welcomed.* United Nations. Retrieved January 3, 2020 from https://unric.org/en/17-sustainable-development-goals-are-set-and-welcomed-2/

United Nations. (2015b). *The Millennium Development Goals Report 2015.* United Nations. Retrieved January 6, 2020 from https://sustainabledevelopment.un.org/content/documents/2036MDG%202015%20rev%20(July%201).pdf

United Nations. (2016). *Integrated Food Security Phase.* United Nations Classification. https://www.un.org/sustainabledevelopment/blog/2016/10/press-release-united-nations-urges-commitment-to-fight-humiliation-and-exclusion-to-end-poverty/

United Nations. (2018). *Fast-Forward Progress: Leveraging Tech to Achieve the Global Goals.* United Nations International Telecommunication Union. https://www.itu.int/en/sustainable-world/Documents/Fast-forward_progress_report_414709%20FINAL.pdf (156pp.)

Vladimirova, K., & Le Blanc, D. (2016). Exploring Links Between Education and Sustainable Development Goals through the Lens of UN Flagship Reports. *Sustainable Development, 24*(4), 254–271.

WEF. (2019). *The Global Risks Report 2019, 14th Edition*. World Economic Forum. https://www.weforum.org/reports/the-global-risks-report-2019 (114pp.).

Weitz, N., Carlsen, H., Nilsson, M., & Skånberg, K. (2018). Towards Systemic and Contextual Priority Setting for Implementing the 2030 Agenda. *Sustainability Science, 13*(2), 531–548.

Weitz, N., Nilsson, M., & Davis, M. (2014). A Nexus Approach to the Post-2015 Agenda: Formulating Integrated Water, Energy, and Food SDGs. *The SAIS Review of International Affairs, 34*(2), 37–50. https://www.jstor.org/stable/27000956

Wodon, Q., & Blackden, C. M. (Eds.). (2006). *Gender, Time Use, and Poverty in Sub-Saharan Africa*. The World Bank.

World Bank. (2016). *Poverty and Shared Prosperity 2016: Taking on Inequality*.

Yumkella, K. K., & Yillia, P. T. (2015). Framing the Water-Energy Nexus for the Post-2015 Development Agenda. *Aquatic Procedia, 5*, 8–12.

15

Ethical Issues with Social Impact Measurement

Claire Paterson-Young and Richard Hazenberg

15.1 Ethics in Social Impact Measurement

Social impact measurement has received increasing attention, with organisations under pressure to produce reports that evidence the outcomes and impact of activities (specifically, activities aligned with SDGs). Social impact involves evaluating the scope of activities (*outputs);* the positive and negative outcomes experienced by beneficiaries (*outcomes*); long-term changes in beneficiaries and society (*impacts*); the role of other stakeholders/partners in this change (alternative attribution); and the changes that would have occurred anyway (deadweight/control group) (Paterson-Young & Hazenberg, 2021). Measuring social impact relies on understanding, not only the financial impact of activities, but the softer outcomes (for example, wellbeing) and falls in the arena of evaluation

C. Paterson-Young (✉) • R. Hazenberg
Institute for Social Innovation and Impact, University of Northampton, Northampton, UK
e-mail: claire.paterson-young@northampton.ac.uk; richard.hazenberg@northampton.ac.uk

R. Hazenberg, C. Paterson-Young (eds.), *Social Impact Measurement for a Sustainable Future*, https://doi.org/10.1007/978-3-030-83152-3_15

research (Paterson-Young & Hazenberg, 2021). Simons (2006) outlines the differences in evaluation research and traditional research, noting that evaluation research intends to report on the value of activities and/or programmes rather than generate knowledge. Evaluation research has an ethical blind spot (Newman & Brown, 1996; Morris, 2015), with detailed ethical reviews rarely sought unless evaluations are conducted by universities and/or conducted in specific environments (for example, health services). This chapter identifies the fundamental ethical principles in evaluation research and the ethical challenges in conducting social impact evaluations. It will explore the decision processes guiding ethical research and current ethical frameworks in evaluation research. The chapter ends with the outlining of an ethical framework for social impact measurement.

15.2 Ethics: The Fundamental Principles for Social Impact Measurement

Ethical dilemmas in evaluation research arise from conflicting values and principles (Newman & Brown, 1996), illustrating the need for understanding and addressing ethical issues. Ethics are a set of moral principles and rules that, in research, involves the promotion of fair and respectful principles that prevent harm (Sieber, 1993). The Economic and Social Research Council Framework for Research Ethics (ESRC, 2015), on the other hand, defines ethics as the guiding principles for research. Others associate ethics with behaviours that are right or wrong (Newman & Brown, 1996) or behaviours that are fair and just (Simons, 2006). Research conducted by Williams (2016) noted several issues in defining ethics from acknowledging the diversity of relationships and behaviours in the evaluation process to acknowledging the complexities in decisions and judgements based on individual circumstances.

Ethical theories, from deontology to consequentialism, provide different perspectives on research ethics. Deontological ethics is acknowledging the relationships duty and morality play in human behaviours and/or action (Darwall, 2002; Rawls, 1971). It places emphasis on the characteristics of actions rather than the consequences of the action (Darwall, 2002; Biagetti et al., 2019). General examples of deontological ethics can be found in the ideas proposed by Thomas Aquinas (do good, avoid evil) and Immanuel Kant (universal law of nature) (Darwall, 2002; Rawls, 1971). Deontological ethics do, however, offer guidance on how to regulate behaviour from the perspective of doing no harm (Biagetti et al., 2019). Consequentialist ethics is founded on universal values, promoting the values associated with moral behaviour (Rawls, 1971). Moral behaviour has no specific norms and values, however, operates under the assumptions that all actions should serve the common good – the greatest good for the greatest number (Biagetti et al., 2019).

Consequentialist ethics are founded under the principles of the common good, consequences, utility, hedonism and universality, which consider whether actions are good based on the consequences (Biagetti et al., 2019). While consequentialist ethics promote specific values, deontological ethics promote the honouring of values (Pettit, 1991). Deontological and consequentialist ethics offer general ideas on ethics but have limited applicability in research evaluation if adopted independently (Biagetti et al., 2019). Biagetti et al. (2019) recommend a mixed-approach to managing ethics in research evaluation, combining deontological and consequentialist approaches. This mixed-approach balances the challenges presented by deontological and consequential ethics by acknowledging the ethical issues associated with actions and consequences (see Biagetti et al., 2019). It encompasses the norms and principles associated with the common good, notions of right and wrong (subject specific), and stakeholder involvement in considering the common good (Biagetti et al., 2019).

Ethical issues in evaluation research focus on the challenges of conducting said research (Morris, 2008, 2015; Williams 2016), offering insight on evaluation experience (de Montclos, 2012; Hendricks & Bamberger, 2010; Klerman, 2010; Trimble et al., 2012; Buchanan & MacDonald, 2011; Morris & Clark, 2013). Newman and Brown (1996) conducted research with evaluators, finding that evaluators consistently responded to queries on ethics with questions such as "What? Ethics? What does ethics have to do with evaluation?". Research conducted by Honea (1992) found that ethics were often overlooked in evaluation and policy analysis. Indeed, ethical issues in evaluation research exist at several points in the research process, from entry/contracting to utilisation of results (Morris, 2008). This ethical blind spot may have reduced over time (Morris, 2015), however, a survey conducted with members from the American Evaluation Association, the Australasian Evaluation Society and the Canadian Evaluation Society found that over 60% of respondents reported experiencing ethical challenges in evaluation research (Buchanan & MacDonald, 2011).

15.3 Ethical Issues in Evaluation Research

Ethical issues in evaluation research are diverse, with research (Morris, 2015; Mathison, 2005; Williams, 2016) identifying issues associated with conflict of interest, informed consent, and stakeholder expectations. Acknowledging the benefits and interests of beneficiaries, stakeholders and society is essential in evaluation research. No generic guidelines exist in accessing the benefits and/or risks associated with conflicts of interest, however, evaluators should consider conflicts of interest through the evaluation process. Conflicts of interest occur in the presence of personal or financial relationships that influence the purpose, design, conduct or reporting of evaluation research (Mathison, 2005). Research evaluations are *often* described as independent, however, recognising *potential* conflicts of interest is imperative to ensuring evaluations are reliable and valid (Mathison, 2005). Morris (2015) acknowledged the issues associated with conflicts of interest in evaluation, stating that evaluators can approach this situation by acknowledging the existence of conflicts. Another fundamental issue associated with conflicts of interest relate to the evaluator's presentation of findings, especially in the presentation of findings that disagree with key stakeholder views (Greene & Lee, 2006). This is evident in research conducted by Morris and Clark (2013) who found 40% of evaluators felt that stakeholders actively pressured them to misrepresent results. The American Evaluation Association Guiding Principles (2018) provide recommendation on dealing with conflict of interest, stating that all conflicts of interest should be disclosed to ensure the evaluation process and results are not compromised.

Stakeholder involvement is imperative in social impact measurement; however, the involvement of beneficiaries, stakeholders, and society creates unique ethical issues (Morris, 2015). Stakeholders are defined by the American Evaluation Association (2018) as individuals, groups and organisations with legitimate interest in evaluations and/or research. This includes beneficiaries who are the direct recipients of activities and/or interventions (for example, young people engaged on employability programmes). Good practice guidance on stakeholder involvement exists (Cartland et al., 2012), however, stakeholder involvement is *often* tokenistic, which creates further ethical challenges (Kara, 2018). Research conducted by Morris (2008) found common ethical challenges in navigating the expectation of stakeholders. This research found that stakeholders often have conflicting expectations on the purpose and direction of evaluation, which create challenges for evaluators (Morris, 2008). Furthermore, evaluators reported receiving pressure from stakeholders to misrepresent findings and/or violate confidentiality which, if rejected, led to suppression or the burying of findings (Morris, 2008; Morris & Clark, 2013). Fleischer and Christie (2009) found that 29% of members' surveys from the American Evaluation Association Evaluation Use Topical Interest Group stated that evaluation results were intentionally misrepresented or misused. Issues associated with misuse were noted in around one-third of respondents, however, over two-thirds noted that evaluation results were not actually published or disseminated. The tension in evaluation research was also explored by Azzam (2010), who surveyed a random sample of American Evaluation Association members, finding that stakeholder influence was the main factor in willingness to alter evaluation design. These tensions illustrate the challenges in balancing professional standards that acknowledge stakeholder concerns and the quality of the evaluation (Morris, 2008).

Research outlining the ethical challenges associated with evaluation research *often* focused on issues associated with participants (Morris, 2015). Participants require information on the purpose of research evaluations, the benefits and/or risk to participation, right to withdraw and limits of confidentiality to make an informed decision on participation in research valuations (Kara, 2018). Informed consent is the process of obtaining permission for the involvement of individuals in research evaluations. Research conducted by Walker et al. (2008), on the implementation of informed consent in evaluation research, found that although informed consent was generally acknowledged, there was an overestimation of the extent beneficiaries understood services and support. Other research, conducted by Lakes et al. (2012), found that informed consent in evaluation research relies on ensuring participants received adequate information on the perceived risks and burden of participation. Specific questions, outlined by Morris (2015), in understanding informed consent include:

- Are standard informed consent procedures appropriate for evaluation research?
- Are participants able to weigh risks and burden of participation in evaluation research?
- Are participants provided with sufficient information to provide informed consent?

Active consent (opt-in) requires an investment of time and resources, which results in evaluators *often* opting for passive consent (opt-out) (Morris, 2015). Researchers (Johnson et al., 1999; Leakey et al., 2004) acknowledge the issues associated with obtaining active consent, specifically in employing effective strategies that promote active consent. Employing techniques that ensure active consent is imperative for ensuring the true wishes of participants are considered (Johnson et al., 1999).

15.4 Guidance for Evaluation Research

The United Nations Evaluation Group (2008) Ethical Guidelines expand on the Ethical Code of Conduct for Evaluation, outlining the purpose of adopting an ethical code for evaluation research associated with: responsible use of power, ensuring credibility, and responsible use of resources (The United Nations Evaluation Group, 2008). The guidance is applicable to United Nations staff, contractors and subcontractors. It defines the ethical principles in evaluation through The United Nations Evaluation Group (2008, pp. 6–10), including:

1. Evaluation should enable organisations to address and serve the needs of beneficiaries and stakeholders;
2. Evaluation should minimise disruption, invasion of privacy and explore to risks;
3. Evaluation should provide comprehensive and balanced presentation of findings;
4. Evaluation should be free of bias, credible and reliable;
5. Evaluators should respect the rights of participants, ensuring participants are aware of the scope and purpose of research, the benefits and risks of participation and the limits of confidentiality;
6. Evaluators should respect cultural differences, local customs and practices;
7. Evaluators should minimise disruption to participants, organisations and other stakeholders;
8. Evaluators should ensure all reports and presentations provide accurate, reliable and valid information.

Professional standards and ethical principles should guide all individuals and organisations engaged in research evaluation, with The United Nations Evaluation Group (2008) proposing a shared approach to research evaluation.

The Department for International Development (DFID) (2019) Ethical Guidance for Research, Evaluation and Monitoring Activities sets out guidance for conducting research, evaluation and monitoring. The guidance acknowledges the ethical dilemmas associated with research, evaluation and monitoring and is applicable to DFID staff, contractors and subcontractors. The guidance outlines the ethical standards, principles and expectations for each cycle in the evaluation process (DFID, 2019):

1. Commissioning, planning and design (Stage One);
2. Data collection and analysis (Stage Two);
3. Reporting, dissemination and use of evidence (Stage Three); and
4. Monitoring, follow-up and data use (Stage Four).

The ethical principles outlined by DFID (2019) are based on *maximising* benefit and *minimising* harm, respecting people's rights and dignity, acting with honesty and accountability, and delivering evaluations with integrity and credibility. Table 15.1 summaries the core ethical principles associated with The United Nations Evaluation Group (2008) Ethical Guidelines and the DFID (2019) Ethical Guidance for Research, Evaluation and Monitoring Activities.

Guidelines from The United Nations Evaluation Group (2008) and DFID (2019) are summarised under eight core ethical principles: Utility and Necessity; Independence, Impartiality and Conflict of Interest; Honesty, Integrity and Accountability; Respect for Dignity and Diversity; Rights and Confidentiality; Avoidance of Harm; Accuracy, Completeness and Reliability; and Transparency, Omissions and Wrongdoing (The United Nations Evaluation Group, 2008; DFID, 2019) (Table 15.2).

15.5 An Ethical Framework for Social Impact Measurement

Sustainability has strong grounding in ethics, with the Brundtland Report (1987) outlining the fundamental principles for sustainability based on social justice, poverty and equality. The focus on sustainability has grown since the Brundtland Report (1987), accumulating in the development of the Millennium Development Goals and The United Nations Sustainable Development Goals (SDGs). The SDGs were introduced to promote a sustainable, peaceful and prosperous planet for all, through the development of 17 core goals (United Nations 2015). Promotion of the SDG agenda creates pressure for organisation to develop activities and programmes that address the systemic barriers recognised in the goals (Paterson-Young & Hazenberg, 2021). This pressure creates an opportunity for organisations to align impact measurement with the SDGs to demonstrate local, national and global impact (Paterson-Young & Hazenberg, 2021). Understanding the ethical implications associated with social impact measurement is crucial for understanding the impact of programmes and interventions in alleviating societal problems.

Research shows that, despite the existence of ethical frameworks for evaluation research, these frameworks vary in usefulness and rigor

Table 15.1 Ethical principles in evaluation research

The United Nations Evaluation Group (2008) Ethical Guidelines	The DFID (2019) Ethical Guidance for Research, Evaluation and Monitoring Activities
Evaluation design should help organisations serve stakeholders needs.	Evaluation should generate evidence that is of utility to different stakeholders.
Evaluation should be necessary and justified with benefits outweighing.	Evaluation should be useful, necessary and feasible.
Evaluation should be independent and free from bias.	Evaluation should be preserved against bias or external influence.
Evaluations should be impartial and credible, with information on the strengths and weaknesses balanced.	Evaluation should be aligned with principles of impartiality, credibility and objectivity.
Evaluators should acknowledge and disclose conflicts of interest (in writing) to ensure credibility.	Evaluators should ensure information is shared to help identify and mitigate conflicts of interest.
Evaluators should ensure honesty and integrity.	Evaluation should preserve the integrity of evidence.
Evaluators should ensure completion of evaluation within agreed timeframes, noting changes to plans or risks.	Evaluation has been implemented, delivered and disseminated in accordance with agreed timeframes and/or contracts.
Evaluators should respect culture, local customs, personal characteristics and practices; minimise disruption; and ensure participants rights to privacy.	Evaluators should provide accurate and sufficient information on participants rights (confidentiality, privacy etc.) to ensure informed consent.
Evaluators should ensure participants rights, fair representation and compliance.	Evaluators should ensure participants rights and dignity, promoting equitable participation.
Evaluators should respect participants rights to confidentiality, explaining any limits of confidentiality.	Evaluators should ensure participants are provided with accurate information on arrangements for guarding confidentiality.
Evaluators should minimise the risk of harm and negative consequences of participation.	Evaluators should acknowledge any risk of harm to participants and the wider society.
Evaluators should ensure the accurate, complete and reliable presentation of evaluation reports.	Evaluators should consult on risks, benefits and mitigations to ensure accuracy and completeness.
Evaluators should disclose wrongdoings or omissions uncovered through the evaluation.	Evaluators should have clear processes for reporting and/or disclosing wrongdoing.

Table 15.2 Core principles in evaluation research

Core principles	Description
Utility and necessity	Evaluations should serve the needs of beneficiaries, stakeholders and society. Evaluations should be necessary, useful and justified. The benefits of evaluation should outweigh the risks.
Independence, impartiality and conflict of interest	Evaluation should be independent, preserved against bias or external influence. Evaluators should acknowledge and disclose conflicts of interest (in writing) to ensure credibility and mitigate concerns. It should be aligned with principles of impartiality, credibility and objectivity.
Honesty, integrity and accountability	Evaluators should ensure honesty and integrity, preserving the integrity of evidence and conclusions. They should ensure completion of evaluations within agreed timeframes, noting any developments or changes.
Respect for dignity and diversity	Evaluators should respect culture, local customs, personal characteristics and practices; minimise disruption to participants and organisations; and ensure participants rights to privacy.
Rights and confidentiality	Evaluators should respect participants rights to confidentiality, explaining the arrangements for guarding confidentiality.
Avoidance of harm	Evaluators should minimise the risk of harm and negative consequences of participation to participants and the wider society.
Accuracy, completeness and reliability	Evaluators should ensure the accurate, complete and reliable presentation of evaluation reports. They should consult on risks, benefits and mitigations to ensure accuracy and completeness.
Transparency, omissions and wrongdoing	Evaluators should disclose any wrongdoings and/or omissions uncovered through the evaluation. They should have clear processes for reporting and/or disclosing wrongdoing.

(Williams, 2016). Adopting an ethical framework for measuring social impact, aligned with the SDGs, will allow evaluators and researchers to ensure professional standards in evaluation research. Figure 15.1 provides an overview of an 'Ethical Framework for Social Impact Measurement' evaluation and/or research. The 'Ethical Framework for Social Impact Measurement' draws on core ethical principles outlined by The United

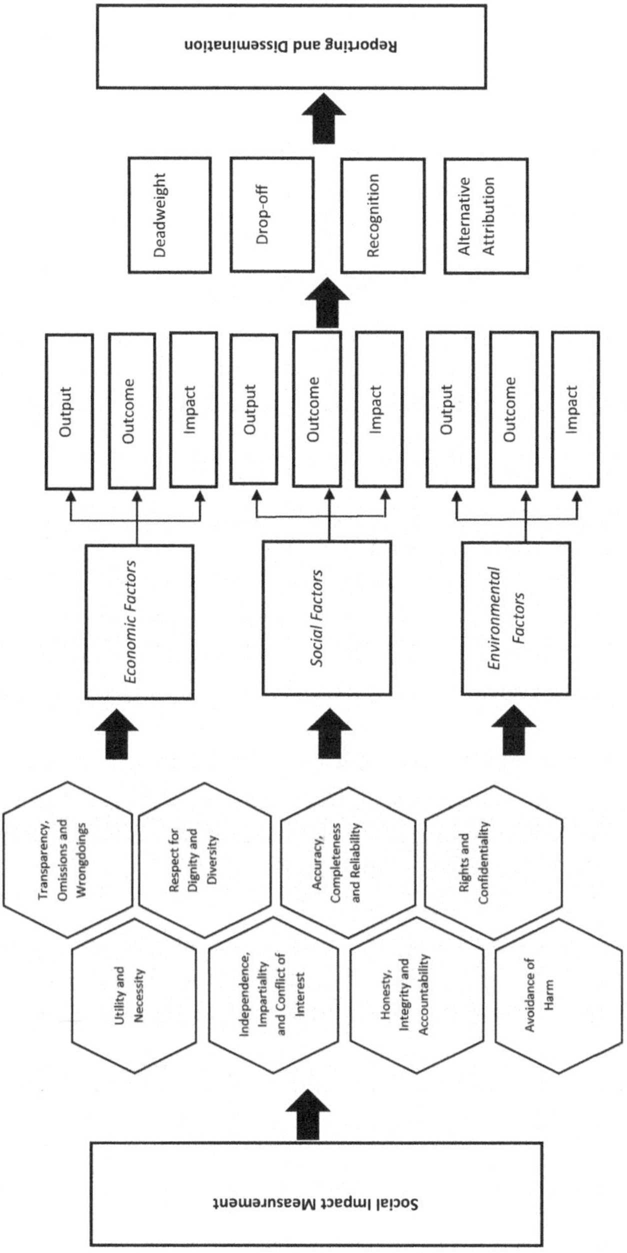

Fig. 15.1 Ethical Framework for Social Impact Measurement

Nations Evaluation Group (2008) Ethical Guidelines and the DFID (2019) Ethical Guidance for Research, Evaluation and Monitoring Activities. It embeds the scope of activities (*outputs);* the positive and negative outcomes experienced by beneficiaries (*outcomes*); long-term changes in beneficiaries and society (*impacts*) (Clifford et al., 2014; McLoughlin et al., 2009; Paterson-Young & Hazenberg, 2021) with the role of other stakeholders/partners in this change (alternative attribution); the changes that would have occurred anyway (deadweight) and the changes declining over time (*drop-off*) (Clifford et al., 2014; Paterson-Young & Hazenberg, 2021). It also acknowledges the dissemination and reporting of the evaluation, externally and internally, to ensure transparency (Clifford et al., 2014; The United Nations Evaluation Group, 2008; DFID, 2019).

15.6 Ethics and Impact

Effective reporting of social impact measurement, aligned with the United Nations' SDGs, is pivotal for allowing us to better understand the impact of programmes and interventions in alleviating societal problems. Ethical issues in evaluation research focus on the challenges of conducting evaluation research (Morris, 2008, 2015; Williams, 2016), offering insight on evaluation experience (de Montclos, 2012; Hendricks & Bamberger, 2010; Klerman, 2010; Trimble et al., 2012; Buchanan & MacDonald, 2011; Morris & Clark, 2013).

Social impact measurement, and evaluation research, can result in ethical violations that directly impact beneficiaries, stakeholders and society (Morris, 2015; Williams, 2016). Acknowledging the ethical issues (for example, informed consent, stakeholder expectations, conflicts of interest) associated with social impact measurement is imperative in ensuring evaluation research is reliable and valid. It empowers organisations in evaluating the social impact of activities and helps position the theoretical within the practical, especially in tackling the SDGs.

References

American Evaluation Association. (2018). *Guiding Principles*. Online at https://freshspectrum.com/wp-content/uploads/2020/06/Evaluation-Guiding-Principles-American-Evaluation-Association-2018.pdf. Accessed on 01 Feb 2021.

Azzam, T. (2010). Evaluator Responsiveness to Stakeholders. *American Journal of Evaluation, 31*, 45–65.

Biagetti, M. T., Gedutis, A., & Ma, L. (2019). Ethical Theories in Research Evaluation: An Exploratory Approach. *Scholarly Assessment Reports, 2*(1), 11. https://doi.org/10.29024/sar.19

Brundtland, G. H. (1987). *Our Common Future*. Report of the World Commission on Environment and Development. United Nation.

Buchanan, H., & MacDonald, W. (2011). *Anytime, Anywhere, Evaluation Ethics do Matter*! Paper Presented at the Meeting of the American Evaluation Association, Anaheim, Capabilities Approach.

Cartland, J., Ruch-Ross, H., & Mason, M. (2012). Engaging Community Researchers in Evaluation: Looking at the Experiences of Community Partners in School-Based Projects in the US. In L. Goodson & J. Phillimore (Eds.), *Community Research for Participation: From Theory to Method* (pp. 169–184). Policy Press.

Clifford, J., Hehenberger, L., & Fantini, M. (2014). *Proposed Approaches to Social Impact Measurement in European Commission Legislation and in Practice Relating to: EuSEFs and the EaSI*. European Commission Report 140605 (June 2014). Available online at http://ec.europa.eu/internal_market/social_business/docs/expert-group/social_impact/140605-sub-group-report_en.pdf and http://ec.europa.eu/social/main.jsp?catId=738&langId=en&pubId=7735&type=2&furtherPubs=yes

Darwall, S. (Ed.). (2002). *Deontology*. Hoboken, N. J.: Wiley-Blackwell.

de Montclos, M. P. (2012). Humanitarian Action in Developing Countries: Who Evaluates Who? *Evaluation and Program Planning, 35*, 154–160.

Department for International Development (DFID). (2019). *Ethical Guidance for Research, Evaluation and Monitoring Activities*. Online at: https://assets.publishing.service.gov.uk/government/uploads/system/uploads/attachment_data/file/838106/DFID-Ethics-Guidance-Oct2019.pdf. Accessed on 02 Febr 2021.

Economic and Social Research Council (ESRC). (2015). *Framework for Research Ethics*. Economic and Social Research Council.

Fleischer, D. N., & Christie, C. A. (2009). Evaluation use: Results from a survey of U.S. American Evaluation Association members. *American Journal of Evaluation, 30*, 158–175.

Greene, J. C., & Lee, J. (2006). Quieting Education Reform . . . with Educational Reform. *American Journal of Evaluation, 27*, 337–352.

Hendricks, M., & Bamberger, M. (2010). The Ethical Implications of Underfunding Development Evaluations. *American Journal of Evaluation, 31*(00), 549–556.

Honea, G. E. (1992). *Ethics and Public Sector Evaluators: Nine Case Studies.* Unpublished Doctoral Dissertation, University of Virginia.

Johnson, K., Bryant, D., Rockwell, E., Moore, M., Straub, B. W., Cummings, P., & Wilson, C. (1999). Obtaining Active Parental Consent for Evaluation Research: A Case Study. *American Journal of Evaluation, 20*, 239–249.

Kara, H. (2018). *Research Ethics in the Real World: Euro-Western and Indigenous Perspectives.* Policy Press.

Klerman, J. A. (2010). Contracting for Independent Evaluation: Approaches to an Inherent Tension. *Evaluation Review, 34*, 299–333.

Lakes, K. D., Vaughan, E., Jones, M., Burke, W., Baker, D., & Swanson, J. M. (2012). Diverse Perceptions of the Informed Consent Process: Implications for the Recruitment and Participation of Diverse Communities in the National Children's Study. *American Journal of Community Psychology, 49*, 215–232.

Leakey, T., Lunde, K. B., Koga, K., & Glanz, K. (2004). Written Parental Consent and the Use of Incentives in a Youth Smoking Prevention Trial: A Case Study from Project SPLASH. *American Journal of Evaluation, 25*, 509–523.

Mathison, S. (2005). *Encyclopaedia of Evaluation* (Vols. 1–0). Sage Publications, Inc. https://doi.org/10.4135/9781412950558.

McLoughlin, J., Kaminski, J., Sodagar, B., Khan, S., Harris, R., Arnaudo, G., & McBrearty, S. (2009). A Strategic Approach to Social Impact Measurement of Social Enterprises: The SIMPLE Methodology. *Social Enterprise Journal, 5*(2), 154–178.

Morris, M. (2008). *Evaluation Ethics for Best Practices. Cases and Commentaries.* Guilford Press.

Morris, M. (2015). Research on Evaluation Ethics: Reflections and an Agenda. In P. Brandon (Ed.), *Research on Evaluation: New Directions for Evaluation* (pp. 31–42). Wiley.

Morris, M., & Clark, B. (2013). You Want me to Do What? Evaluators and the Pressure to Misrepresent Findings. *American Journal of Evaluation, 34*, 57–70.

Newman, D., & Brown, R. (1996). *Applied Ethics for Program Evaluation*. SAGE Publications.

Paterson-Young, C., & Hazenberg, R. (2021). Transformative Outcomes: The Use of Social Impact Measurement. In F. W. Leal, A. M. Azul, L. Brandli, S. A. Lange, P. G. Özuyar, & T. Wall (Eds.), *Peace, Justice and Strong Institutions* (Encyclopaedia of the UN Sustainable Development Goals). Springer.

Pettit, P. (1991). Consequentialism. In S. Darwall (Ed.), *Deontology* (2002). Wiley-Blackwell.

Rawls, J. (1971). *A Theory of Justice*. Harvard University Press.

Sieber, J. (1993). The Ethics and Politics of Sensitive Research. In C. Renzetti & R. Lee (Eds.), *Researching Sensitive Topics*. Sage.

Simons, H. (2006). Ethics in Evaluation. In I. Shaw, J. C. Greene, & M. M. Mark (Eds.), *The SAGE Handbook of Evaluation* (pp. 244–266). SAGE Publications.

Trimble, J., Trickett, E., Fisher, C., & Goodyear, L. (2012). A Conversation on Multicultural Competence in Evaluation. *American Journal of Evaluation, 33*, 112–123.

United Nations. (2015). *Transforming Our World: The 2030 Agenda for Sustainable Development*. https://sustainabledevelopment.un.org/post2015/transformingourworldDate. Accessed 9 April 2021.

United Nations Evaluation Group. (2008). *Ethical Guidelines for Evaluation*. Online at: http://uneval.org/document/download/548. Accessed on 02 Feb 2021.

Walker, R., Hoggart, L., & Hamilton, G. (2008). Random Assignment and Informed Consent: A Case Study of Multiple Perspectives. *American Journal of Evaluation, 29*, 156–174.

Williams, L. (2016). Ethics in International Development Evaluation and Research: What Is the Problem, Why Does It Matter and What Can We Do About It? *Journal of Development Effectiveness, 8*(4), 535–552. https://doi.org/10.1080/19439342.2016.1244700

16

Impact in the Twenty-First Century: Utilising Measurement to Empower the Disadvantaged

Richard Hazenberg and Claire Paterson-Young

16.1 Impact Must Empower

The preceding chapters of this book have sought to explore the myriad of challenges facing the field of social impact measurement at the present time. These include defining impact measurement, revealing how approaches to designing such measurement should (and must) include the very beneficiaries of the programmes being evaluated, and exploring the increasingly powerful impact of top-down frameworks on the impact landscape. The book has been framed around the United Nation's Sustainable Development Goal (SDGs) framework, in an attempt to show the interconnectedness of SDG focused approaches, but also if we are honest as a means to critique the current normative discussions around impact measurement. Certainly, there is much to be celebrated in

R. Hazenberg (✉) • C. Paterson-Young
Institute for Social Innovation and Impact, University of Northampton, Northampton, UK
e-mail: richard.hazenberg@northampton.ac.uk; claire.paterson-young@northampton.ac.uk

R. Hazenberg, C. Paterson-Young (eds.), *Social Impact Measurement for a Sustainable Future*, https://doi.org/10.1007/978-3-030-83152-3_16

the SDG approach, with their ability to coalesce action around seventeen core areas, to shape discussion globally around sustainable development and to provide mechanisms for measuring such change through the underlying 169 indicators. Further, they have created a meta-narrative around sustainability that just did not exist to the same degree twenty (or even ten) years ago.

Yet these clear positives belie the fact that the SDG framework and the corresponding meta-impact methodologies that have gained prominence over the last decade, present a top-down vision of how to drive and measure social impact, that does not always understand local context, cultures or the needs of disempowered individuals particularly in the developing world. What then to make of this dichotomy between bottom-up need and voice, and the necessity (at least to some degree) for top-down validation of global policy and programmes of development? Whilst we live in an age where the search for simplistic explanations represents somewhat of a zeitgeist, it remains important to recognise that this is a complex area, both in terms of the measurement frameworks themselves and the tensions inherent between top-down and bottom-up approaches. There is a need for both bottom-up social innovation across the world and also top-down approaches to measure their impacts, whilst acknowledging that such bottom-up initiatives can be informed by global knowledge transfer and that top-down approaches must react flexibly to local conditions and the needs of the marginalised. The question remains though how to ensure that this flexibility of approach is enabled and that the right things are measured; and how do we safeguard against social impact measurement frameworks becoming tools that distract from impact that only serve the interests of people in power?

The key arguments made throughout this book by all of the different authors make the answer to these questions exceptionally clear. The solution is to reframe the purpose of impact measurement, the approaches undertaken, and outcomes sought, so that impact measurement becomes a tool for highlighting inequality, empowering those that are most disadvantaged, and providing ethical protection for these same groups. Impact measurement that merely seeks to monetise specific outcomes or demonstrate the efficacy of large-scale programmes (however well-intentioned), will not drive the type of change that the world needs. To quote the late

Oscar Wilde, *"A cynic is a man who knows the price of everything but the value of nothing"*; a lament that has a specific resonance in the field of impact measurement. Impact measurement should be as much (no more) about providing a voice to the marginalised, as it is about evidencing the return on investment of an international NGO's support programme. This is the key message of this book and one that we will explore in this chapter, shaped around the four key themes of the book, namely: 'The how, what, why and whom of Social Impact Measurement', 'Agency, expertise and partnerships', 'Politics and public good', and 'Power, accountability and ethics'. In doing so we aim to demonstrate how social impact measurement can be a tool of empowerment.

16.2 The How, What, Why and Whom...

Throughout the book, as well as in the wider literature, the plethora of different approaches to social impact measurement have been illustrated. These methodological approaches include (not exclusively): Social Return on Investment (SROI); the Global Impact Investment Rating System (GIIRS); IRIS+; Social Impact Assessment (SIA); Stakeholder Value Added (SVA); Outcomes Star; Balanced Scorecard; Local Economic Multiplier; and Social Accounting and Audit (SAA) (Maas & Liket, 2011; Noya, 2015). This creates a veritable minefield for academics, practitioners and policy-makers in understanding which tools to use, what are best for demonstrating different types of impact and how to implement these in different contexts.

There has been somewhat greater success at the meta-level in defining what can be described as gold-standard approaches to social impact measurement; that is, not specific methodologies, but the types of best practice best implemented in evaluation of social impact (see Chap. 2). The GECES framework (Clifford et al., 2014), and to some extent the United Nations Sustainable Development Goals, have both been extensively discussed in this book and held up as meta-narratives that can promote positive change through impact measurement globally. The flipside to this though is that such approaches ignore local context and can fail to understand the conditions for social value creation on the ground. This is why the anthropological critiques presented in this book (see Chap. 3) focused on placing people at the centre of social impact measurement approaches, are so central to the ideas of empowerment inherent to this text, and to social innovation more widely (Mulgan, 2019). As Max Weber (1978) argued, empowerment is a prerequisite for engaging in meaningful social action, and power is relational (Giddens, 2016).

Participatory methods in social impact measurement are insufficient on their own however to ensure that the outcomes of said measurement do not reinforce inequalities or serve the needs of the powerful. Impact measurement approaches and the outcomes and impacts that are identified have to be viewed within wider systems of cause and effect (Capra & Luisi, 2014), whereby social impact and change occurs at different levels, geographies, and timescales, as well as being culturally relativistic. Here, the SDGs can provide a distraction, as it is too easy to view each SDG as an isolated island of impact, with no interrelation, when the reality is that they are all interconnected. For instance, it is difficult to separate out SDG5: Gender Equality from SDG10: Reduced Inequalities, nor to remove these from SDG11: Sustainable Cities and Communities or SDG16: Peace, Justice and Strong Institutions. This lack of joined-up thinking can be found in many sectors utilising impact measurement but was succinctly highlighted in Chap. 6 as a key problem in the impact investment sector.

In physics, the action of measurement itself changes observed outcomes at the quantum level and it can be argued that this is also the case with social impact measurement. Indeed, by defining what we believe the perceived outcomes should be (as we see with the indicators within each SDG), we create incentives for individuals and organisations to achieve these outcomes. Here quantum weirdness is replaced by human predictability in the form of actor-network theory (Justesen & Mouritsen, 2011; Latour, 2005), whereby the existence of powerful, normative assumptions for impact as codified in frameworks such as the SDGs drives behaviour and impact down a predetermined pathway. Now, this can be beneficial when trying to drive sustainable development globally, but it can also be problematic when seeking to deliver positive impact for disadvantaged groups at local levels, for whom the SDG indicators (or other meta-narrative approaches) may not be relevant. Effectively in these cases, institutional and societal power drives impact homogeneity in a world of complex, heterogenic systems. Awareness of this in designing impact measurement approaches and implementing them in the real-world is critical to ensuring that impact measurement serves the correct masters (the disadvantaged) and does not perversely incentivise sub-optimal programmes of work.

16.3 Human Agency, Knowledge and Collaboration

Whilst the discussion above focuses on best practice approaches, frameworks and methodologies, it is also important to recognise the human factors at play here, both in how we approach measurement and knowledge, but also how we view disadvantage. In the same way that our arguments are focused on understanding the heterogeneity of social systems and the many different underlying causes of social problems, we must also acknowledge that the socially disadvantaged are not homogeneous either (this can be split along many lines including gender, ethnicity, religion, socioeconomic status, age etc.) (see Chap. 14). Understanding different individuals/groups trust in and experience of formal institutions can help us to understand their agency and how social impact measurement can support them. Further, as was shown in Chap. 5 with regards to gender, adopting approaches such as the Capability Approach (Sen, 1992) can allow researchers to understand the starting positions and end-goals/desired outcomes of different groups. What we are therefore again faced with here, is a need to acknowledge the complexity of disadvantage and its relationship with social problems.

Knowledge and our approach to it is also shaped by the dominant narratives that exist globally. Discourse here is key, with the language used within dominant frameworks such as the SDGs acting as powerful determinants of future impact measurement approaches, and not always supporting the partnership working that is a critical underpinning of the transdisciplinary nature of impact measurement (Liket et al., 2014; Ormiston, 2019). Indeed, it is partnership based approaches, embedded in the transdisciplinary nature of impact measurement, that makes multi-stakeholder approaches to impact measurement so crucial in bringing together stakeholders from the third, public and private sectors (see Chaps. 7 and 9). So far we have highlighted the need for beneficiaries to be at the centre of impact measurement approaches, but this still needs to be supported through the engagement of other key stakeholders surrounding this work.

One also needs to be able to understand the needs of Non-Government Organisations, policy-makers, investors, and governments, to be able to make impact measurement relevant to them. Indeed, given the overt focus within outcomes and impacts of stakeholder perspective, multi-stakeholder approaches are a prerequisite for effective impact measurement (Costa, 2021; Costa & Pesci, 2016). It is only by carrying out this engagement that impact measurement approaches can develop the evidence required to drive the systemic changes that reduce inequality and disadvantage; by engaging in multi-stakeholder approaches with the disadvantaged beneficiaries at the centre, impact measurement can become a tool for giving voice to the disenfranchised in a way that powerful actors/institutions can understand. In this way impact measurement becomes a form of transformative participatory evaluation (King et al., 2007), which can enable socially relevant knowledge to be created that enables human agency and social action amongst the disadvantaged.

16.4 The Politics of Value

This exploration of the contextual nature of knowledge and evidence in social impact measurement, and the role that dominant narratives and institutions can have on human agency within the impact measurement sphere, leads us inevitably into discussions around the politics of value, whereby the social is inherently political. In this book our contributors have discussed this need to understand context and politics in detail (see Chaps. 8 and 10 for examples), with an acknowledgement that individuals conducting impact measurement do so within spatial, temporal, cultural and socio-political contexts; contexts that shape their behaviour as researchers, but also that they then shape through the 'evidence' that they produce (Welter & Baker, 2020). This brings us to arguments that have existed in social science for decades on value neutrality and objectivity (Hammersley, 2017). It is not the purpose of this chapter to go over these in detail, but it is important that these tensions are acknowledged, as the pressure to conduct impact measurement research that is contextually and culturally relevant, but also value neutral and objective is one that cannot easily be bridged. This is where meta-narratives and guides such as the SDG framework and GECES guidelines can be instructive, in providing a global architecture for core values and measurement that can then be adapted for use in different cultural contexts.

In discussing the concept of power in social impact measurement, it would be remiss to not focus on the monetisation of social value, a central component of social critiques of impact measurement. Certainly, the ubiquitous presence of financial proxy values in impact measurement (most notably in methodologies such as Social Return On Investment) demonstrates where the power lies in impact measurement. After all, how many beneficiaries in disadvantaged communities would seek to articulate (or want to know) how many USD$ a community initiative had produced; rather, they would care about how many lives in their communities had been positively impacted. This perhaps goes back to wider arguments in the third sector (where arguably impact measurement has its greatest place) around neoliberal attempts to monetise the social and whether this a positive or negative (McKay et al., 2015; Han, 2017). However, perhaps more than this it reflects a wider systemic drive in society globally to commodify everything, what can be seen as Polanyi's (1944) 'fictitious commodification' (see Chap. 11). After all, if 'money is power' as the saying goes, then the prevalence of financial metrics for measuring social value shows that the power in impact measurement perhaps lies with governments, investors and funders who all have a vested interest to see such commodification.

Whilst a recurrent theme of this chapter might be a perceived desire to compromise in these areas, to sit on the fence so to speak between top-down monetised approaches to impact measurement and bottom-up approaches that are beneficiary focused, we argue that this is a necessity when conducting impact measurement. Epistemologically, it can be argued that impact measurement best aligns with critical realist approaches, in which the researcher seeks to merge different ontological realities into a coherent research approach. After all, the arguments made throughout this book have shown the need for impact measurement to explain and evidence Bhaskar's (1975) causal mechanisms and to bridge the 'real' with the social.[1] This certainly provides tensions in research approaches, whilst it is perhaps this need within impact measurement for ontological flexibility that makes impact measurement as a field such a contested space, and one that is often distrusted by a variety of different stakeholder groups (especially disadvantaged groups), as the theoretical compromises are not often easily embedded in practice.

Whilst we remain steadfast in our belief that the disadvantaged beneficiary voice remains the most fundamental in impact measurement, we also concede that for impact measurement to be able to drive real-world change and social value creation, it needs to also produce evidence that is recognised as valid by powerful stakeholders. Chapter 12 provides an interesting overview of how this could be done in practice, through the example of economic modelling in social care, presenting a case for how financial metrics can be utilised for beneficiary empowerment, albeit with significant tensions between economic metrics and user engagement in practice. In making these arguments, we as editors and the chapter authors are not suggesting that top-down, monetised approaches should be the be-all and end-all in impact measurement; rather, we are arguing that it is naïve to believe that impact measurement can focus *only* on beneficiary engagement and coproduction. Instead, the solution to improving impact measurement is to ensure that disadvantaged communities are placed at the centre of evaluations, as the key coproducers within a wider multi-stakeholder approach, but in a wider impact framework that also acknowledges the reporting needs of powerful stakeholders (i.e. government). The challenges of exploring data validity, risk-management and end-user voice [the Ladder of Citizen Participation (Arnstein, 1969)] are also discussed in Chap. 13. Certainly, this is no easy task and one that can produce numerous methodological and ethical conundrums for the researcher.

[1] We use the term 'real' here flexibly, and not from any positivistic stance that a truly real world exists.

16.5 Ethical Evidence as Power

When exploring the role of disadvantaged beneficiaries and communities in impact measurement, ethical considerations naturally come to the fore. The topics that have been discussed in this chapter so far centred on the complex systems underpinning disadvantage and social problems, the interconnected nature of the SDGs, the role of power and the engagement of beneficiaries as coproducers in impact measurement, and the need to produce valid and reliable evidence that can drive social change, all have ethical implications to them. Only by understanding the complex interactions within systems and engaging in multi-stakeholder partnerships to design and gather effective impact tools/data, can programmes/organisations be sure that they are delivering positive impact and not causing unintended harm. This is particularly pertinent with the SDGs, where failure to do so can lead to incoherent policies and siloed working within specific SDGs (Boas et al., 2016; Nilsson et al., 2016) (see Chap. 14). What is therefore required in addition to the best practice approaches outlined earlier in this section, are clear guiding ethical principles for impact measurement that place the wellbeing of beneficiaries and the integrity of the data gathered at the forefront of impact measurement work.

Ethics in social impact measurement research is something of a weakness, given that much of it is evaluative and conducted by non-academic organisations that may not have access to in-depth ethical advice and scrutiny (Newman & Brown, 1996). As was noted in Chap. 15, the United Nations' Evaluation Group (2008, pp. 6–10) guidance focuses on eight core principles (see Sect. 15.4), of which four are focused on the perspectives, rights and privacies of the participants; whilst a further one seeks to acknowledge the importance of respecting 'cultural differences, local customs and practices'. However, the issues highlighted throughout the book centred on a lack of engagement with disadvantaged beneficiaries, overt focus on indicators that are not necessarily relevant to communities (i.e. monetised returns on impact), and the use of broad frameworks that do not seek to understand the needs of disenfranchised communities, point to an ethical dilemma in social impact measurement that may lead to ethical violations (Morris, 2008; 2015; Williams, 2016). There is a clear need to ensure that issues such as informed consent, stakeholder expectations, and conflicts of interest are dealt with thoroughly and in partnership with all stakeholders (including beneficiaries), if the efficacy of impact measurement is to stand up to scrutiny.

The development of these types of enhanced ethical frameworks (as outlined in Table 15.1), provide a means to protect the disadvantaged and ensure that they do not become what Chouinard and Milley (2018) termed 'data sources'. In adopting these practices, many of the issues that have been highlighted throughout this book could be minimised, whether that be in relation to beneficiary coproduction, wider stakeholder engagement, best practice in producing impact data, utilising valid data to drive sustainable change, or protecting the rights of individuals engaged through sustainable development work and/or impact evaluations.

16.6 Final Thoughts: Ensuring Inclusive Impact Measurement

At the start of this book we discussed the need to move impact measurement debates beyond considerations of methodology, towards also considering the wider impacts of the measurement process, particularly with regards to disadvantaged and disenfranchised communities globally, who are most in need of impactful sustainable development and have had negative experiences of 'being researched' previously. We believe that this text has, through the expert contributions made by our contributors, made this case with regards to the importance of considering the effect of agency, collaboration, politics, power and ethics in impact measurement research. This remains an area that is under-developed and that does not receive the attention that it deserves either in academia or policy and practice. Indeed, given the rise of social impact measurement consultancy as a sector, these are issues that urgently need to be considered if the reliability and validity of data, the policies that will be formulated based upon it, and the relevance of the evaluations to vulnerable individuals/communities are to be enhanced. We believe that this book makes an important contribution to kickstarting or furthering these debates.

Given that the main focus of the arguments made throughout the book have really been centred on inclusivity in impact measurement, both for vulnerable beneficiaries but also for wider stakeholder groups, its perhaps pertinent to finish off the book on this topic. In our experience inclusivity in research is an easy thing to promise, but not always an easy task to accomplish. This is not always because the researchers do not seek it but can also be due to a lack of stakeholder engagement including from beneficiaries. This is perhaps understandable given that we have seen how beneficiaries have previously experienced impact measurement as mere 'data sources' (Chouinard & Milley, 2018); where the overt monetisation of impact and desire to demonstrate ever increasing returns has alienated those stakeholders more focused on the social; and where distrust of powerful institutions leads to questions being asked as to the motivations behind impact measurement. For impact measurement to be truly inclusive, there is a need for all stakeholders to engage in the process and where needed for barriers to be removed and bridges built between stakeholder groups. Trust-building is key here, as without trust between the stakeholder groups coproduction is difficult if not impossible. We believe that if the wider impact measurement sector can embrace the principles outlined in this book, and align their work with global best-practice frameworks such as the GECES and SDG frameworks, whilst listening to the needs of local communities, that this trust can be built and that effective impact measurement can support a more rapid transition to a sustainable planet and society.

References

Arnstein, S. R. (1969). A Ladder of Citizen Participation. *Journal of the American Planning Association, 35*(4), 216–224.

Bhaskar, R. (1975). *A Realist Theory of Science*. Verso Publishing.

Boas, I., Biermann, F., & Kanie, N. (2016). Cross-Sectoral Strategies in Global Sustainability Governance: Towards a nexus Approach. *International Environmental Agreements: Politics, Law and Economics, 16*(3), 449–464.

Capra, F., & Luisi, P. L. (2014). *The Systems View of Life – A Unifying Vision*. Cambridge University Press.

Chouinard, J. A., & Milley, P. (2018). Uncovering the Mysteries of Inclusion: Empirical and Methodological Possibilities in Participatory Evaluation in an International Context. *Evaluation and Program Planning, 67*, 70–78. https://doi.org/10.1016/j.evalprogplan.2017.12.001

Clifford, J., Hehenberger, L., & Fantini, M. (2014). *Proposed Approaches to Social Impact Measurement in European Commission Legislation and in Practice Relating to: EuSEFs and the EaSI*, European Commission Report 140605 (June 2014). Available online at http://ec.europa.eu/social/main.jsp?catId=738&langId=en&pubId=7735&type=2&furtherPubs=yes

Costa, E. (2021). Challenges for Social Impact Measurement in the Non-profit Sector. In O. Lehner (Ed.), *A Research Agenda for Social Finance* (pp. 119–144). Edward Elgar Publishing.

Costa, E., & Pesci, C. (2016). Social Impact Measurement: Why Do Stakeholders Matter? *Sustainability Accounting, Management and Policy Journal, 7*(1), 99–124.

Giddens, A. (2016). *Profiles and Critiques in Social Theory*. Macmillan International Higher Education.

Hammersley, M. (2017). On the Role of Values in Social Research: Weber Vindicated? *Sociological Research Online, 22*(1).

Han, J. (2017). Social Marketisation and Policy Influence of Third Sector Organisations: Evidence from the UK. *Voluntas: International Journal of Voluntary and Nonprofit Organizations, 28*, 1209–1225.

Justesen, L., & Mouritsen, J. (2011). Effects of Actor-Network Theory in Accounting Research. *Accounting, Auditing and Accountability Journal, 24*(2), 161–193.

King, J. A., Cousins, J. B., & Whitmore, E. (2007). Making Sense of Participatory Evaluation: Framing Participatory Evaluation. *New Directions for Evaluation, 114*, 83–105.

Latour, B. (2005). *Reassembling the Social: An Introduction to Actor-Network Theory*. Oxford University Press.

Liket, K. C., Rey-Garcia, M., & Maas, K. E. H. (2014). Why Aren't Evaluations Working and What to Do About It: A Framework for Negotiating Meaningful Evaluation in Nonprofits. *American Journal of Evaluation, 35*(2), 171–188.

Maas, K., & Liket, K. (2011). Social Impact Measurement: Classification of Methods. In R. L. Burritt, S. Schaltegger, M. Bennett, T. Pohjola, & M. Csutora (Eds.), *Environmental Management Accounting and Supply Chain Management*. Springer. https://doi.org/10.1007/978-94-007-1390-1_8

McKay, S., Moro, D., Teasdale, S., & Clifford, D. (2015). The Marketisation of Charities in England and Wales. *Voluntas: International Journal of Voluntary and Nonprofit Organizations, 26*, 336–354.

Morris, M. (2008). *Evaluation Ethics for Best Practices. Cases and Commentaries.* Guilford Press.

Morris, M. (2015). Research on evaluation ethics: reflections and an agenda. In Brandon, P. (ed) *Research on evaluation: new directions for evaluation*, 31–42. Hoboken, NJ: Wiley.

Mulgan, G. (2019). *Social Innovation: How Societies Find the Power to Change.* Policy Press.

Newman, D., & Brown, R. (1996). *Applied Ethics for Program Evaluation.* SAGE Publications.

Nilsson, M., Griggs, D., & Visbeck, M. (2016). Policy: Map the Interactions Between Sustainable Development Goals. *Nature News, 534*(7607), 320–322.

Noya, A. (2015). *Policy Brief on Social Impact Measurement for Social Enterprises.* OECD Policies for Social Entrepreneurship. Available online at https://www.oecd.org/social/PB-SIM-Web_FINAL.pdf

Ormiston, J. (2019). Blending Practice Worlds: Impact Assessment as a Transdisciplinary Practice. *Business Ethics: A European Review, 28*(4), 423–440.

Polanyi, K. (1944). *The Great Transformation: The Political and Economic Origins of Our Time* (Second Beacon Paperback Edition Published in 2001). Beacon Press.

Sen, A. (1992). *Inequality Re-Examined.* Oxford University Press.

United Nations Evaluation Group. (2008). *Ethical Guidelines for Evaluation.* Online at: http://uneval.org/document/download/548. Accessed on Feb 02, 2021.

Weber, M. (1978). *Economy and Society: An Outline of Interpretative Sociology.* California University Press.

Welter, F., & Baker, T. (2020). Moving Contexts onto New Roads: Clues from Other Disciplines. *Entrepreneurship Theory and Practice.* https://doi.org/10.1177/1042258720930996

Williams, L. (2016). Ethics in International Development Evaluation and Research: What Is the Problem, Why Does It Matter and What Can We Do About It? *Journal of Development Effectiveness, 8*(4), 535–552. https://doi.org/10.1080/19439342.2016.1244700

Index[1]

[1] Note: Page numbers followed by 'n' refer to notes.

R. Hazenberg, C. Paterson-Young (eds.), *Social Impact Measurement for a Sustainable Future*, https://doi.org/10.1007/978-3-030-83152-3

S

The manufacturer's authorised representative in the EU is Springer Nature Customer Service Centre GmbH, Europaplatz 3, 69115 Heidelberg, Germany. If you have any concerns regarding our products, please contact ProductSafety@springernature.com

Printed and bound by CPI Group (UK) Ltd, Croydon, CR0 4YY

30/09/2026

02225700-0009